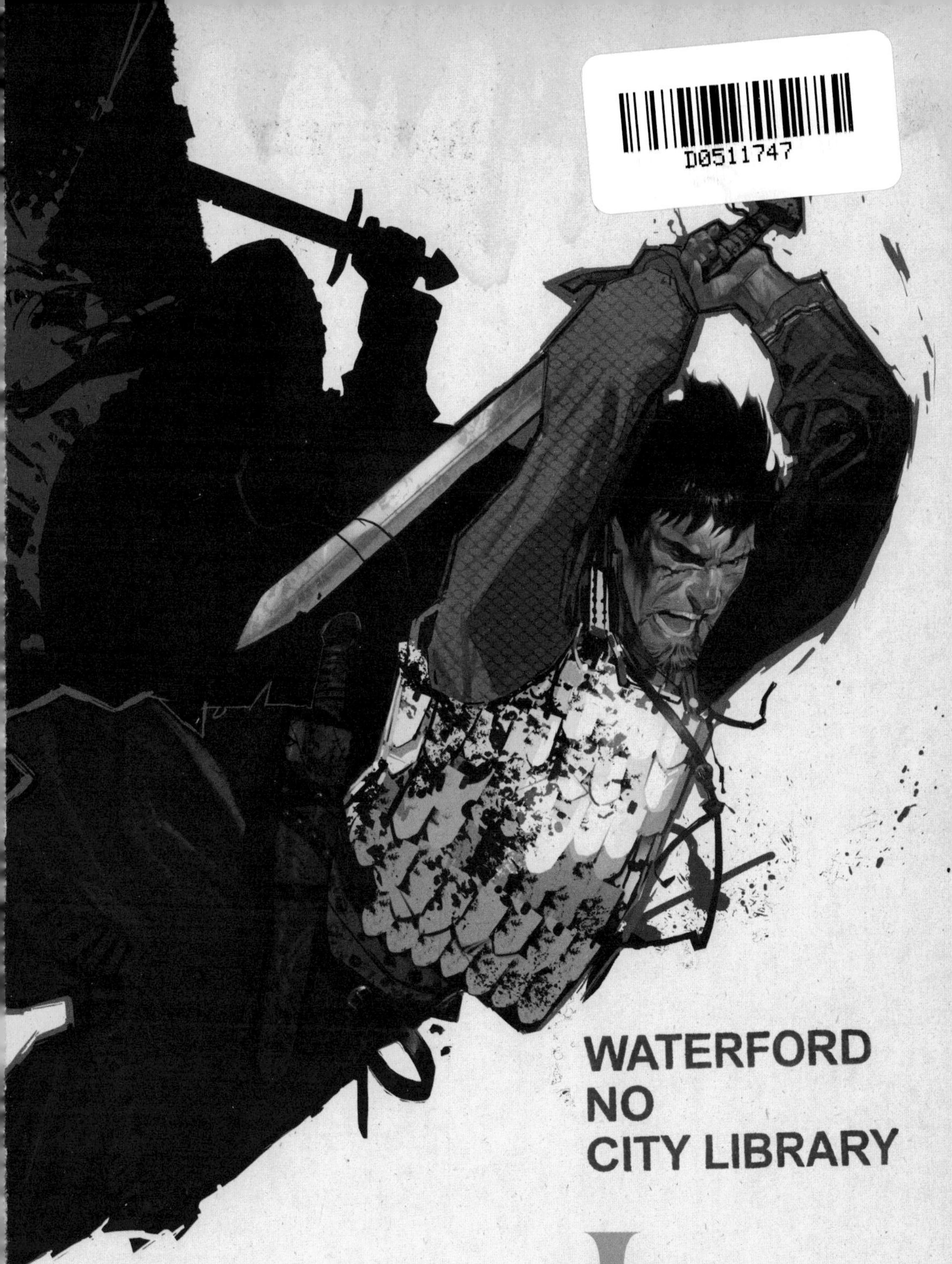

NORTHLANDERS

BOOK ONE: SVEN THE RETURNED

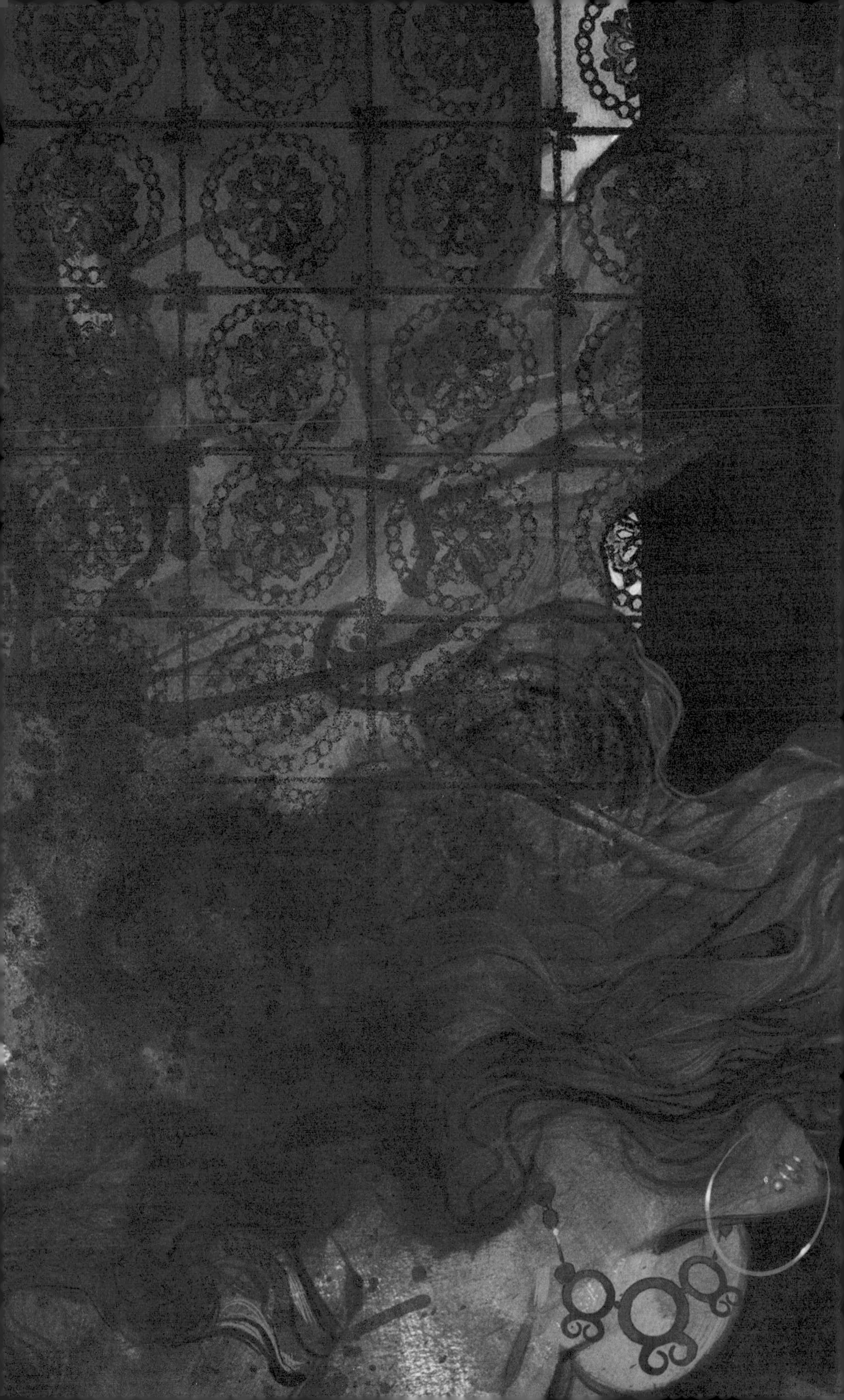

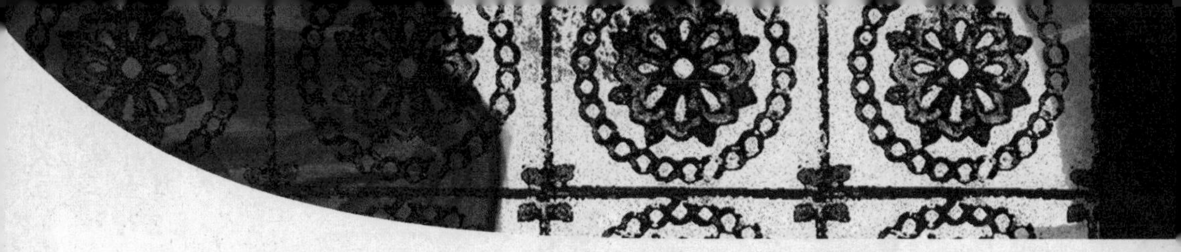

NORTHLANDERS

BOOK ONE: SVEN THE RETURNED

Brian Wood Writer   Davide Gianfelice Artist

Dave McCaig Colorist   Travis Lanham Letterer

Original series covers by Massimo Carnevale

NORTHLANDERS created by Brian Wood

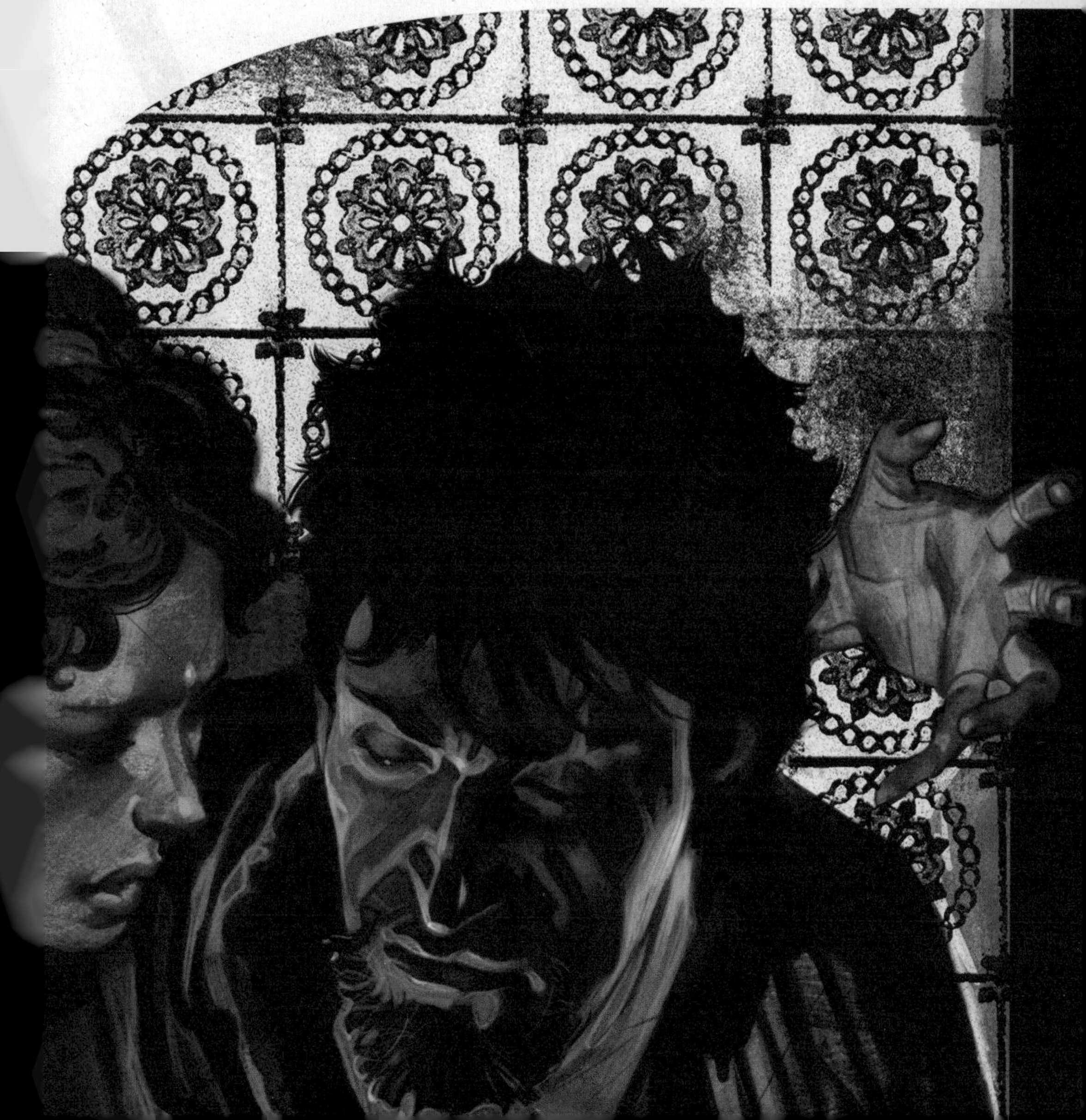

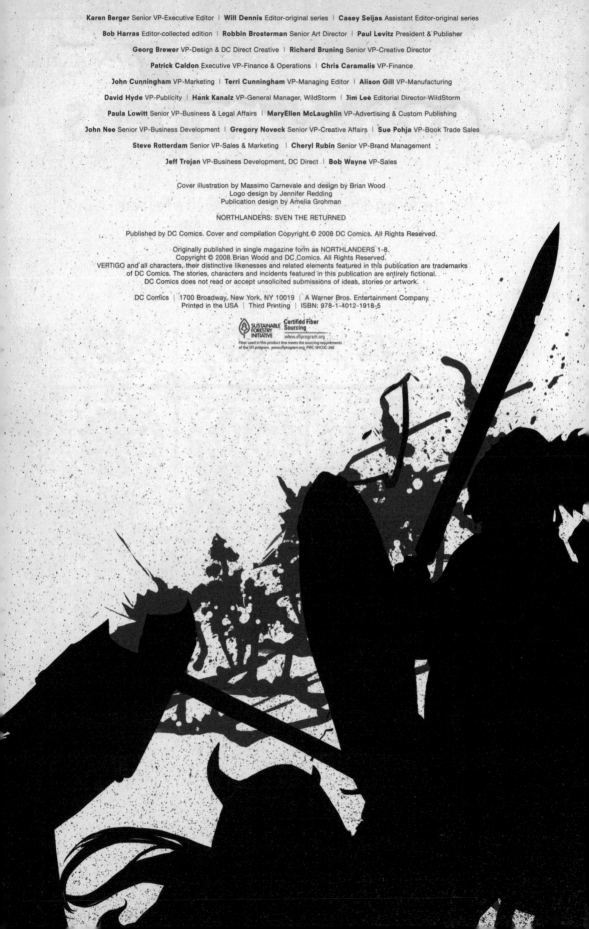

Cover illustration by Massimo Carnevale and design by Brian Wood
Logo design by Jennifer Redding
Publication design by Amelia Grohman

NORTHLANDERS: SVEN THE RETURNED

DC Comics | 1700 Broadway, New York, NY 10019 | A Warner Bros. Entertainment Company
Printed in the USA | Third Printing | ISBN: 978-1-4012-1918-5

SUSTAINABLE FORESTRY INITIATIVE Certified Fiber Sourcing www.sfiprogram.org
Fiber used in this product line meets the sourcing requirements of the SFI program. www.sfiprogram.org PWC-SFICOC-260

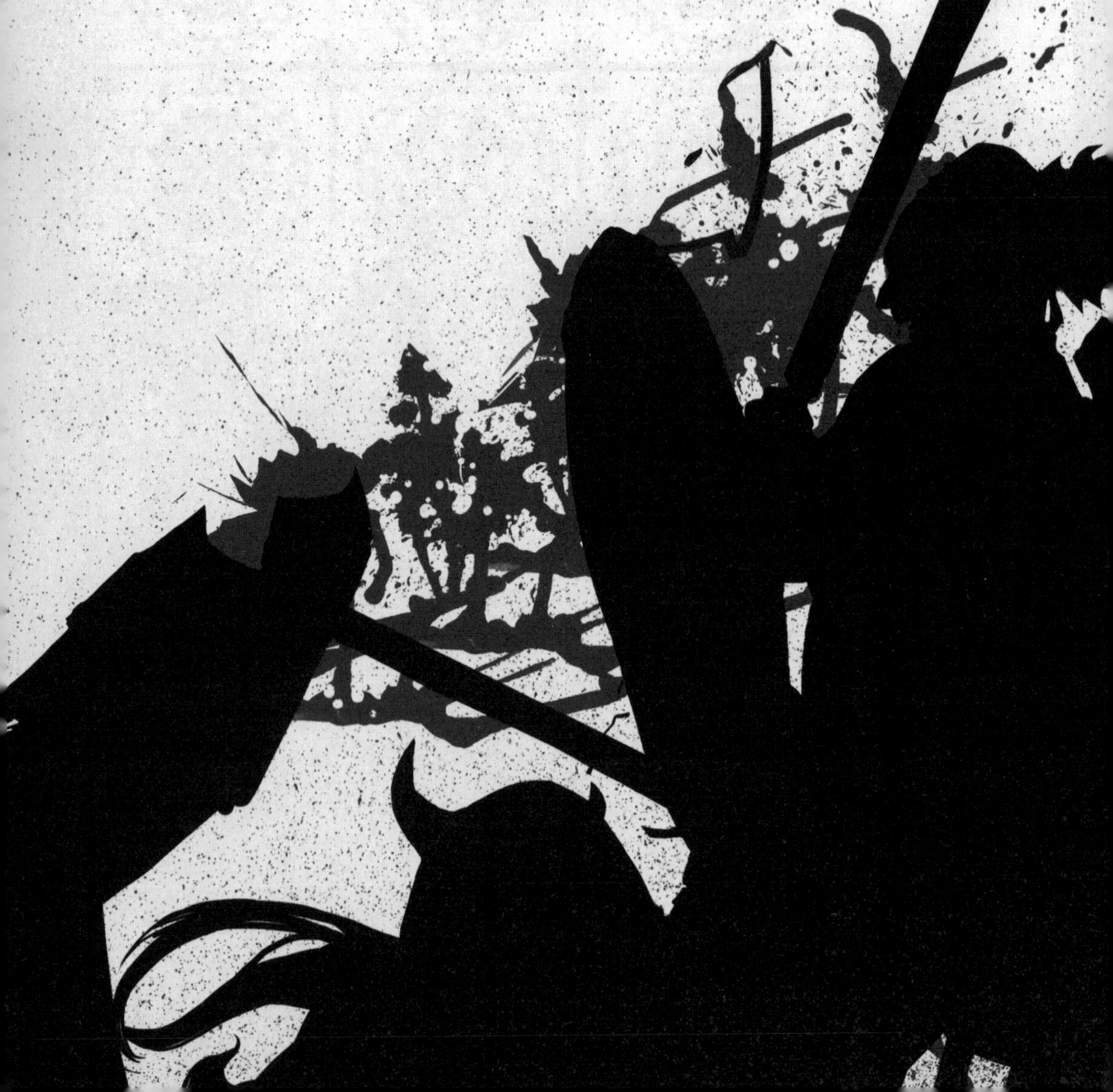

1 As High Summer Passes

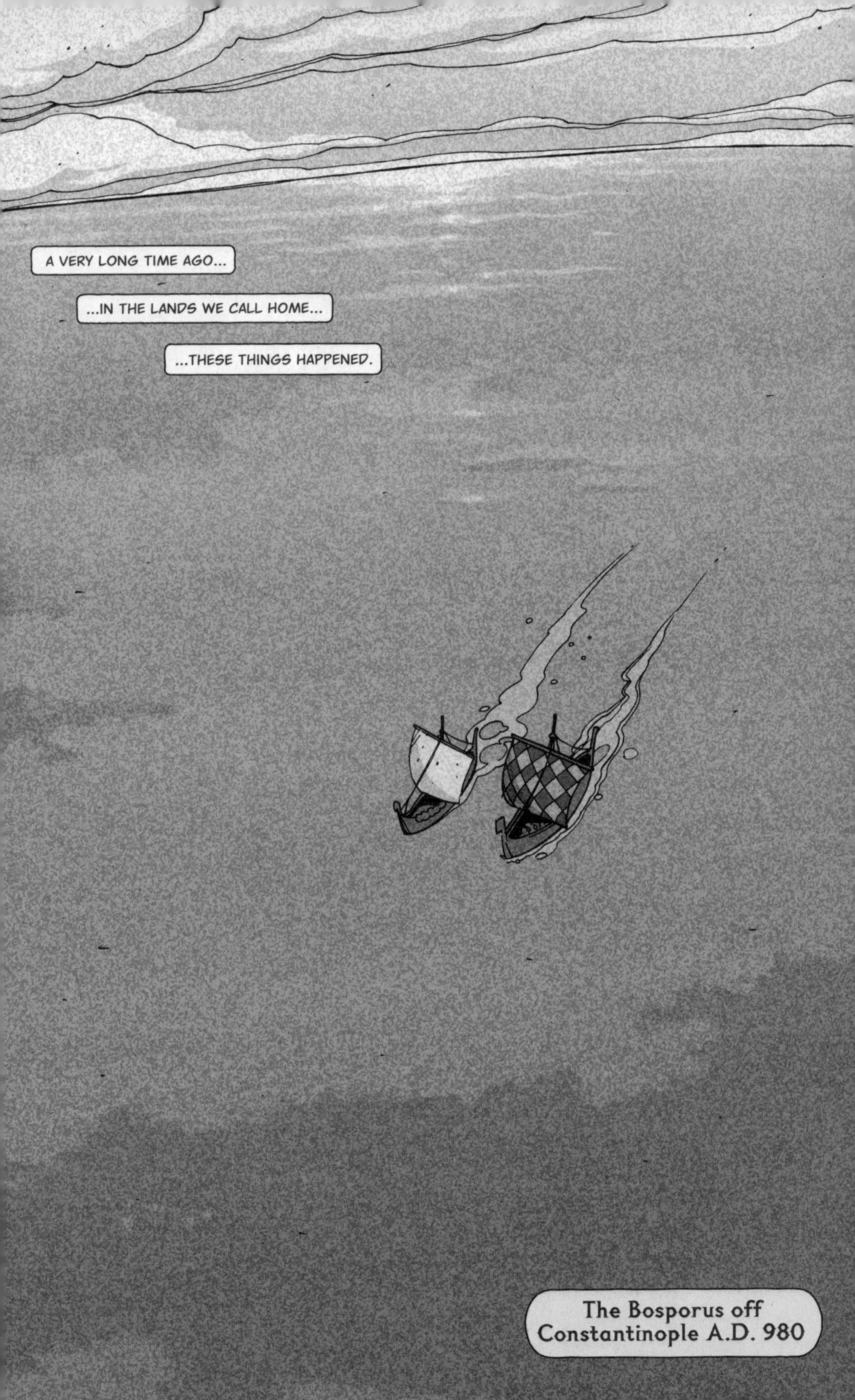
A VERY LONG TIME AGO...
...IN THE LANDS WE CALL HOME...
...THESE THINGS HAPPENED.
The Bosporus off Constantinople A.D. 980

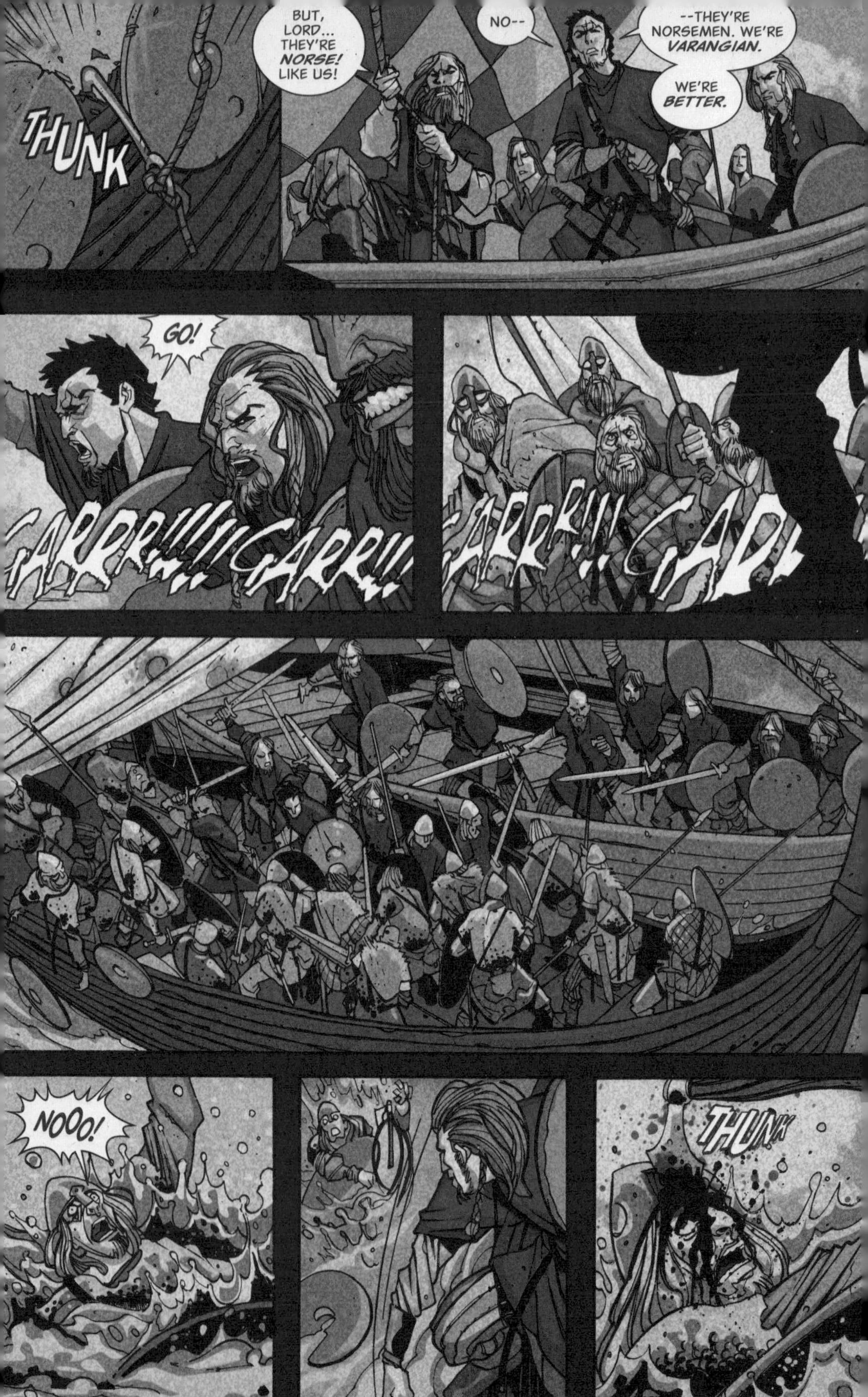
THUNK
BUT, LORD... THEY'RE NORSE! LIKE US!
NO--
--THEY'RE NORSEMEN. WE'RE VARANGIAN.
WE'RE BETTER.
GO!
GARRR!!! GARRR!!!
GARRR!!! GARR
NOOO!
THUNK

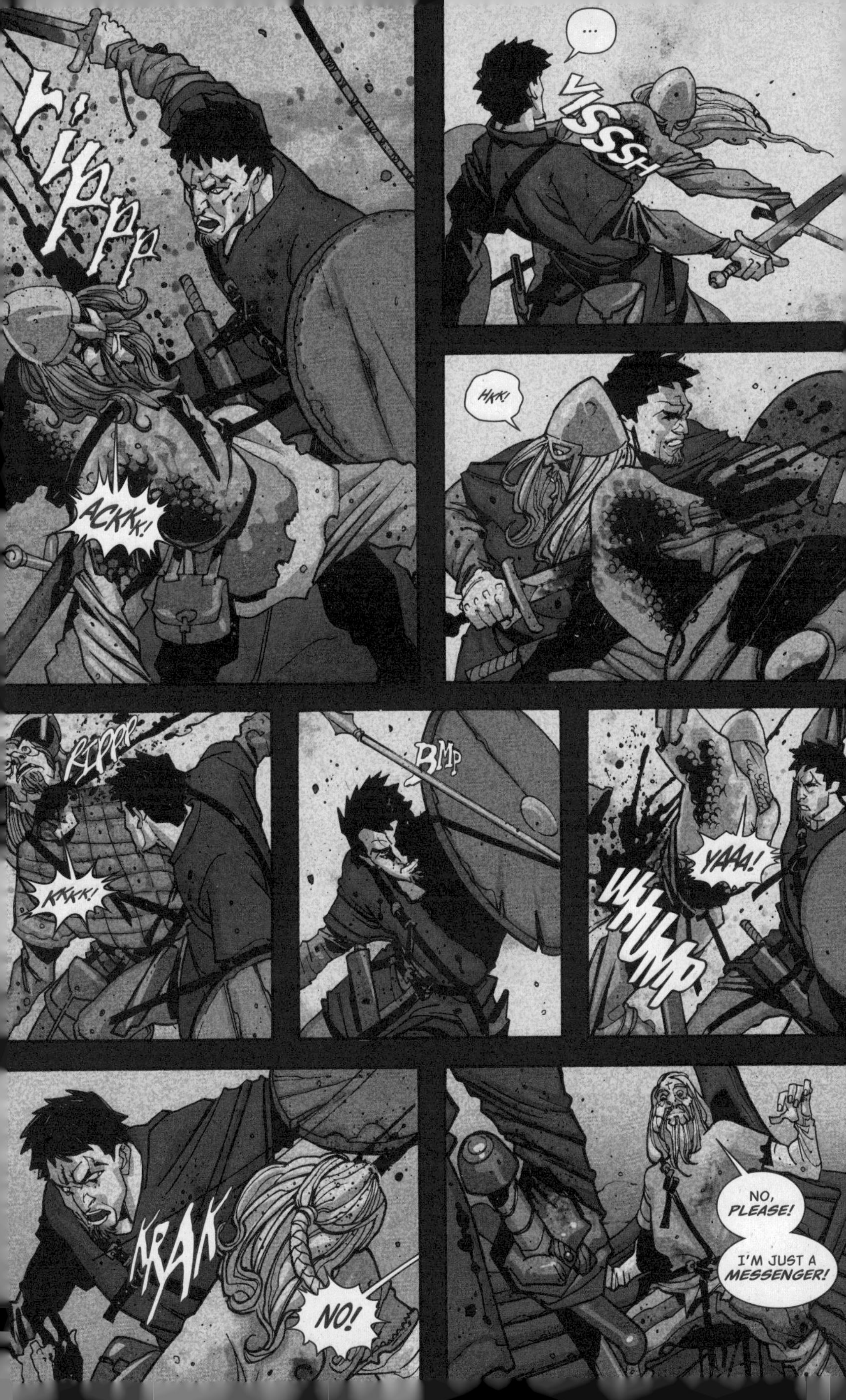

RIPPP
ACKKK!
...
VISSSH
HKK!
RIPPP
KKKK!
BMP
YAAA!
WHUMP
KRAK
NO!
NO, PLEASE!
I'M JUST A MESSENGER!

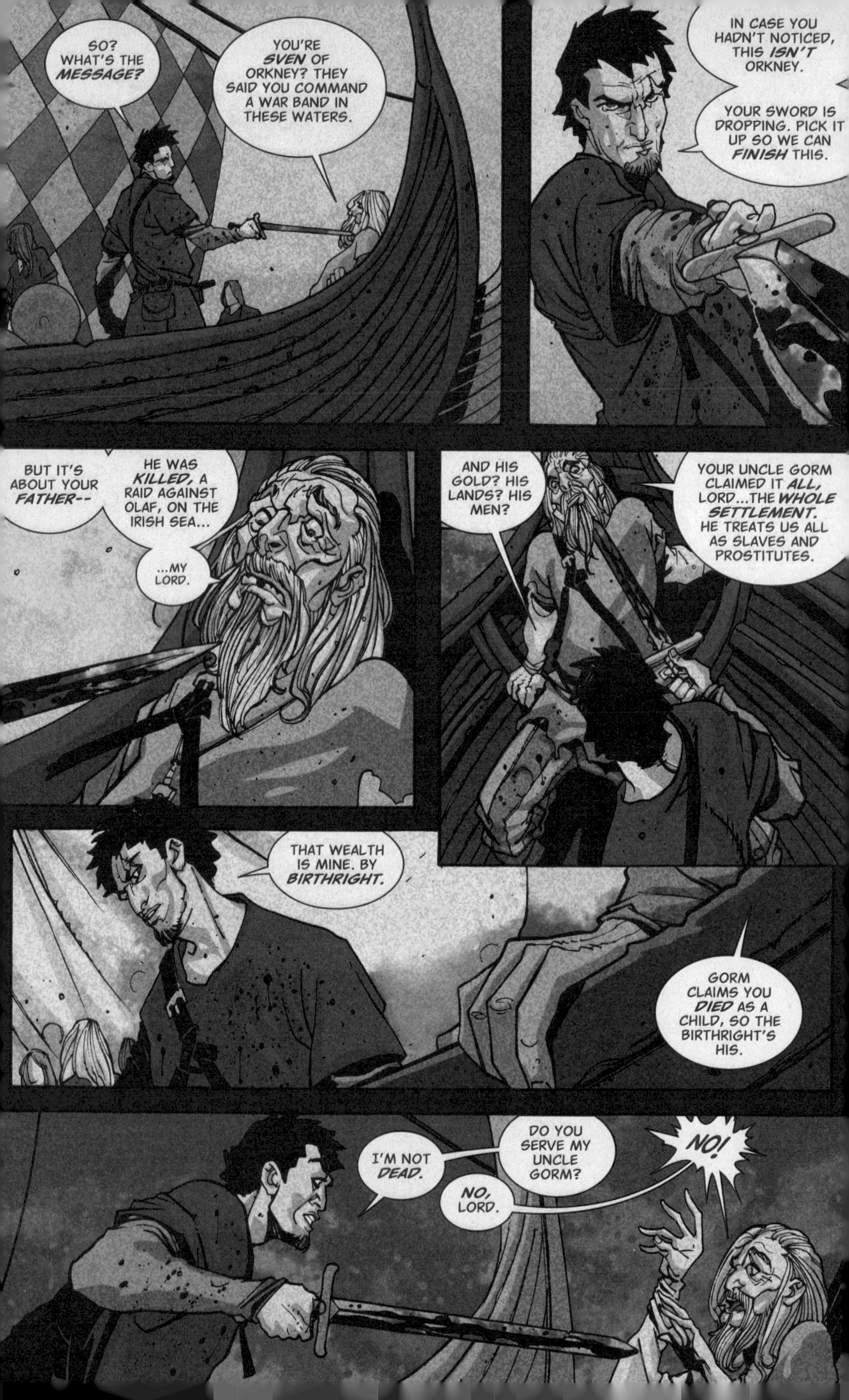
SO? WHAT'S THE *MESSAGE?*
YOU'RE *SVEN* OF ORKNEY? THEY SAID YOU COMMAND A WAR BAND IN THESE WATERS.
IN CASE YOU HADN'T NOTICED, THIS *ISN'T* ORKNEY.
YOUR SWORD IS DROPPING. PICK IT UP SO WE CAN *FINISH* THIS.
BUT IT'S ABOUT YOUR *FATHER--*
HE WAS *KILLED,* A RAID AGAINST OLAF, ON THE IRISH SEA...
...MY LORD.
AND HIS GOLD? HIS LANDS? HIS MEN?
YOUR UNCLE GORM CLAIMED IT *ALL,* LORD...THE *WHOLE SETTLEMENT.* HE TREATS US ALL AS SLAVES AND PROSTITUTES.
THAT WEALTH IS MINE. BY *BIRTHRIGHT.*
GORM CLAIMS YOU *DIED* AS A CHILD, SO THE BIRTHRIGHT'S HIS.
I'M NOT *DEAD.*
DO YOU SERVE MY UNCLE GORM?
NO, LORD.
NO!

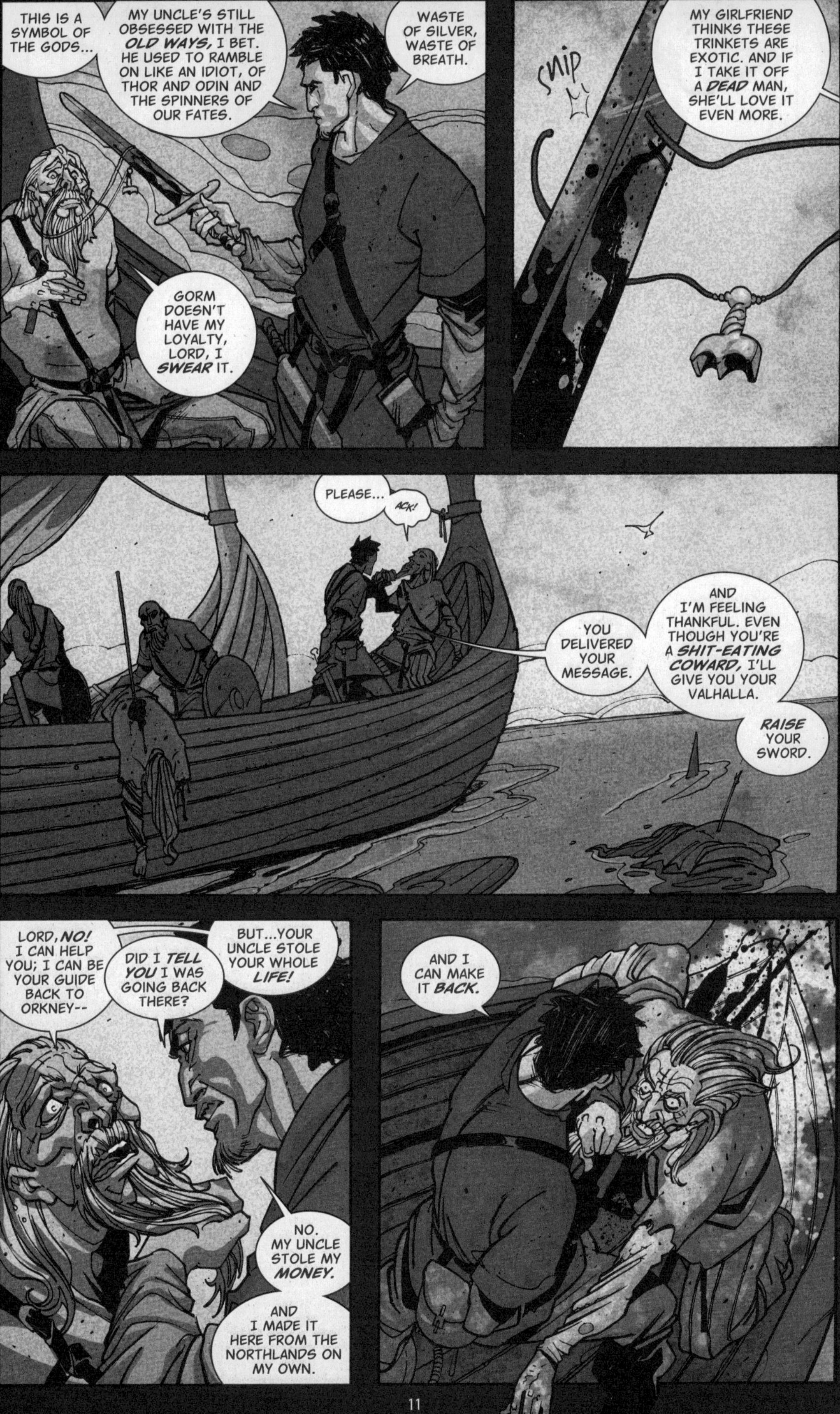
THIS IS A SYMBOL OF THE GODS...
MY UNCLE'S STILL OBSESSED WITH THE OLD WAYS, I BET. HE USED TO RAMBLE ON LIKE AN IDIOT, OF THOR AND ODIN AND THE SPINNERS OF OUR FATES.
WASTE OF SILVER, WASTE OF BREATH.
GORM DOESN'T HAVE MY LOYALTY, LORD, I SWEAR IT.
SNIP
MY GIRLFRIEND THINKS THESE TRINKETS ARE EXOTIC. AND IF I TAKE IT OFF A DEAD MAN, SHE'LL LOVE IT EVEN MORE.
PLEASE...
ACK!
YOU DELIVERED YOUR MESSAGE.
AND I'M FEELING THANKFUL. EVEN THOUGH YOU'RE A SHIT-EATING COWARD, I'LL GIVE YOU YOUR VALHALLA.
RAISE YOUR SWORD.
LORD, NO! I CAN HELP YOU; I CAN BE YOUR GUIDE BACK TO ORKNEY--
DID I TELL YOU I WAS GOING BACK THERE?
BUT...YOUR UNCLE STOLE YOUR WHOLE LIFE!
NO. MY UNCLE STOLE MY MONEY.
AND I MADE IT HERE FROM THE NORTHLANDS ON MY OWN.
AND I CAN MAKE IT BACK.

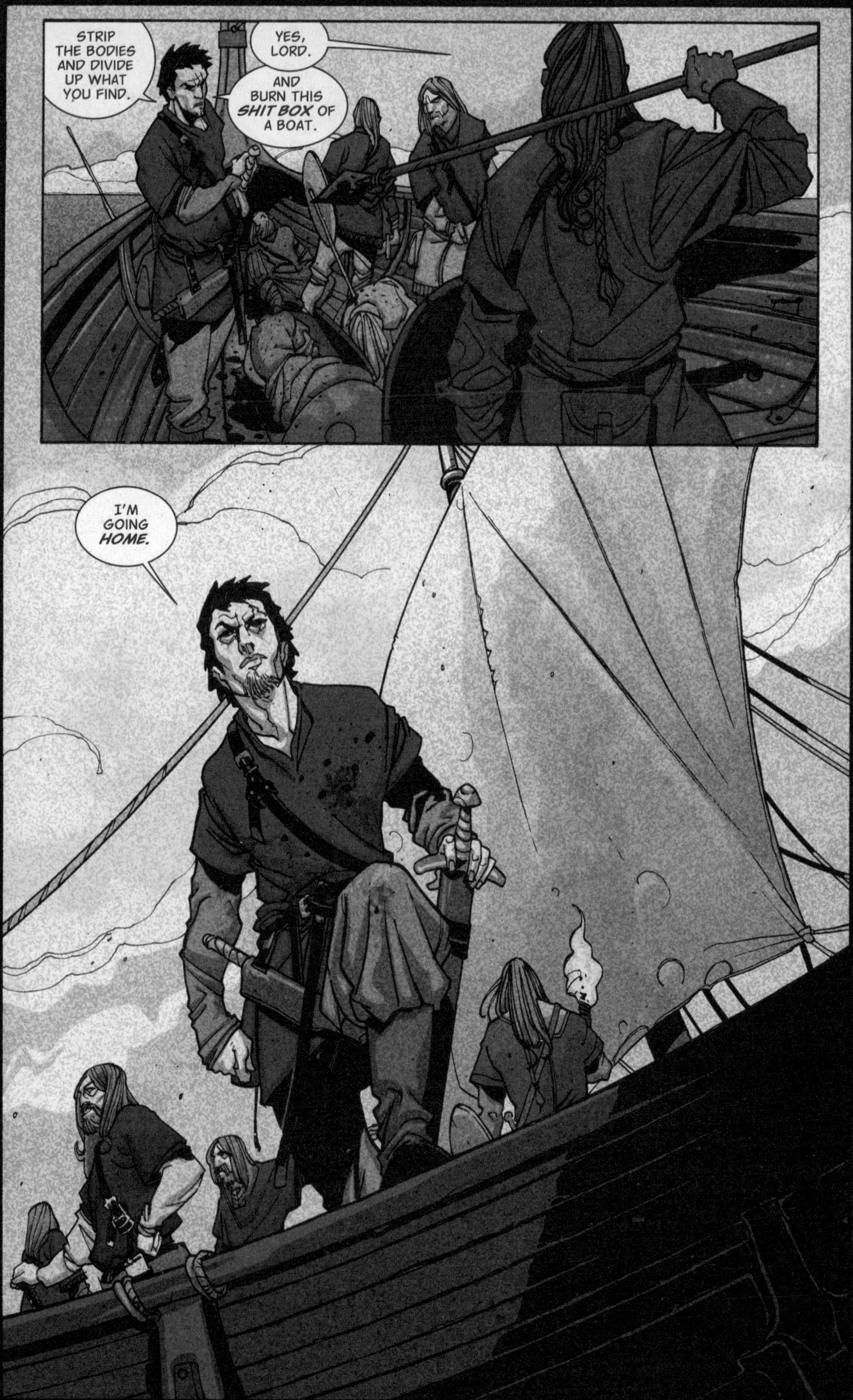
STRIP THE BODIES AND DIVIDE UP WHAT YOU FIND.
YES, LORD.
AND BURN THIS SHIT BOX OF A BOAT.
I'M GOING HOME.

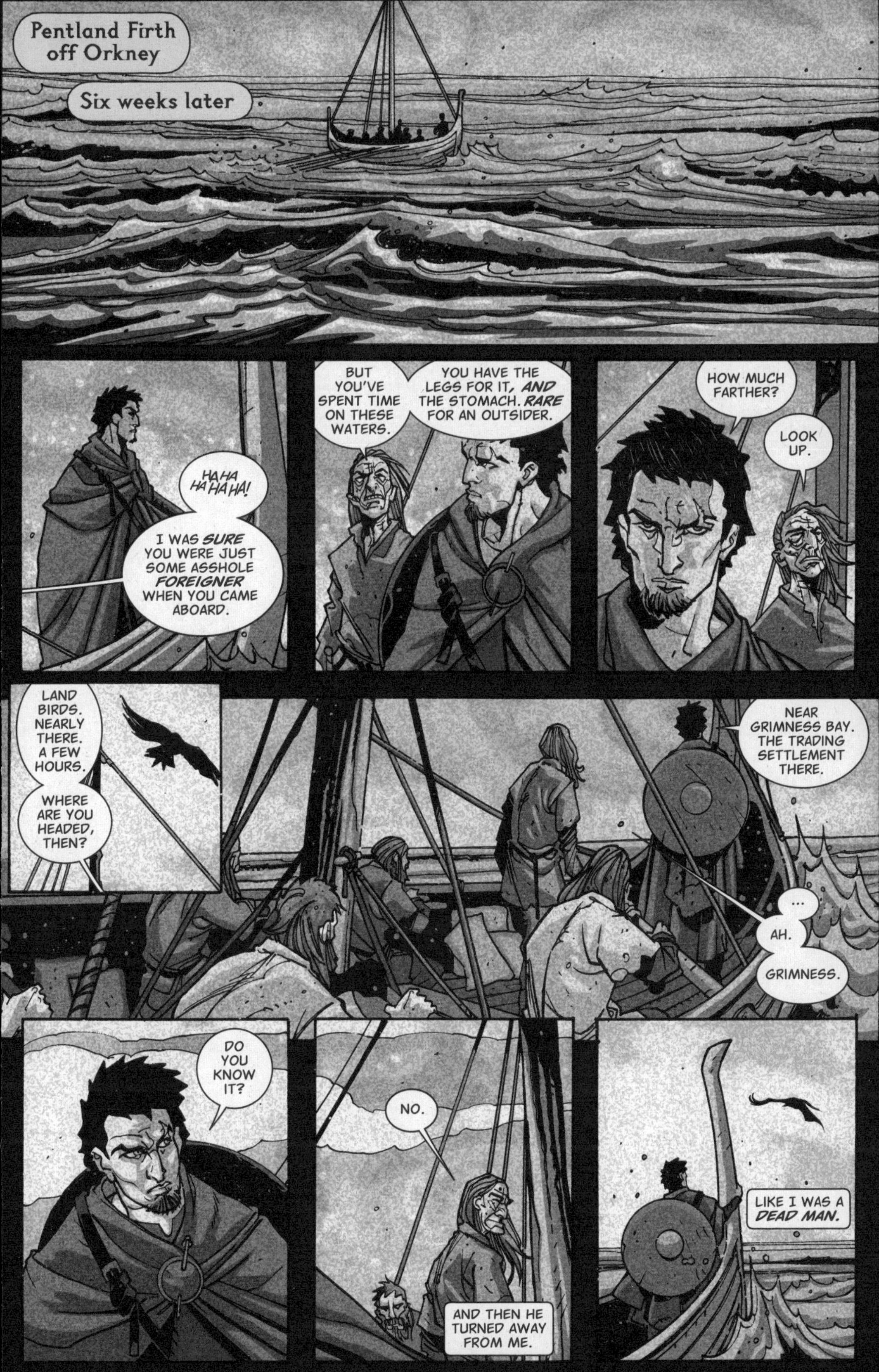
Pentland Firth off Orkney
Six weeks later
HA HA HA HA!
I WAS SURE YOU WERE JUST SOME ASSHOLE FOREIGNER WHEN YOU CAME ABOARD.
BUT YOU'VE SPENT TIME ON THESE WATERS.
YOU HAVE THE LEGS FOR IT, AND THE STOMACH. RARE FOR AN OUTSIDER.
HOW MUCH FARTHER?
LOOK UP.
LAND BIRDS. NEARLY THERE. A FEW HOURS.
WHERE ARE YOU HEADED, THEN?
NEAR GRIMNESS BAY. THE TRADING SETTLEMENT THERE.
...
AH.
GRIMNESS.
DO YOU KNOW IT?
NO.
AND THEN HE TURNED AWAY FROM ME.
LIKE I WAS A DEAD MAN.

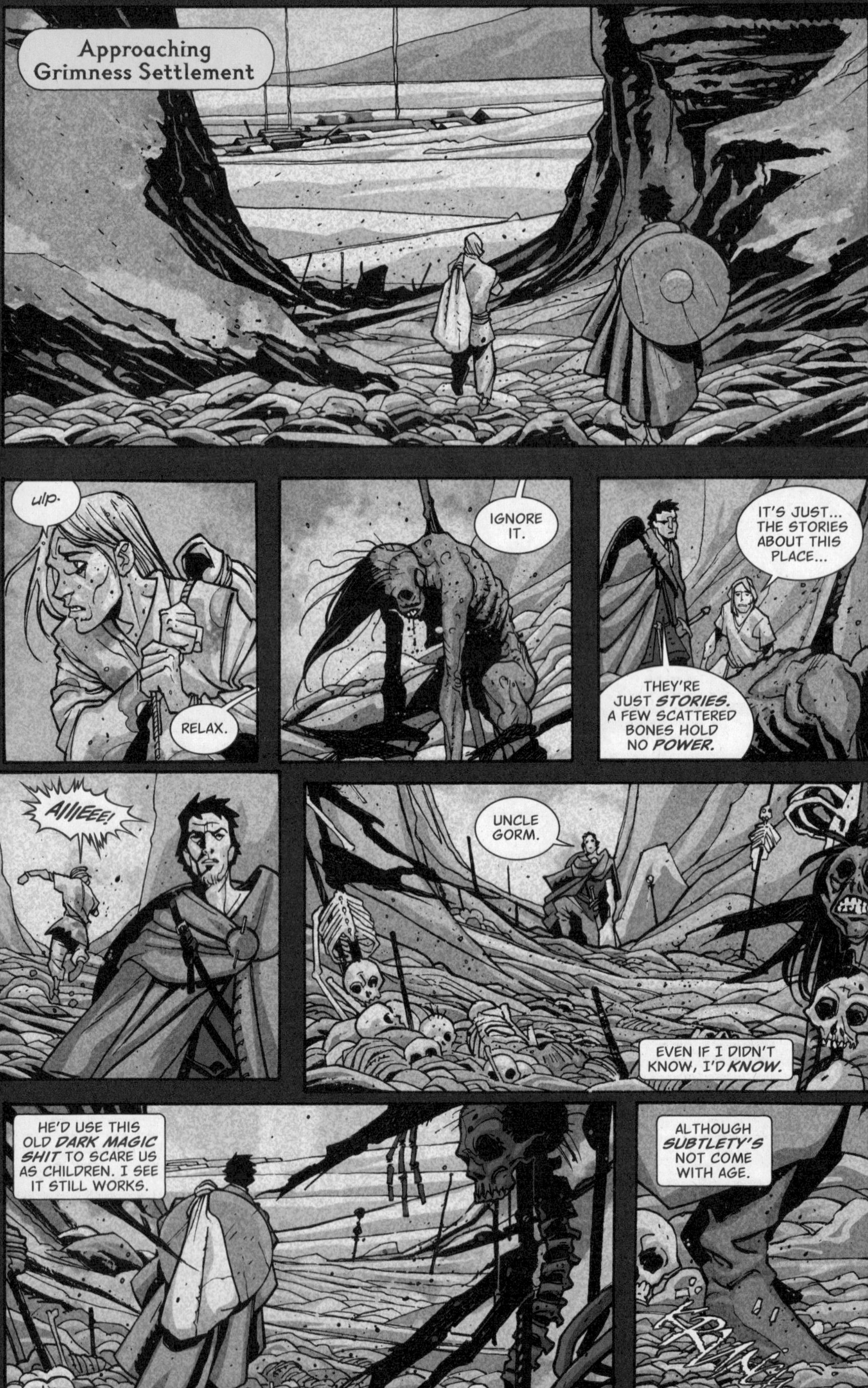
Approaching Grimness Settlement
ulp.
RELAX.
IGNORE IT.
IT'S JUST... THE STORIES ABOUT THIS PLACE...
THEY'RE JUST STORIES. A FEW SCATTERED BONES HOLD NO POWER.
AIIIEEE!
UNCLE GORM.
EVEN IF I DIDN'T KNOW, I'D KNOW.
HE'D USE THIS OLD DARK MAGIC SHIT TO SCARE US AS CHILDREN. I SEE IT STILL WORKS.
ALTHOUGH SUBTLETY'S NOT COME WITH AGE.

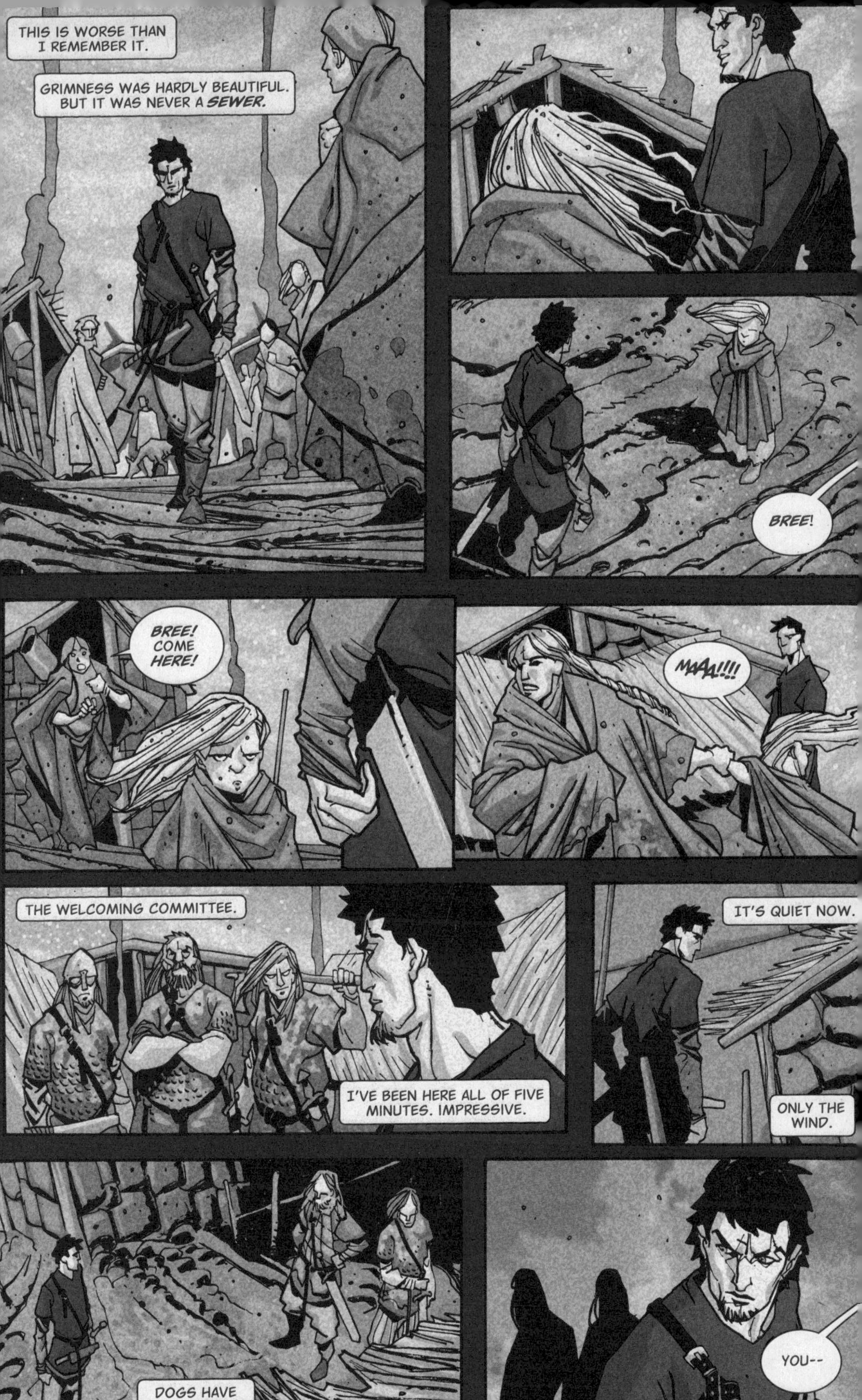

THIS IS WORSE THAN I REMEMBER IT.
GRIMNESS WAS HARDLY BEAUTIFUL. BUT IT WAS NEVER A *SEWER.*
BREE!
BREE! COME HERE!
MAAA!!!!
THE WELCOMING COMMITTEE.
I'VE BEEN HERE ALL OF FIVE MINUTES. IMPRESSIVE.
IT'S QUIET NOW.
ONLY THE WIND.
DOGS HAVE EVEN STOPPED BARKING.
YOU--

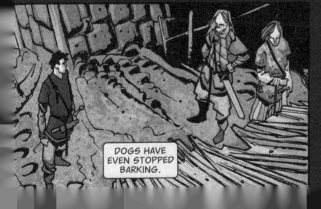

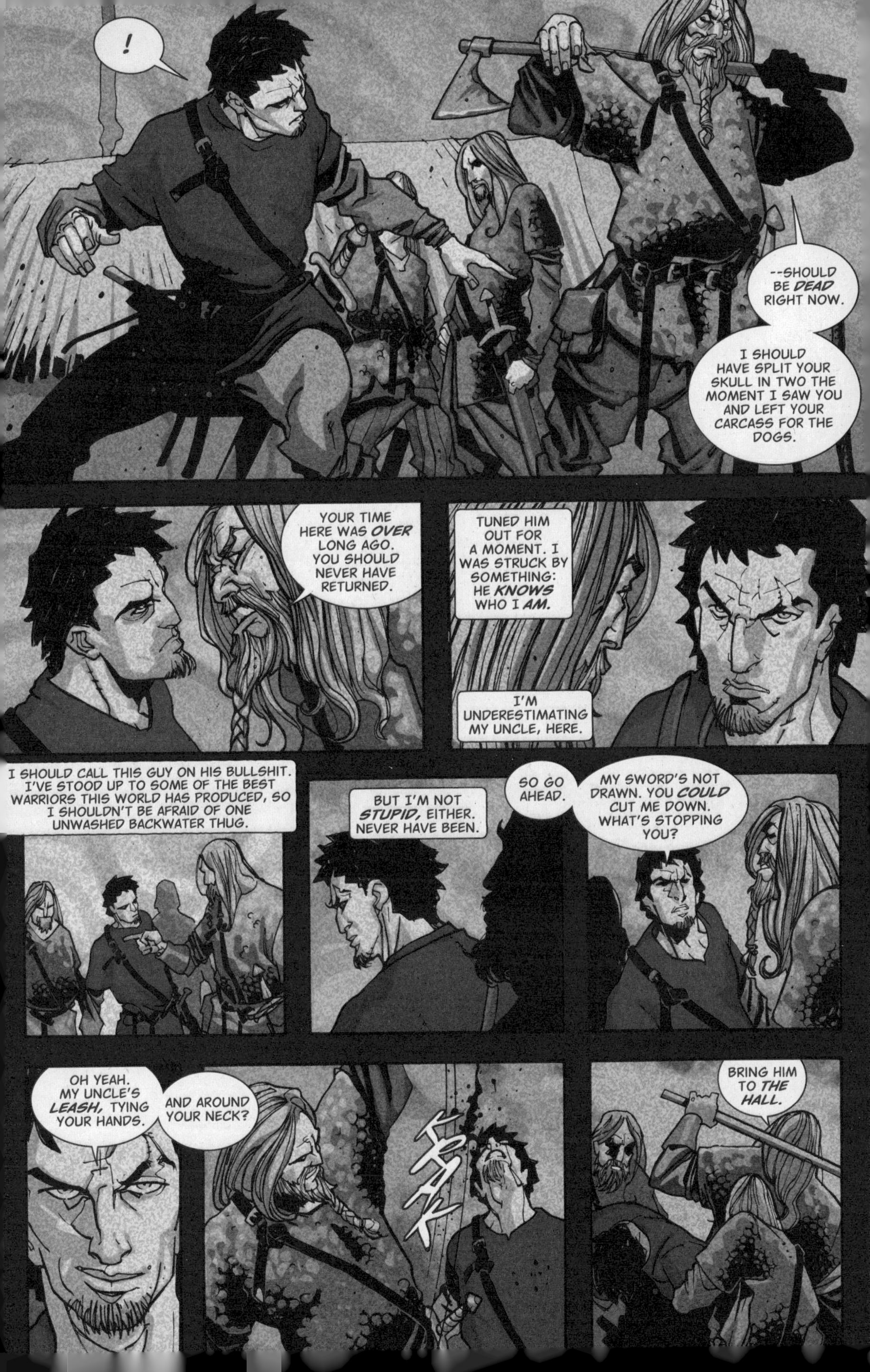
!
--SHOULD BE DEAD RIGHT NOW.
I SHOULD HAVE SPLIT YOUR SKULL IN TWO THE MOMENT I SAW YOU AND LEFT YOUR CARCASS FOR THE DOGS.
YOUR TIME HERE WAS OVER LONG AGO. YOU SHOULD NEVER HAVE RETURNED.
TUNED HIM OUT FOR A MOMENT. I WAS STRUCK BY SOMETHING: HE KNOWS WHO I AM.
I'M UNDERESTIMATING MY UNCLE, HERE.
I SHOULD CALL THIS GUY ON HIS BULLSHIT. I'VE STOOD UP TO SOME OF THE BEST WARRIORS THIS WORLD HAS PRODUCED, SO I SHOULDN'T BE AFRAID OF ONE UNWASHED BACKWATER THUG.
BUT I'M NOT STUPID, EITHER. NEVER HAVE BEEN.
SO GO AHEAD.
MY SWORD'S NOT DRAWN. YOU COULD CUT ME DOWN. WHAT'S STOPPING YOU?
OH YEAH. MY UNCLE'S LEASH, TYING YOUR HANDS.
AND AROUND YOUR NECK?
KRAK
BRING HIM TO THE HALL.

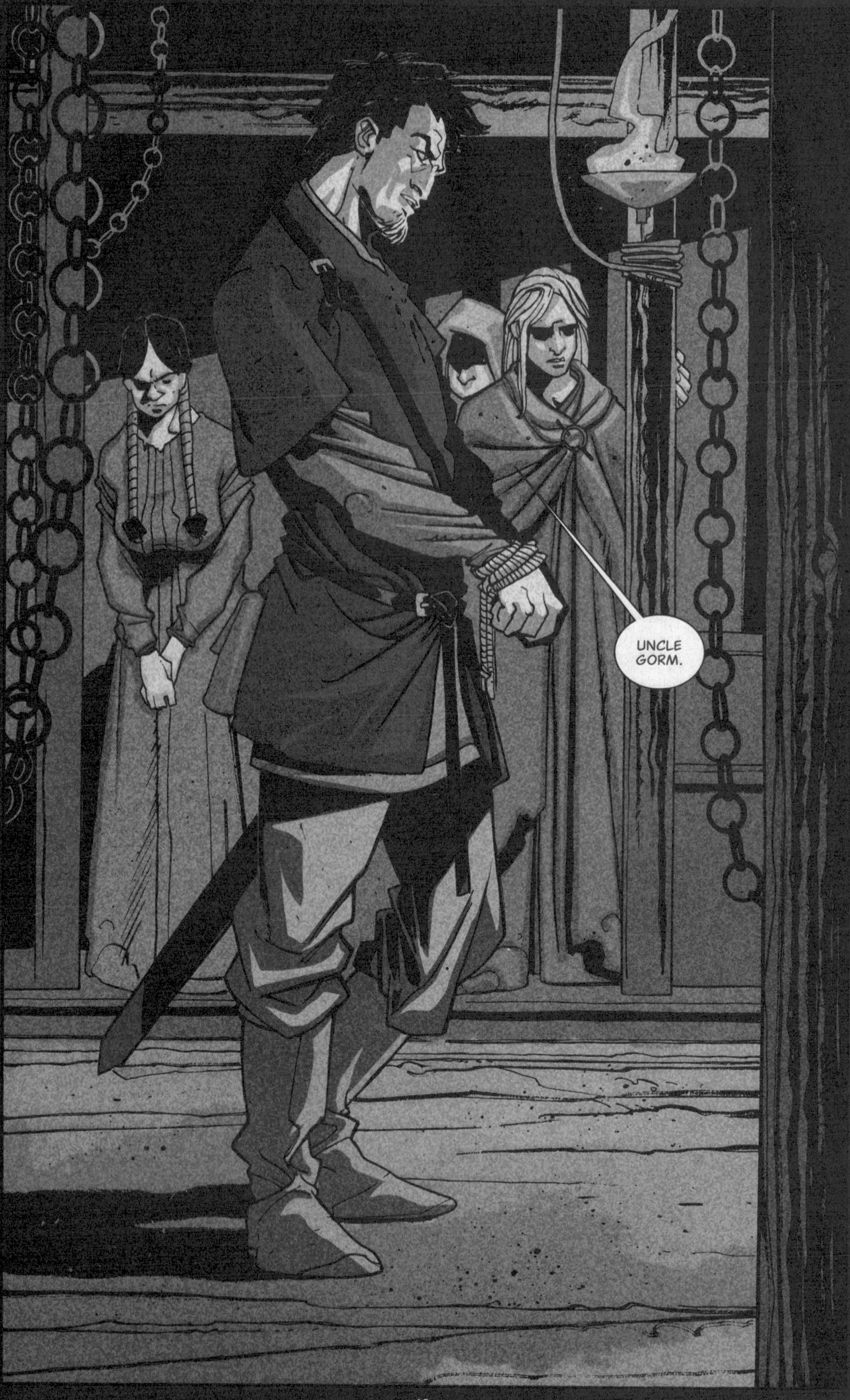
UNCLE GORM.

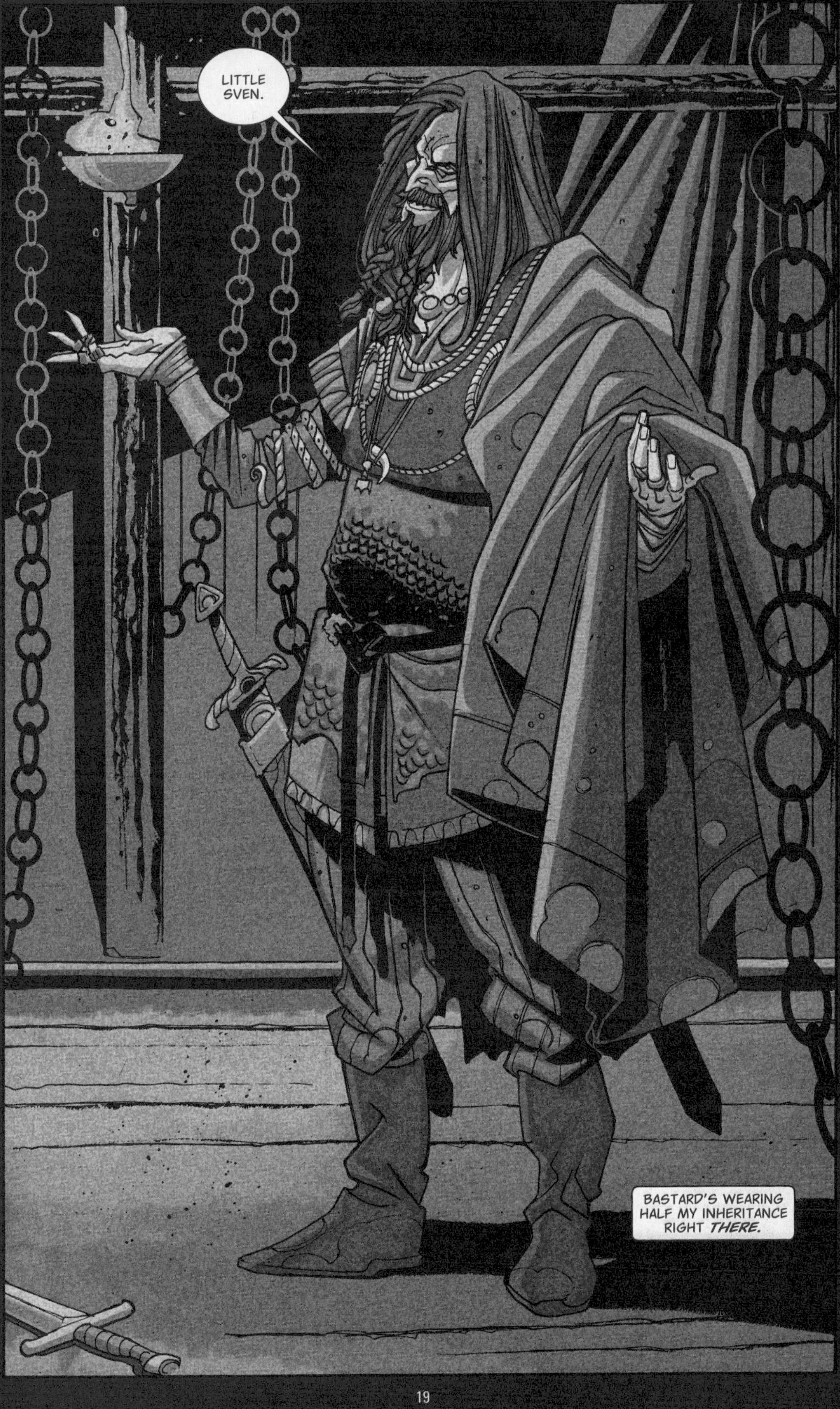
LITTLE SVEN.
BASTARD'S WEARING HALF MY INHERITANCE RIGHT *THERE.*

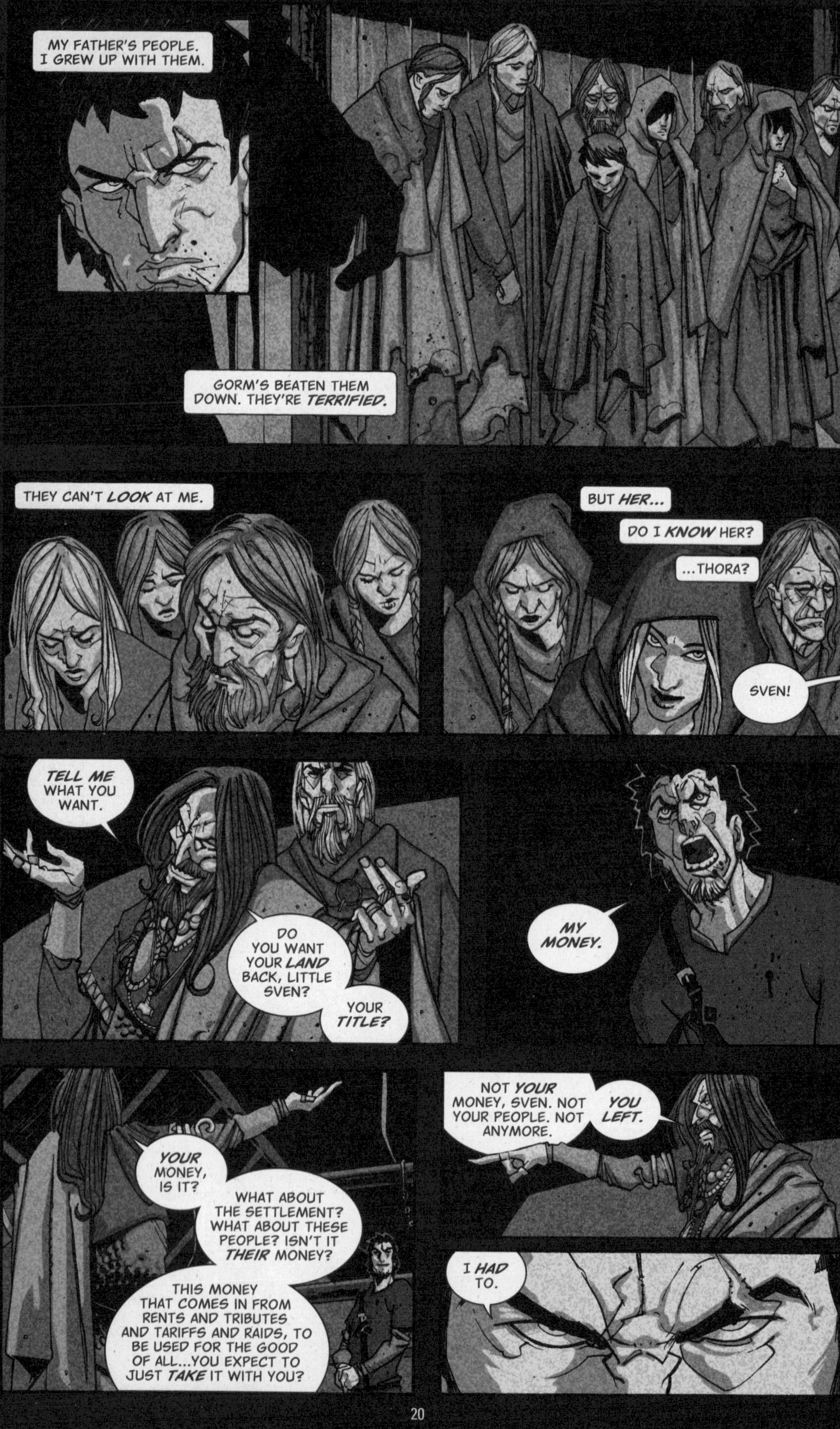
MY FATHER'S PEOPLE. I GREW UP WITH THEM.
GORM'S BEATEN THEM DOWN. THEY'RE TERRIFIED.
THEY CAN'T LOOK AT ME.
BUT HER...
DO I KNOW HER?
...THORA?
SVEN!
TELL ME WHAT YOU WANT.
DO YOU WANT YOUR LAND BACK, LITTLE SVEN?
YOUR TITLE?
MY MONEY.
YOUR MONEY, IS IT?
WHAT ABOUT THE SETTLEMENT? WHAT ABOUT THESE PEOPLE? ISN'T IT THEIR MONEY?
THIS MONEY THAT COMES IN FROM RENTS AND TRIBUTES AND TARIFFS AND RAIDS, TO BE USED FOR THE GOOD OF ALL...YOU EXPECT TO JUST TAKE IT WITH YOU?
NOT YOUR MONEY, SVEN. NOT YOUR PEOPLE. NOT ANYMORE.
YOU LEFT.
I HAD TO.

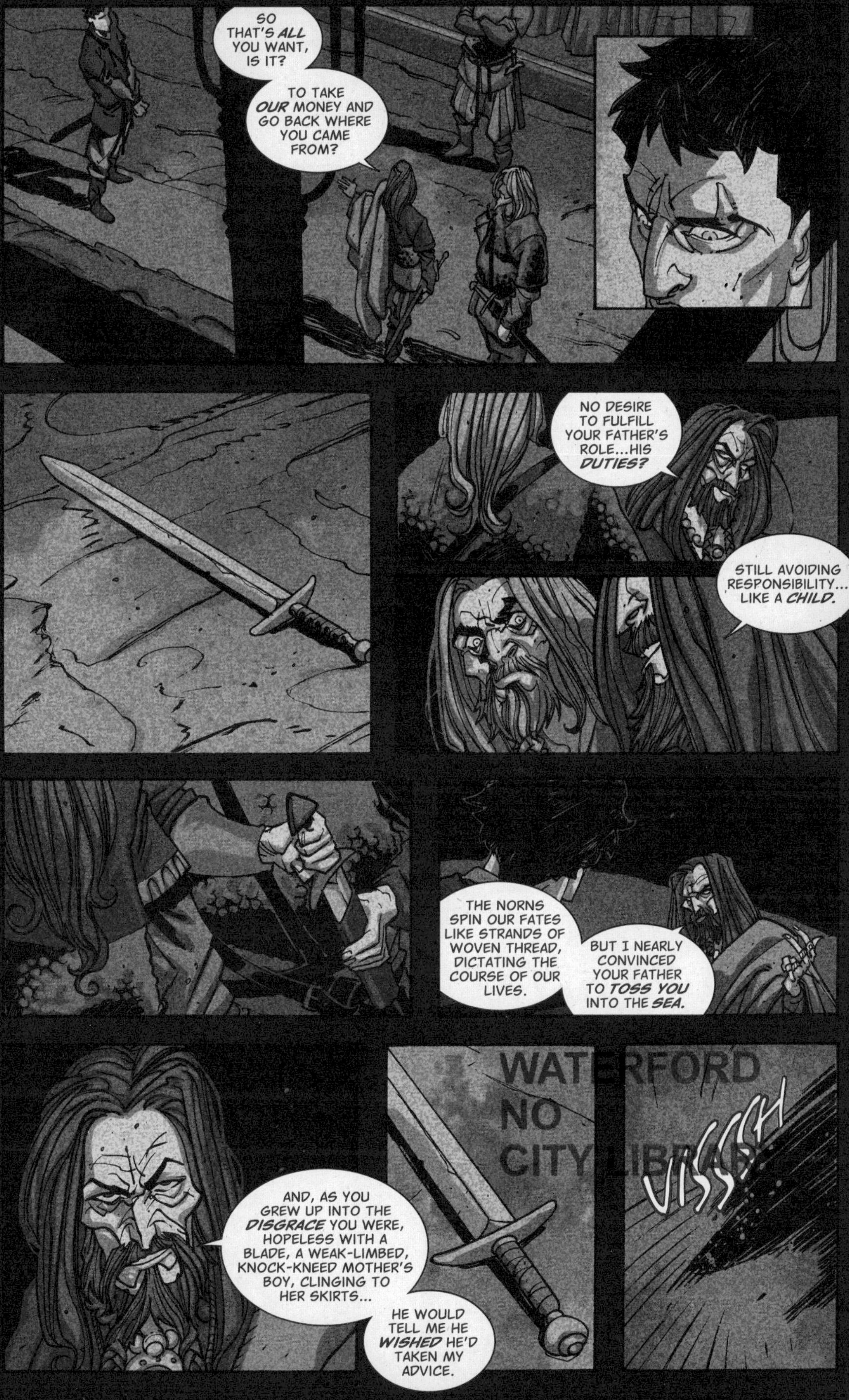
SO THAT'S ALL YOU WANT, IS IT?
TO TAKE OUR MONEY AND GO BACK WHERE YOU CAME FROM?
NO DESIRE TO FULFILL YOUR FATHER'S ROLE...HIS DUTIES?
STILL AVOIDING RESPONSIBILITY... LIKE A CHILD.
THE NORNS SPIN OUR FATES LIKE STRANDS OF WOVEN THREAD, DICTATING THE COURSE OF OUR LIVES.
BUT I NEARLY CONVINCED YOUR FATHER TO TOSS YOU INTO THE SEA.
AND, AS YOU GREW UP INTO THE DISGRACE YOU WERE, HOPELESS WITH A BLADE, A WEAK-LIMBED, KNOCK-KNEED MOTHER'S BOY, CLINGING TO HER SKIRTS...
HE WOULD TELL ME HE WISHED HE'D TAKEN MY ADVICE.

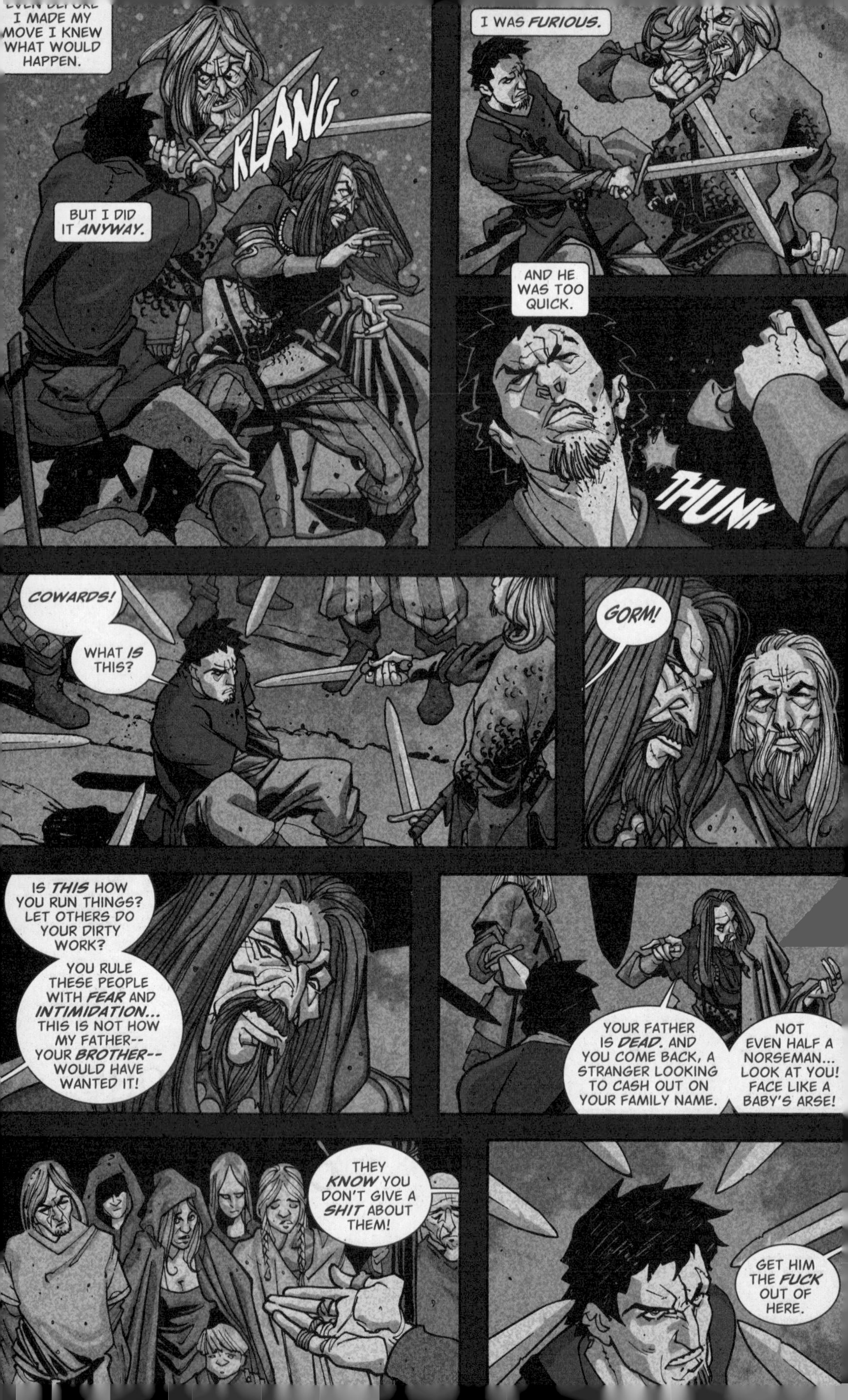
I MADE MY MOVE I KNEW WHAT WOULD HAPPEN.
KLANG
BUT I DID IT ANYWAY.
I WAS FURIOUS.
AND HE WAS TOO QUICK.
THUNK
COWARDS!
WHAT IS THIS?
GORM!
IS THIS HOW YOU RUN THINGS? LET OTHERS DO YOUR DIRTY WORK?
YOU RULE THESE PEOPLE WITH FEAR AND INTIMIDATION... THIS IS NOT HOW MY FATHER-- YOUR BROTHER-- WOULD HAVE WANTED IT!
YOUR FATHER IS DEAD. AND YOU COME BACK, A STRANGER LOOKING TO CASH OUT ON YOUR FAMILY NAME.
NOT EVEN HALF A NORSEMAN... LOOK AT YOU! FACE LIKE A BABY'S ARSE!
THEY KNOW YOU DON'T GIVE A SHIT ABOUT THEM!
GET HIM THE FUCK OUT OF HERE.

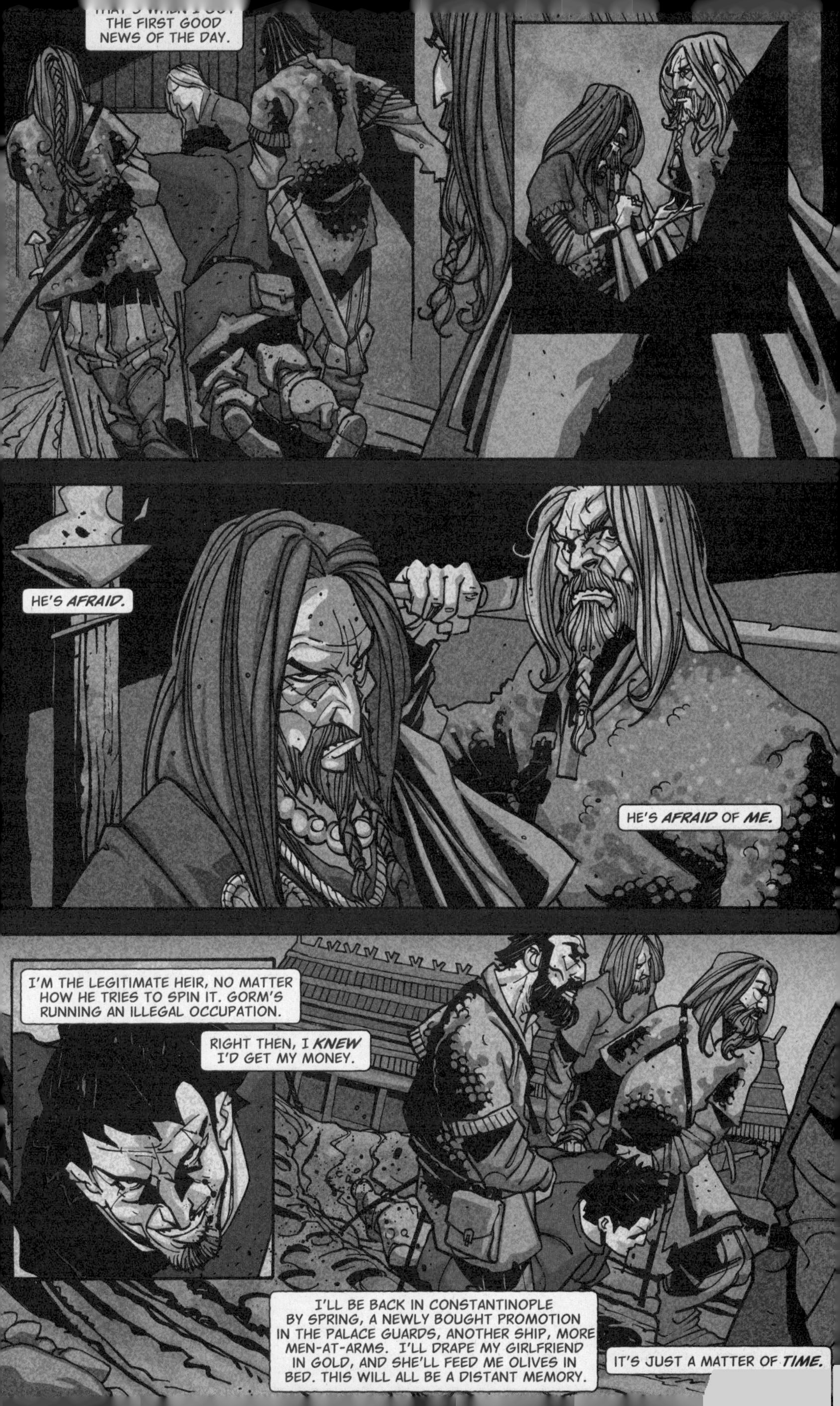

THE FIRST GOOD NEWS OF THE DAY.
HE'S AFRAID.
HE'S AFRAID OF ME.
I'M THE LEGITIMATE HEIR, NO MATTER HOW HE TRIES TO SPIN IT. GORM'S RUNNING AN ILLEGAL OCCUPATION.
RIGHT THEN, I KNEW I'D GET MY MONEY.
I'LL BE BACK IN CONSTANTINOPLE BY SPRING, A NEWLY BOUGHT PROMOTION IN THE PALACE GUARDS, ANOTHER SHIP, MORE MEN-AT-ARMS. I'LL DRAPE MY GIRLFRIEND IN GOLD, AND SHE'LL FEED ME OLIVES IN BED. THIS WILL ALL BE A DISTANT MEMORY.
IT'S JUST A MATTER OF TIME.

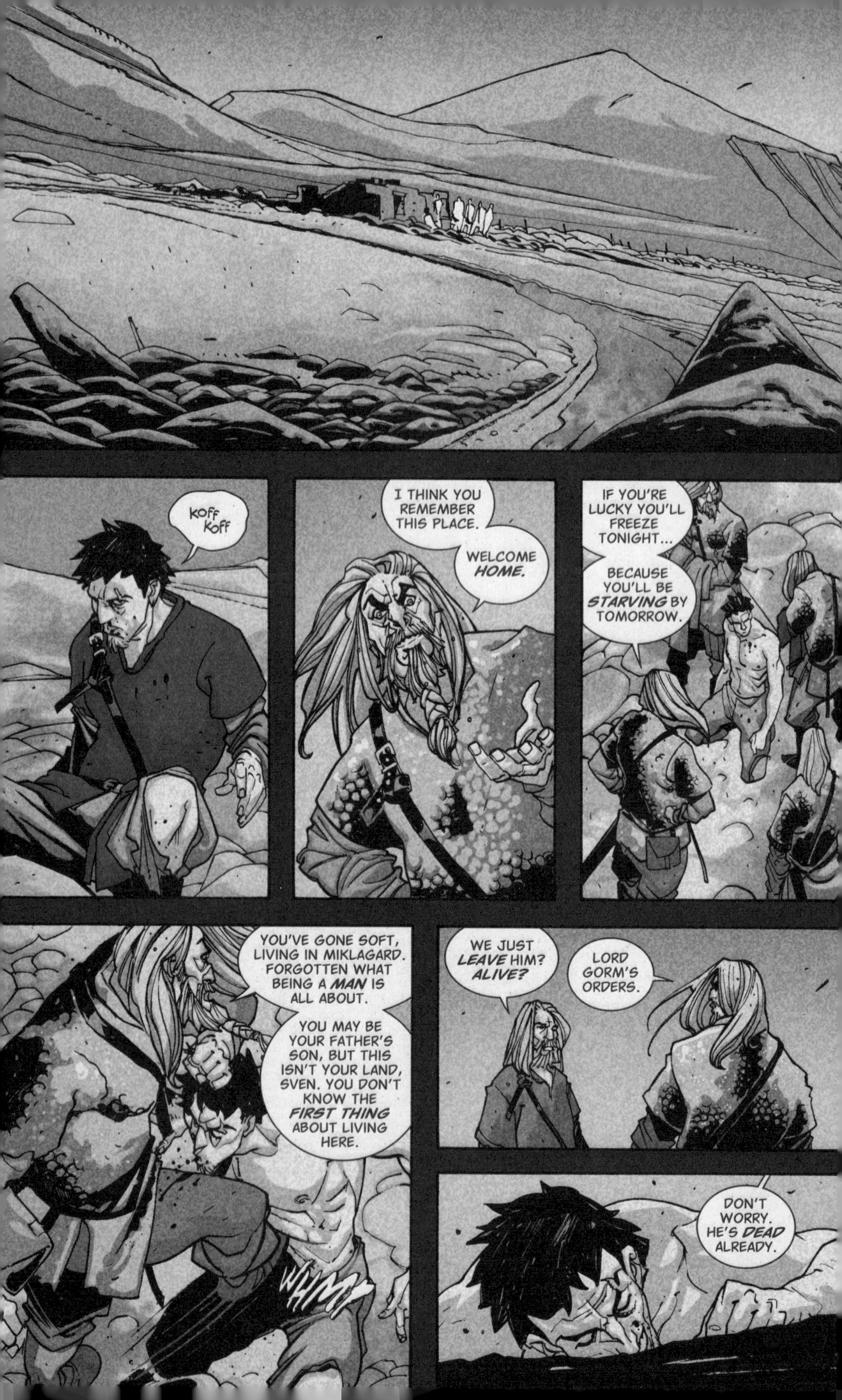
KOFF KOFF
I THINK YOU REMEMBER THIS PLACE.
WELCOME HOME.
IF YOU'RE LUCKY YOU'LL FREEZE TONIGHT...
BECAUSE YOU'LL BE STARVING BY TOMORROW.
YOU'VE GONE SOFT, LIVING IN MIKLAGARD. FORGOTTEN WHAT BEING A MAN IS ALL ABOUT.
YOU MAY BE YOUR FATHER'S SON, BUT THIS ISN'T YOUR LAND, SVEN. YOU DON'T KNOW THE FIRST THING ABOUT LIVING HERE.
WHUMP
WE JUST LEAVE HIM? ALIVE?
LORD GORM'S ORDERS.
DON'T WORRY. HE'S DEAD ALREADY.

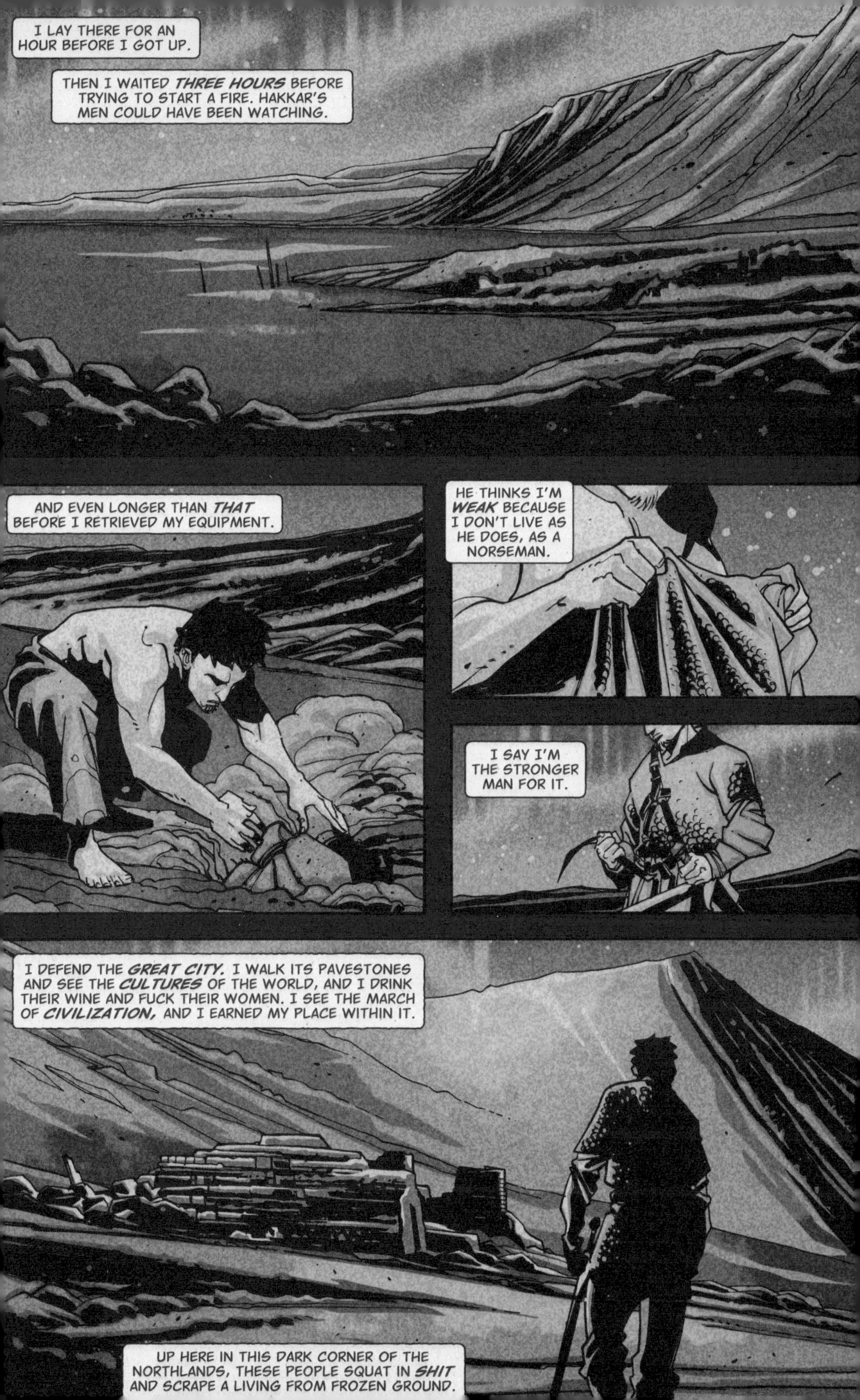
I LAY THERE FOR AN HOUR BEFORE I GOT UP.
THEN I WAITED THREE HOURS BEFORE TRYING TO START A FIRE. HAKKAR'S MEN COULD HAVE BEEN WATCHING.
AND EVEN LONGER THAN THAT BEFORE I RETRIEVED MY EQUIPMENT.
HE THINKS I'M WEAK BECAUSE I DON'T LIVE AS HE DOES, AS A NORSEMAN.
I SAY I'M THE STRONGER MAN FOR IT.
I DEFEND THE GREAT CITY. I WALK ITS PAVESTONES AND SEE THE CULTURES OF THE WORLD, AND I DRINK THEIR WINE AND FUCK THEIR WOMEN. I SEE THE MARCH OF CIVILIZATION, AND I EARNED MY PLACE WITHIN IT.
UP HERE IN THIS DARK CORNER OF THE NORTHLANDS, THESE PEOPLE SQUAT IN SHIT AND SCRAPE A LIVING FROM FROZEN GROUND.

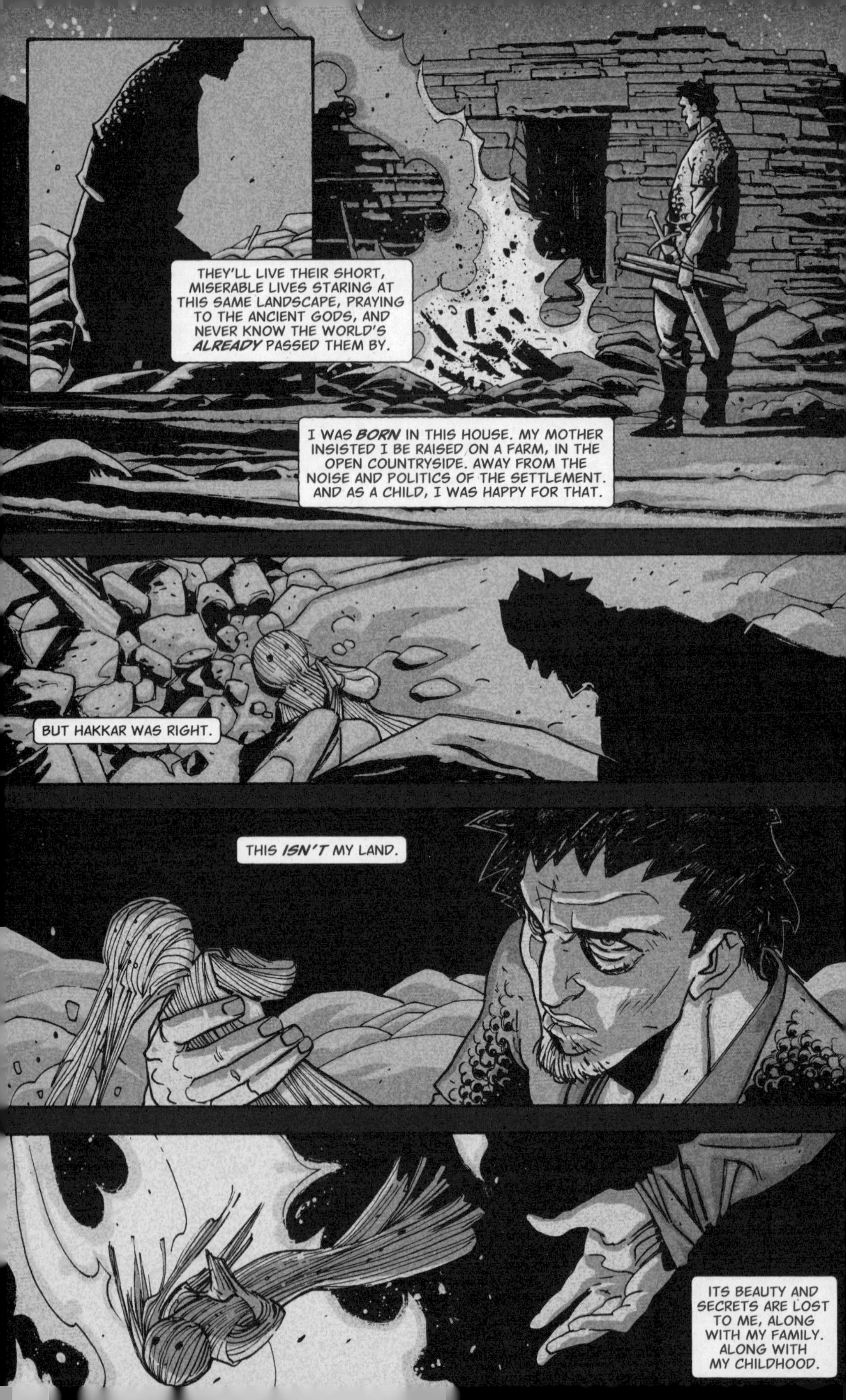
THEY'LL LIVE THEIR SHORT, MISERABLE LIVES STARING AT THIS SAME LANDSCAPE, PRAYING TO THE ANCIENT GODS, AND NEVER KNOW THE WORLD'S *ALREADY* PASSED THEM BY.
I WAS *BORN* IN THIS HOUSE. MY MOTHER INSISTED I BE RAISED ON A FARM, IN THE OPEN COUNTRYSIDE. AWAY FROM THE NOISE AND POLITICS OF THE SETTLEMENT. AND AS A CHILD, I WAS HAPPY FOR THAT.
BUT HAKKAR WAS RIGHT.
THIS *ISN'T* MY LAND.
ITS BEAUTY AND SECRETS ARE LOST TO ME, ALONG WITH MY FAMILY. ALONG WITH MY CHILDHOOD.

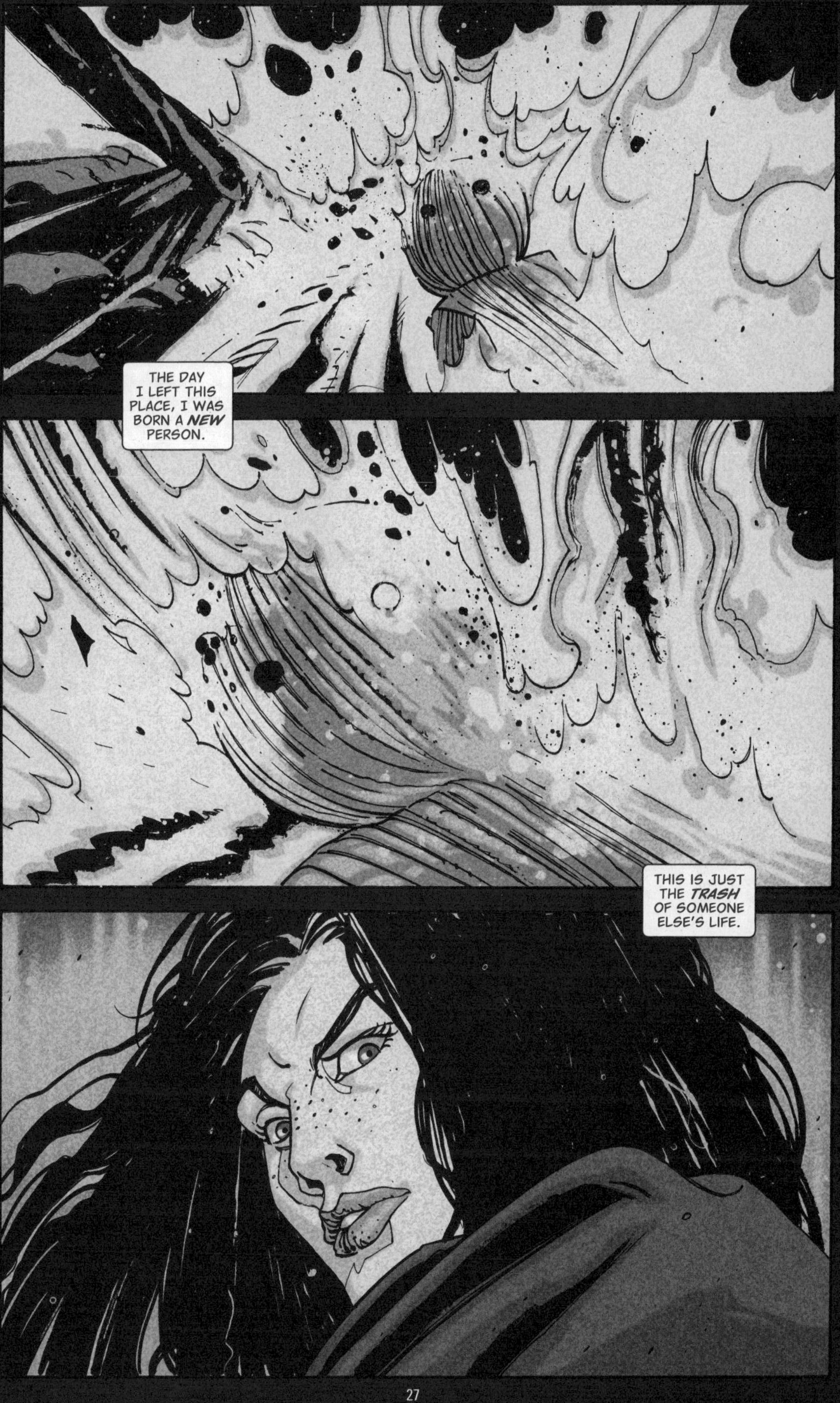
THE DAY I LEFT THIS PLACE, I WAS BORN A NEW PERSON.
THIS IS JUST THE TRASH OF SOMEONE ELSE'S LIFE.

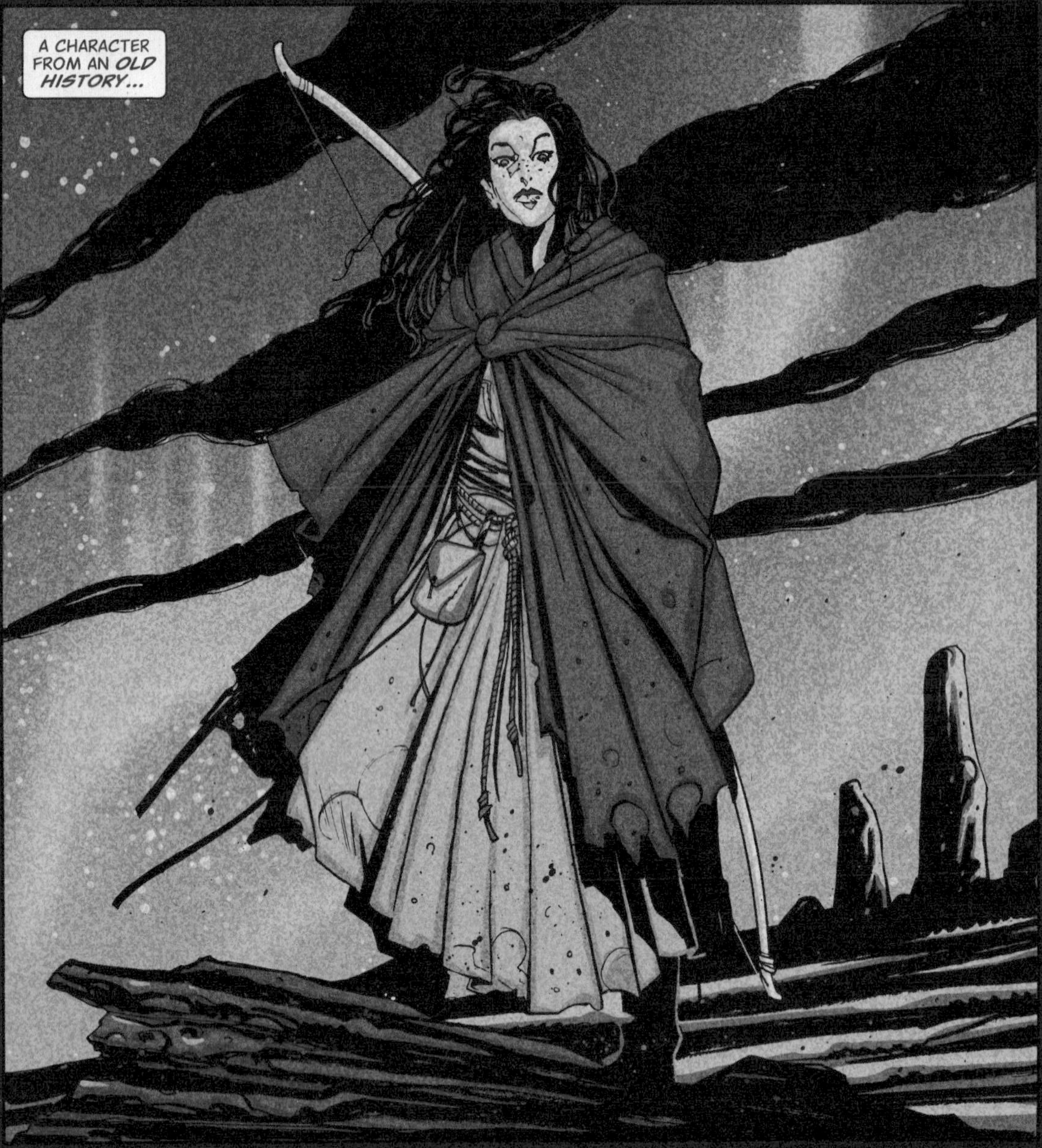
A CHARACTER FROM AN OLD HISTORY...

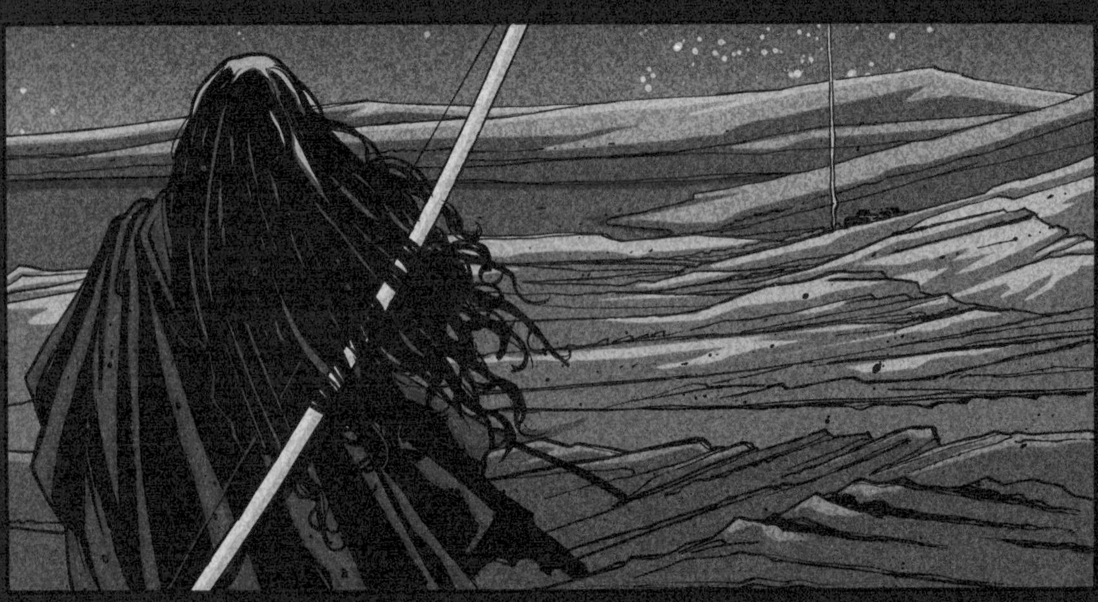

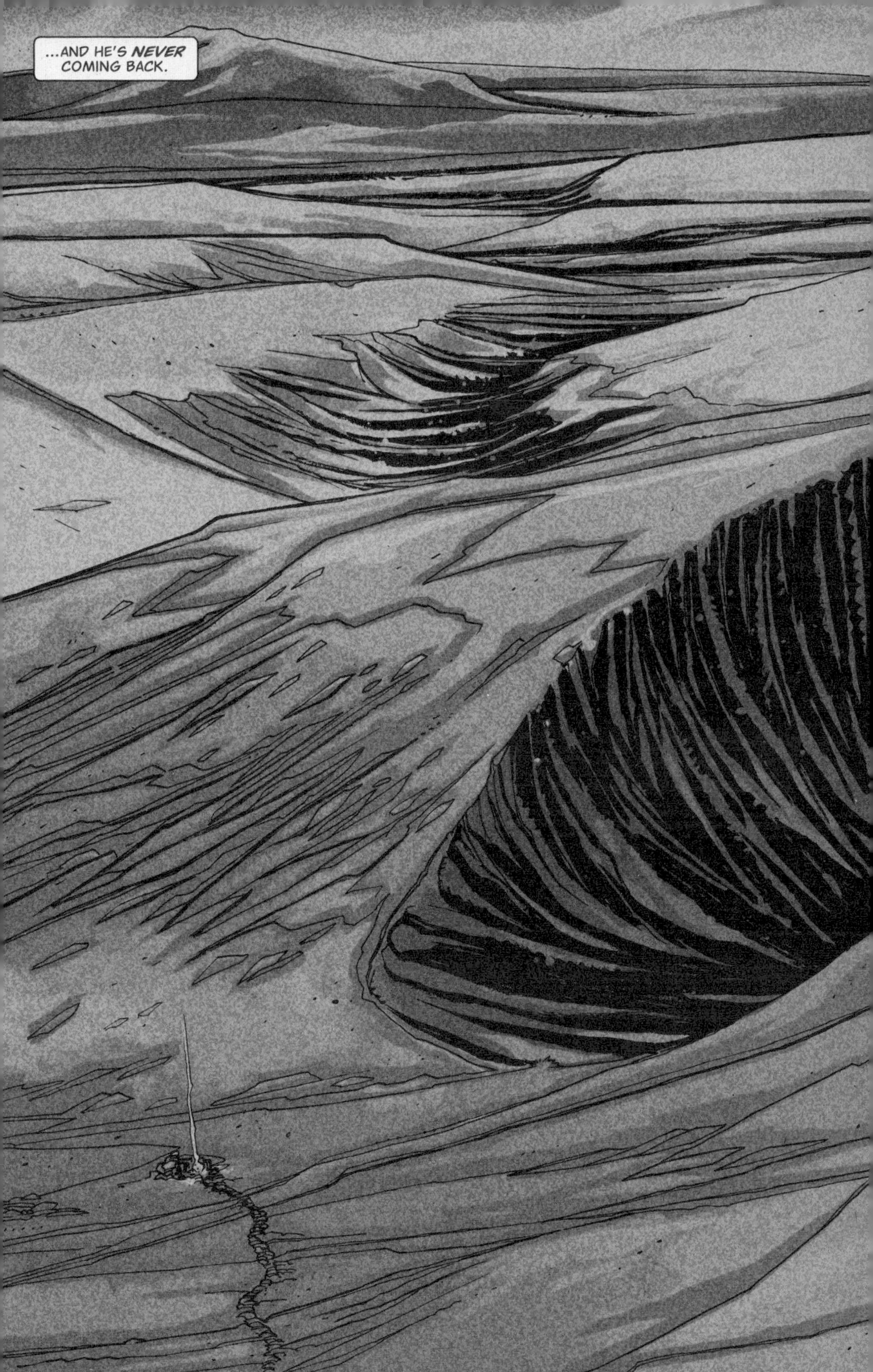
...AND HE'S NEVER COMING BACK.

2 Caledonia's Hardy Sons

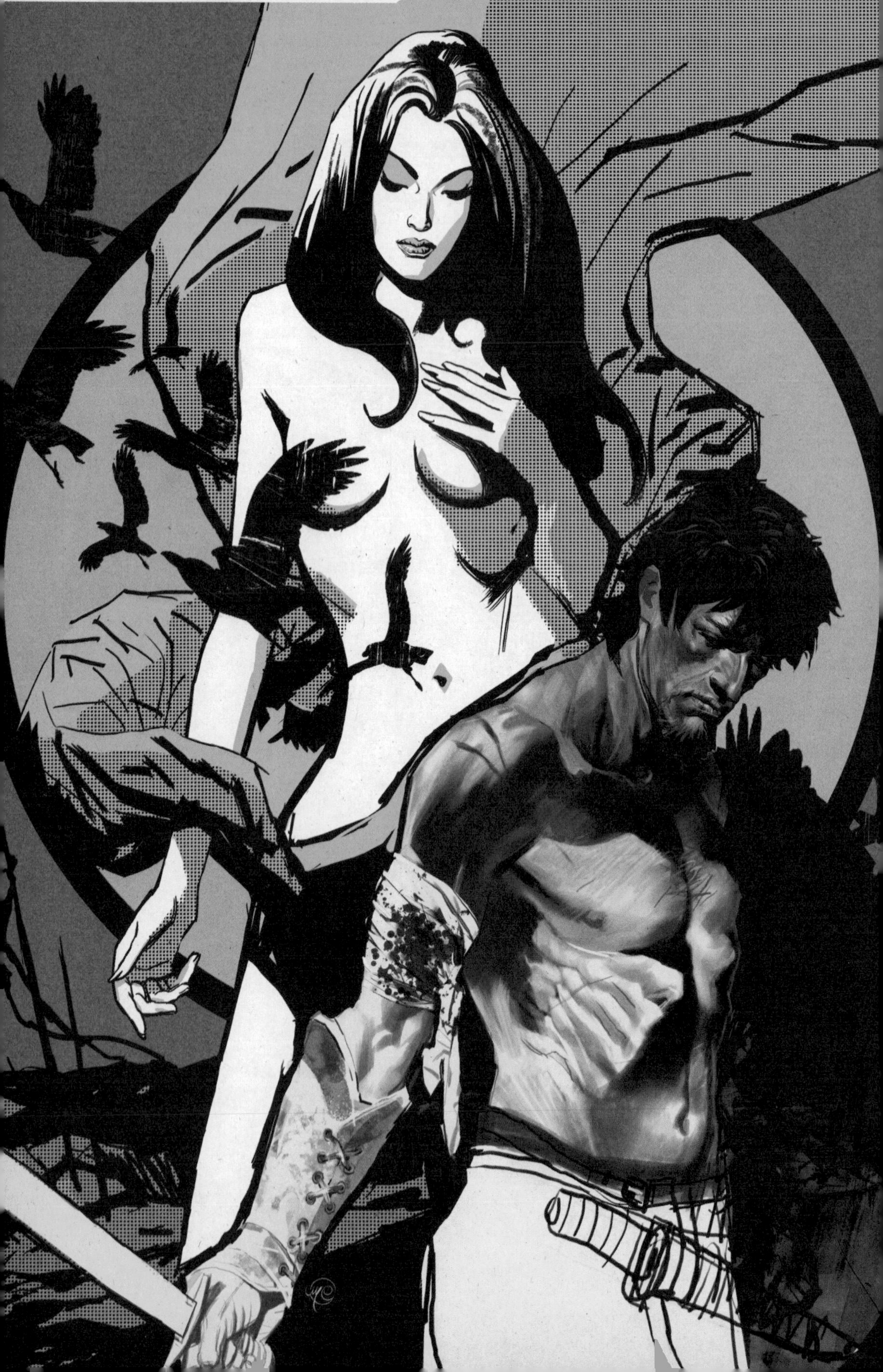

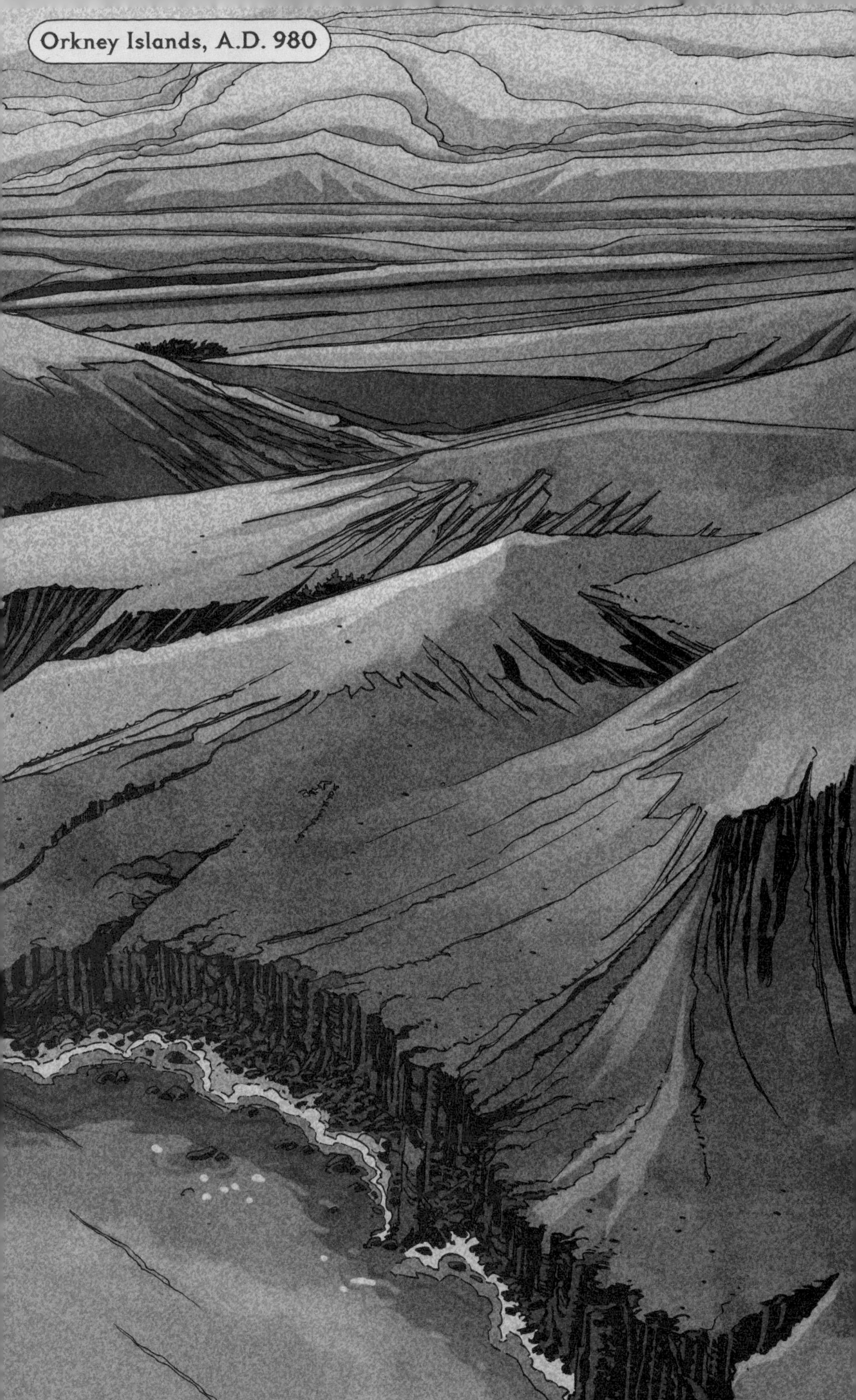

Orkney Islands, A.D. 980

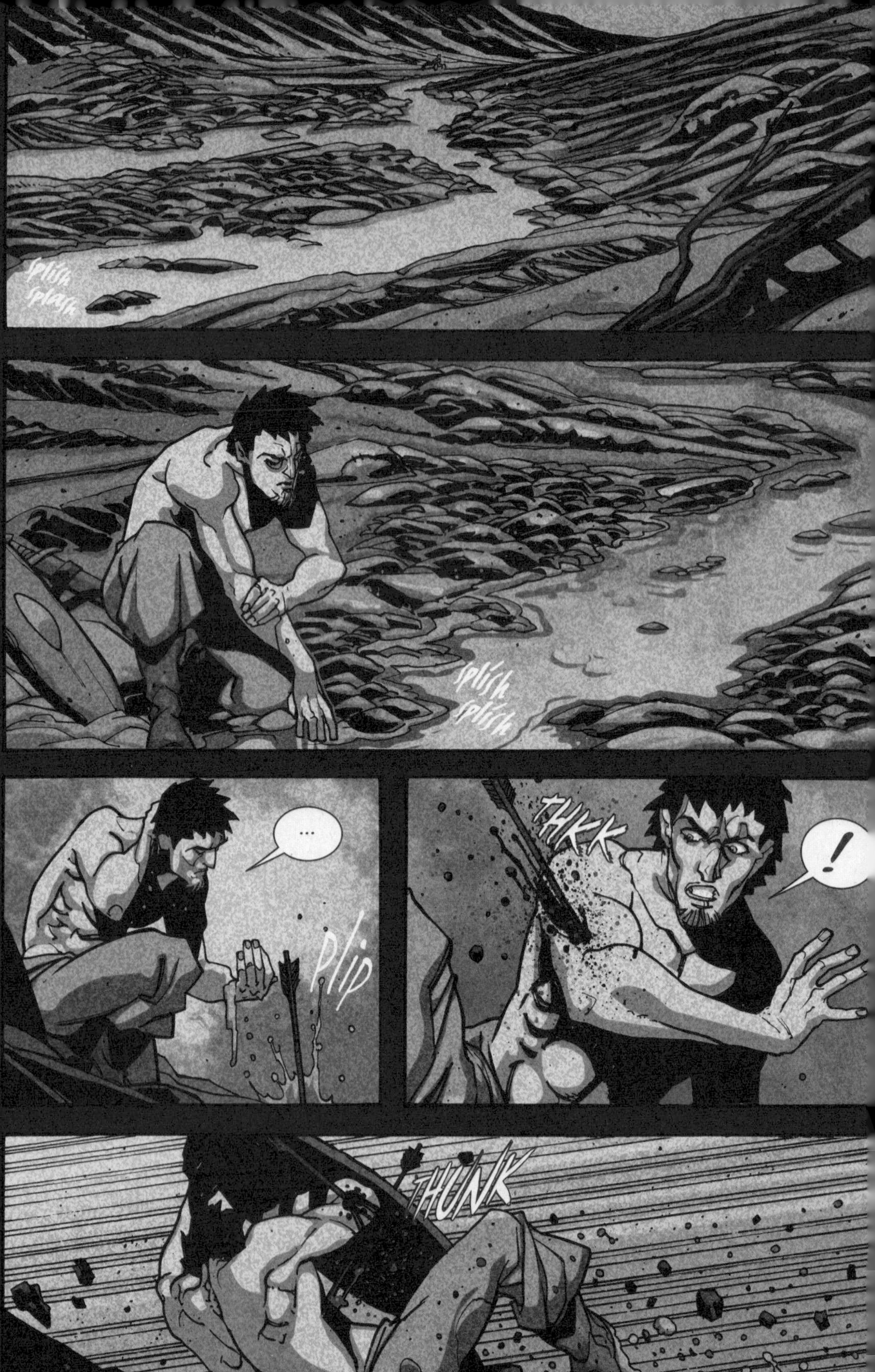
splish
splash
splish
splish
...
plip
THKK
!
THUNK

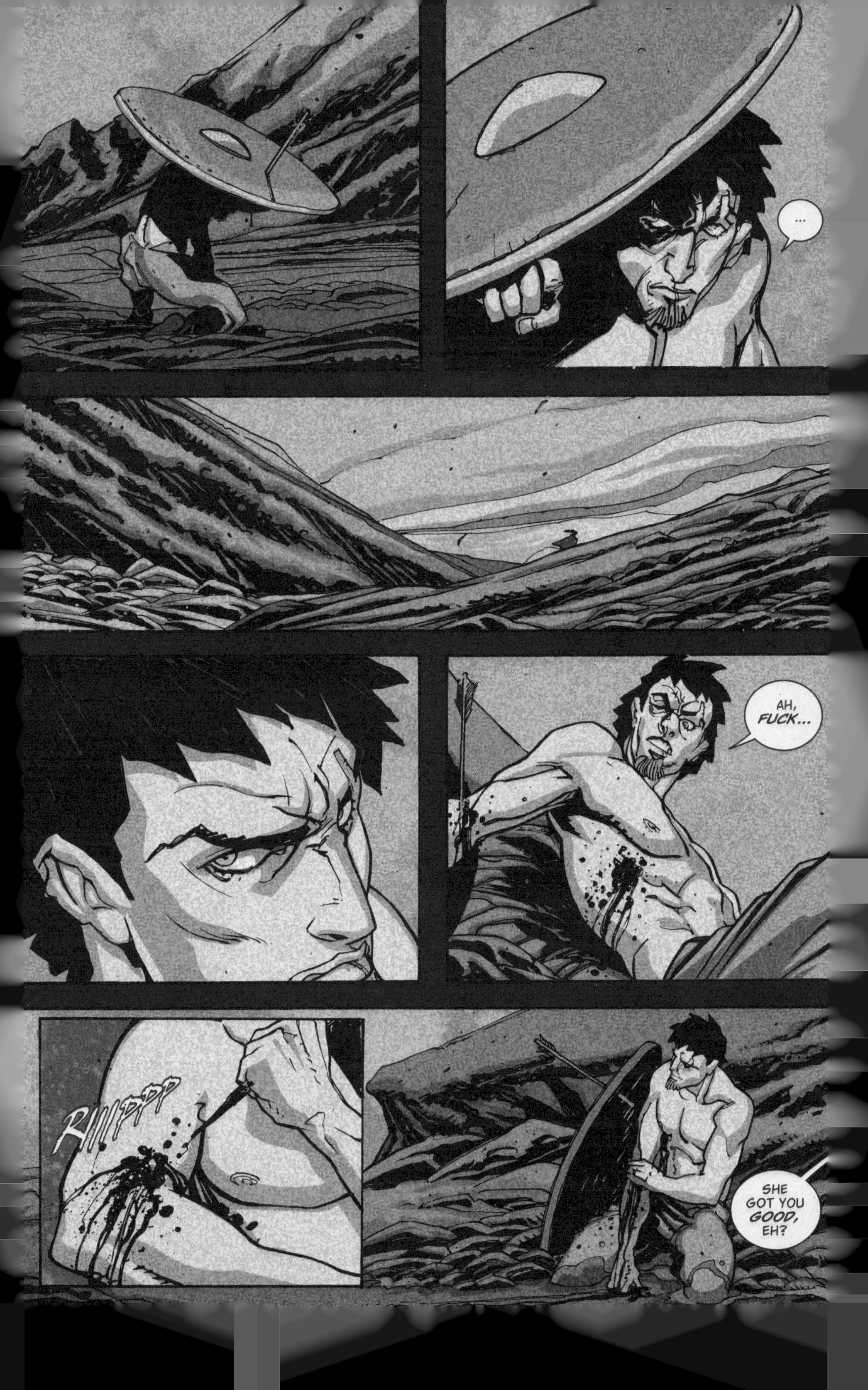
...
AH, FUCK...
RIIIPPP
SHE GOT YOU GOOD, EH?

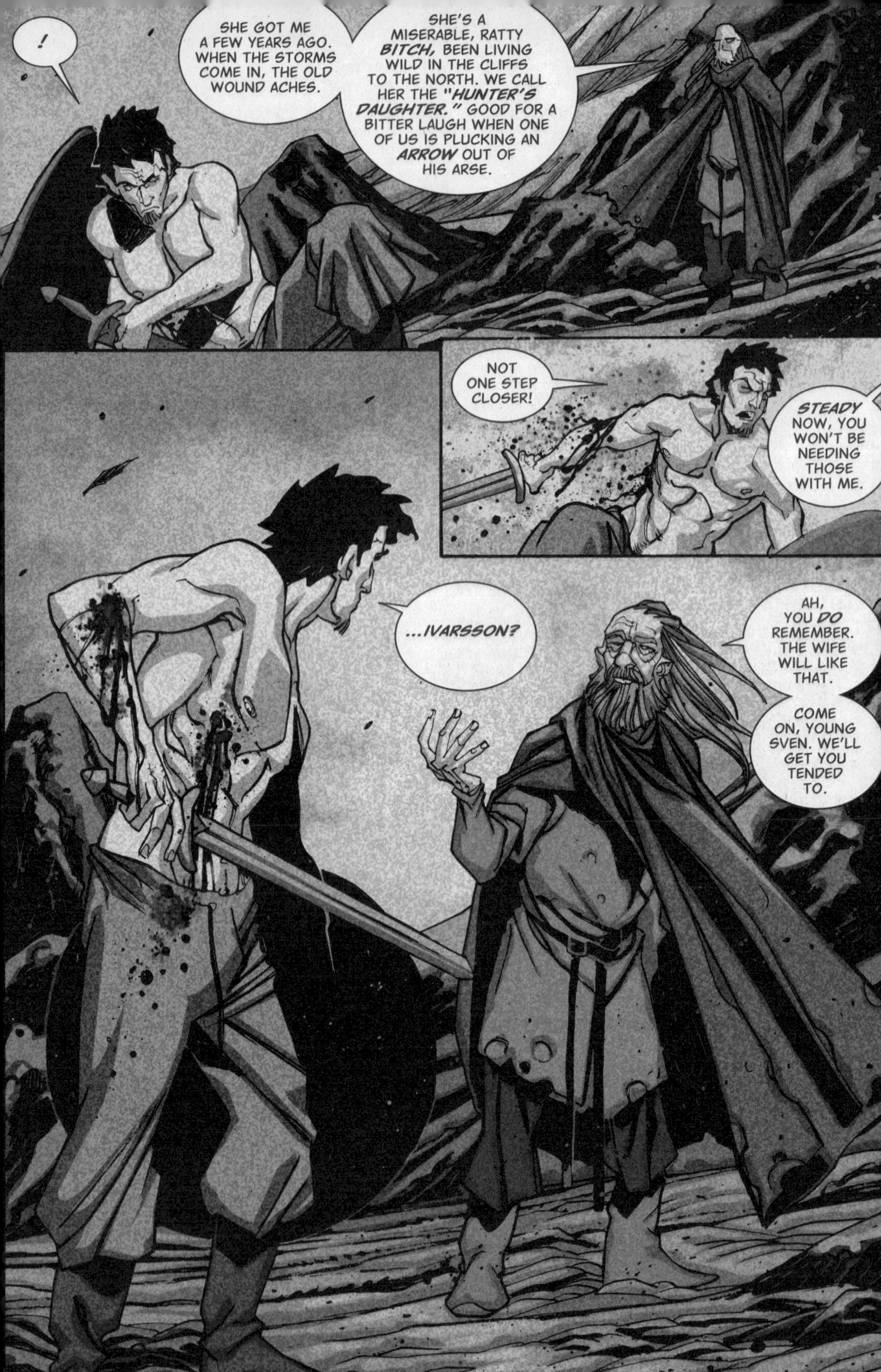
!
SHE GOT ME A FEW YEARS AGO. WHEN THE STORMS COME IN, THE OLD WOUND ACHES.
SHE'S A MISERABLE, RATTY BITCH, BEEN LIVING WILD IN THE CLIFFS TO THE NORTH. WE CALL HER THE "HUNTER'S DAUGHTER." GOOD FOR A BITTER LAUGH WHEN ONE OF US IS PLUCKING AN ARROW OUT OF HIS ARSE.
NOT ONE STEP CLOSER!
STEADY NOW, YOU WON'T BE NEEDING THOSE WITH ME.
...IVARSSON?
AH, YOU DO REMEMBER. THE WIFE WILL LIKE THAT.
COME ON, YOUNG SVEN. WE'LL GET YOU TENDED TO.

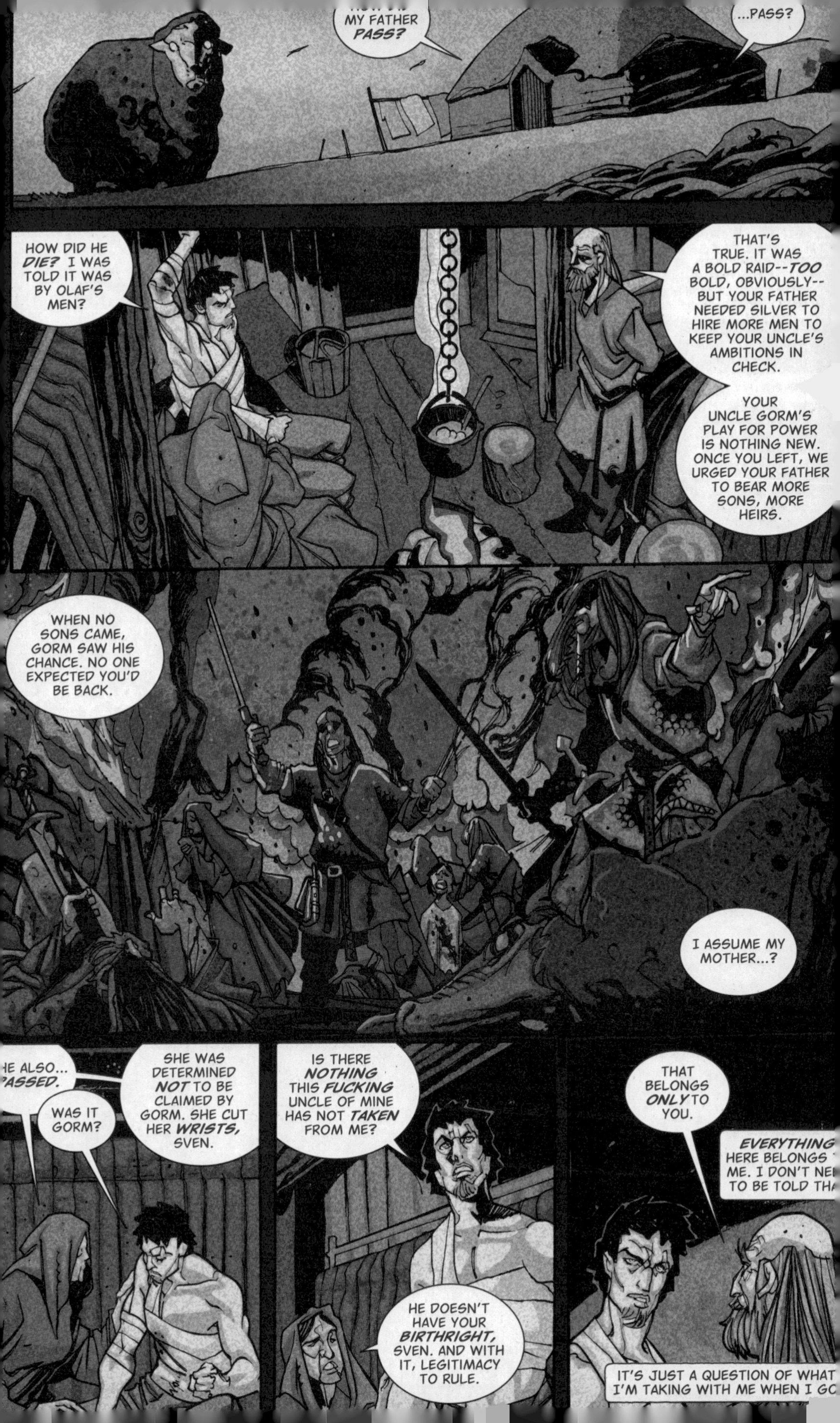

MY FATHER PASS?
...PASS?
HOW DID HE DIE? I WAS TOLD IT WAS BY OLAF'S MEN?
THAT'S TRUE. IT WAS A BOLD RAID--TOO BOLD, OBVIOUSLY--BUT YOUR FATHER NEEDED SILVER TO HIRE MORE MEN TO KEEP YOUR UNCLE'S AMBITIONS IN CHECK.
YOUR UNCLE GORM'S PLAY FOR POWER IS NOTHING NEW. ONCE YOU LEFT, WE URGED YOUR FATHER TO BEAR MORE SONS, MORE HEIRS.
WHEN NO SONS CAME, GORM SAW HIS CHANCE. NO ONE EXPECTED YOU'D BE BACK.
I ASSUME MY MOTHER...?
HE ALSO... PASSED.
WAS IT GORM?
SHE WAS DETERMINED NOT TO BE CLAIMED BY GORM. SHE CUT HER WRISTS, SVEN.
IS THERE NOTHING THIS FUCKING UNCLE OF MINE HAS NOT TAKEN FROM ME?
HE DOESN'T HAVE YOUR BIRTHRIGHT, SVEN. AND WITH IT, LEGITIMACY TO RULE.
THAT BELONGS ONLY TO YOU.
EVERYTHING HERE BELONGS ME. I DON'T NE TO BE TOLD TH
IT'S JUST A QUESTION OF WHAT I'M TAKING WITH ME WHEN I GO

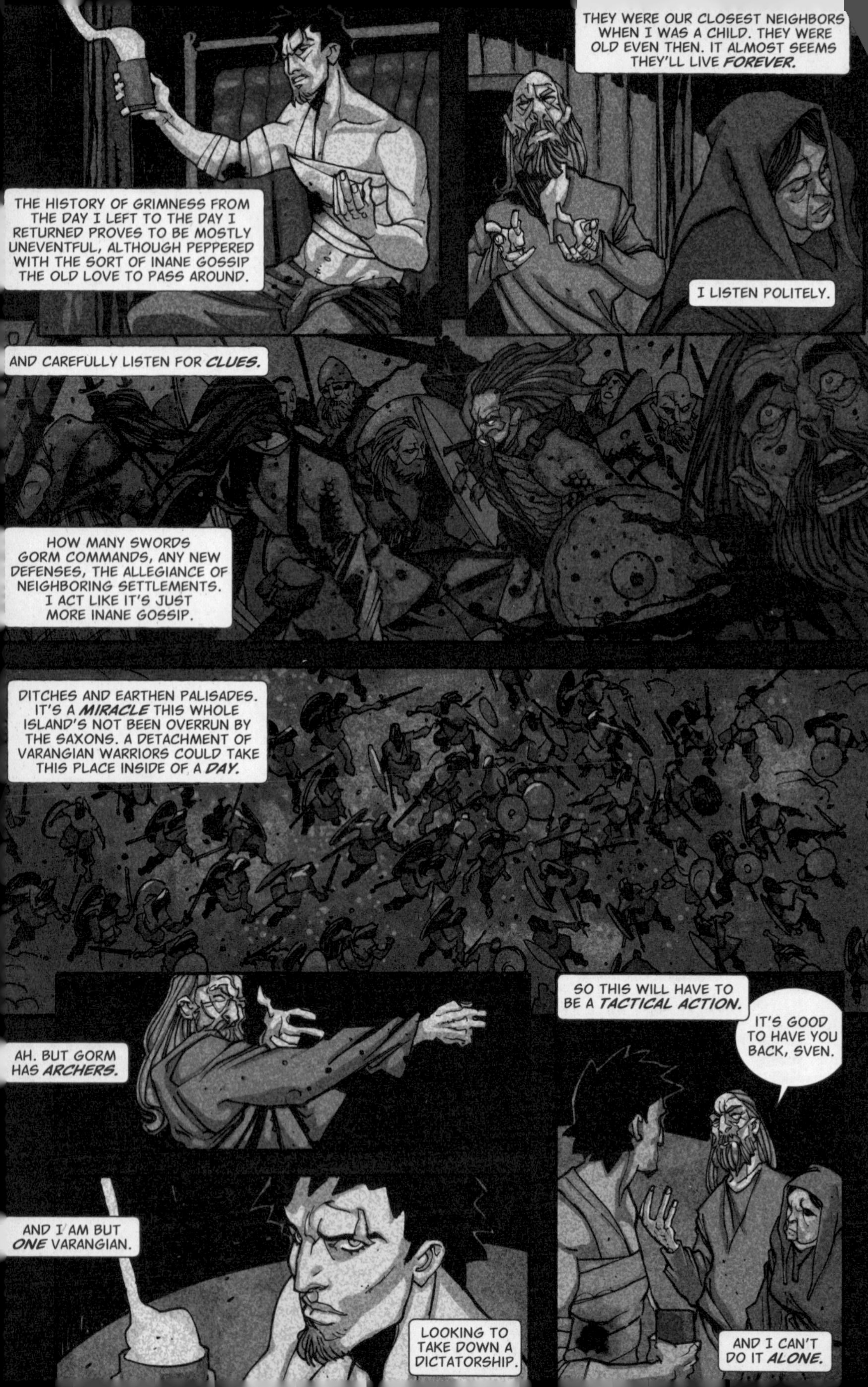
THE HISTORY OF GRIMNESS FROM THE DAY I LEFT TO THE DAY I RETURNED PROVES TO BE MOSTLY UNEVENTFUL, ALTHOUGH PEPPERED WITH THE SORT OF INANE GOSSIP THE OLD LOVE TO PASS AROUND.
THEY WERE OUR CLOSEST NEIGHBORS WHEN I WAS A CHILD. THEY WERE OLD EVEN THEN. IT ALMOST SEEMS THEY'LL LIVE *FOREVER.*
I LISTEN POLITELY.
AND CAREFULLY LISTEN FOR *CLUES.*
HOW MANY SWORDS GORM COMMANDS, ANY NEW DEFENSES, THE ALLEGIANCE OF NEIGHBORING SETTLEMENTS. I ACT LIKE IT'S JUST MORE INANE GOSSIP.
DITCHES AND EARTHEN PALISADES. IT'S A *MIRACLE* THIS WHOLE ISLAND'S NOT BEEN OVERRUN BY THE SAXONS. A DETACHMENT OF VARANGIAN WARRIORS COULD TAKE THIS PLACE INSIDE OF A *DAY.*
AH. BUT GORM HAS *ARCHERS.*
AND I AM BUT *ONE* VARANGIAN.
LOOKING TO TAKE DOWN A DICTATORSHIP.
SO THIS WILL HAVE TO BE A *TACTICAL ACTION.*
IT'S GOOD TO HAVE YOU BACK, SVEN.
AND I CAN'T DO IT *ALONE.*

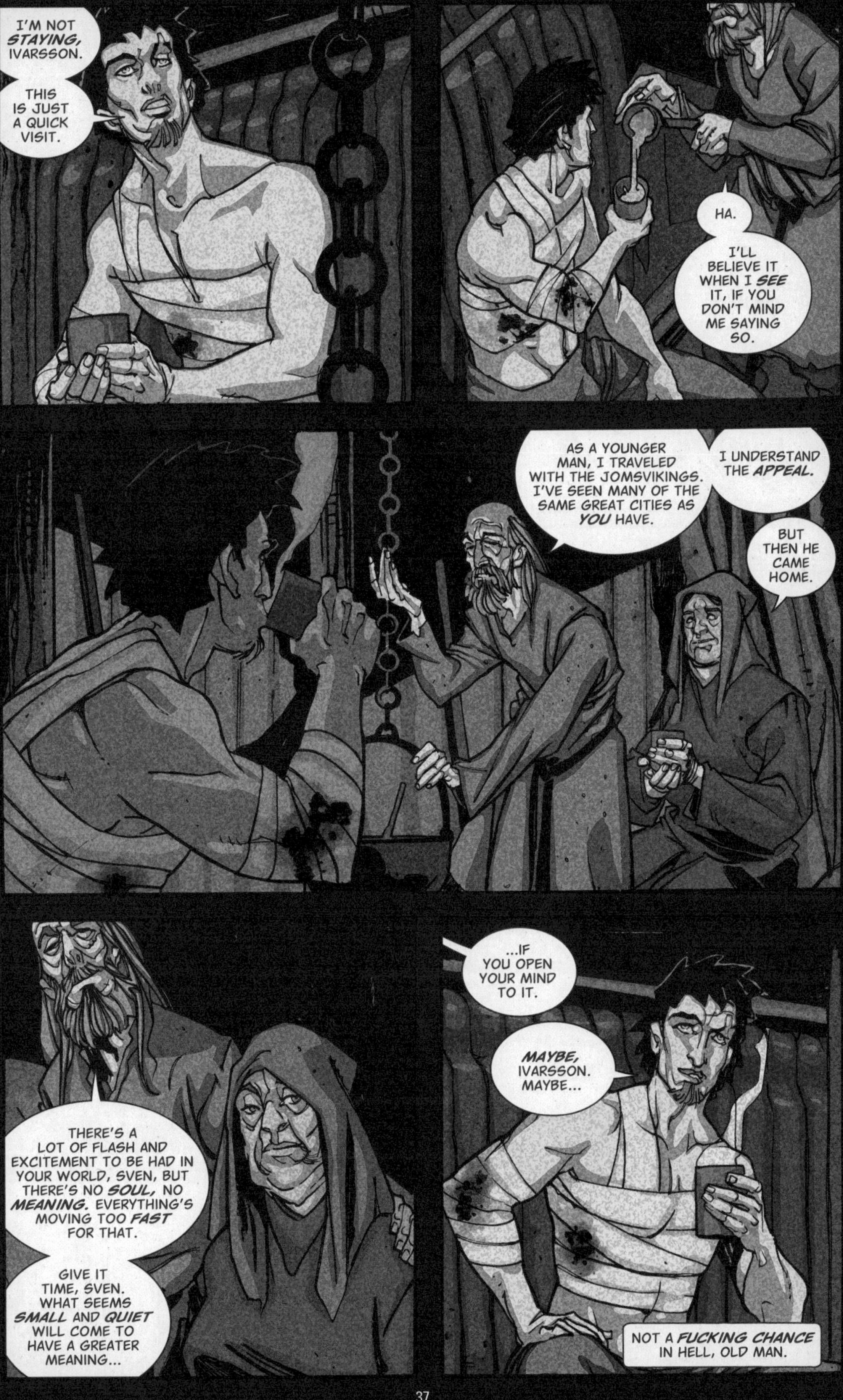
I'M NOT STAYING, IVARSSON.
THIS IS JUST A QUICK VISIT.
HA.
I'LL BELIEVE IT WHEN I SEE IT, IF YOU DON'T MIND ME SAYING SO.
AS A YOUNGER MAN, I TRAVELED WITH THE JOMSVIKINGS. I'VE SEEN MANY OF THE SAME GREAT CITIES AS YOU HAVE.
I UNDERSTAND THE APPEAL.
BUT THEN HE CAME HOME.
THERE'S A LOT OF FLASH AND EXCITEMENT TO BE HAD IN YOUR WORLD, SVEN, BUT THERE'S NO SOUL, NO MEANING. EVERYTHING'S MOVING TOO FAST FOR THAT.
GIVE IT TIME, SVEN. WHAT SEEMS SMALL AND QUIET WILL COME TO HAVE A GREATER MEANING...
...IF YOU OPEN YOUR MIND TO IT.
MAYBE, IVARSSON. MAYBE...
NOT A FUCKING CHANCE IN HELL, OLD MAN.

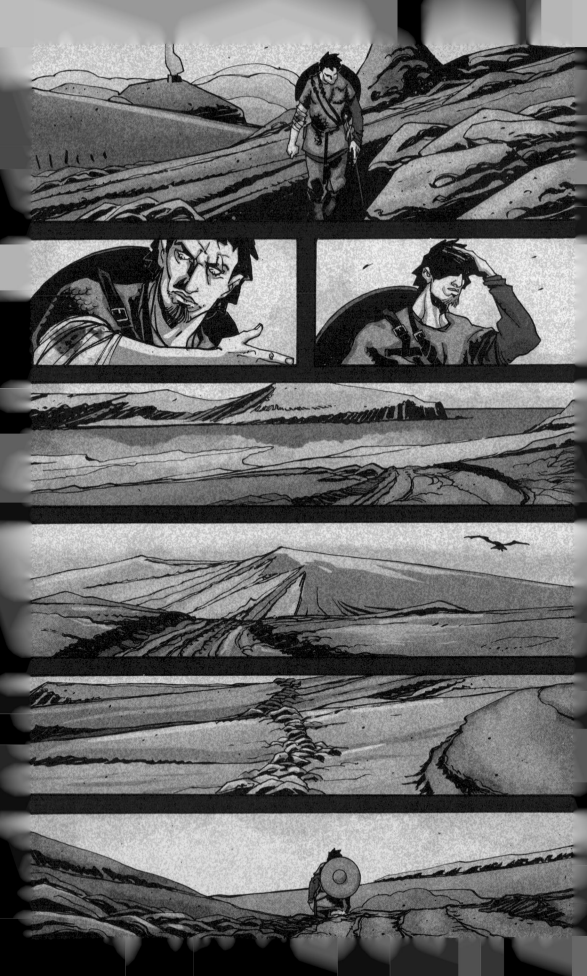

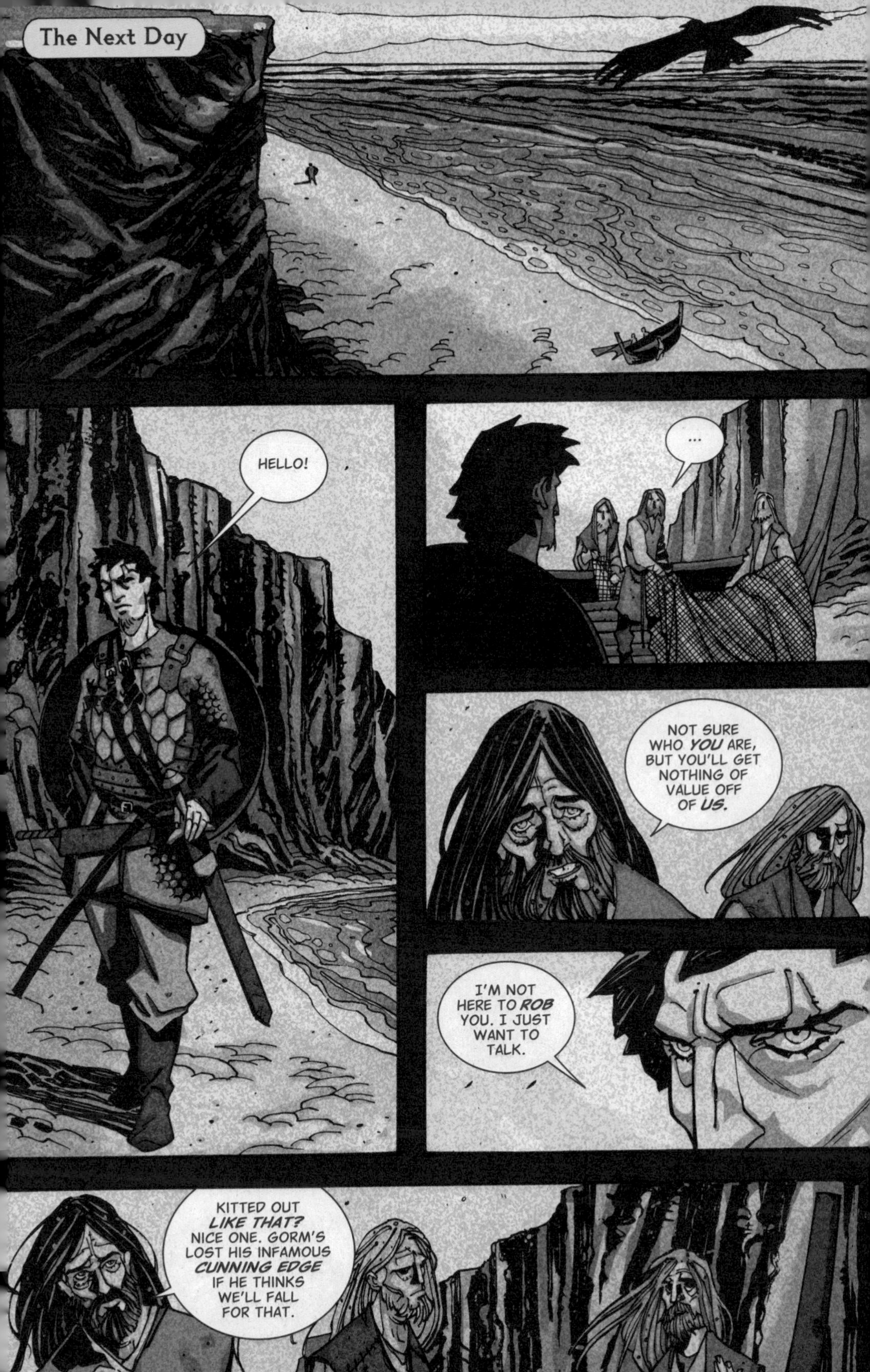

The Next Day
HELLO!
...
NOT SURE WHO YOU ARE, BUT YOU'LL GET NOTHING OF VALUE OFF OF US.
I'M NOT HERE TO ROB YOU. I JUST WANT TO TALK.
KITTED OUT LIKE THAT? NICE ONE. GORM'S LOST HIS INFAMOUS CUNNING EDGE IF HE THINKS WE'LL FALL FOR THAT.

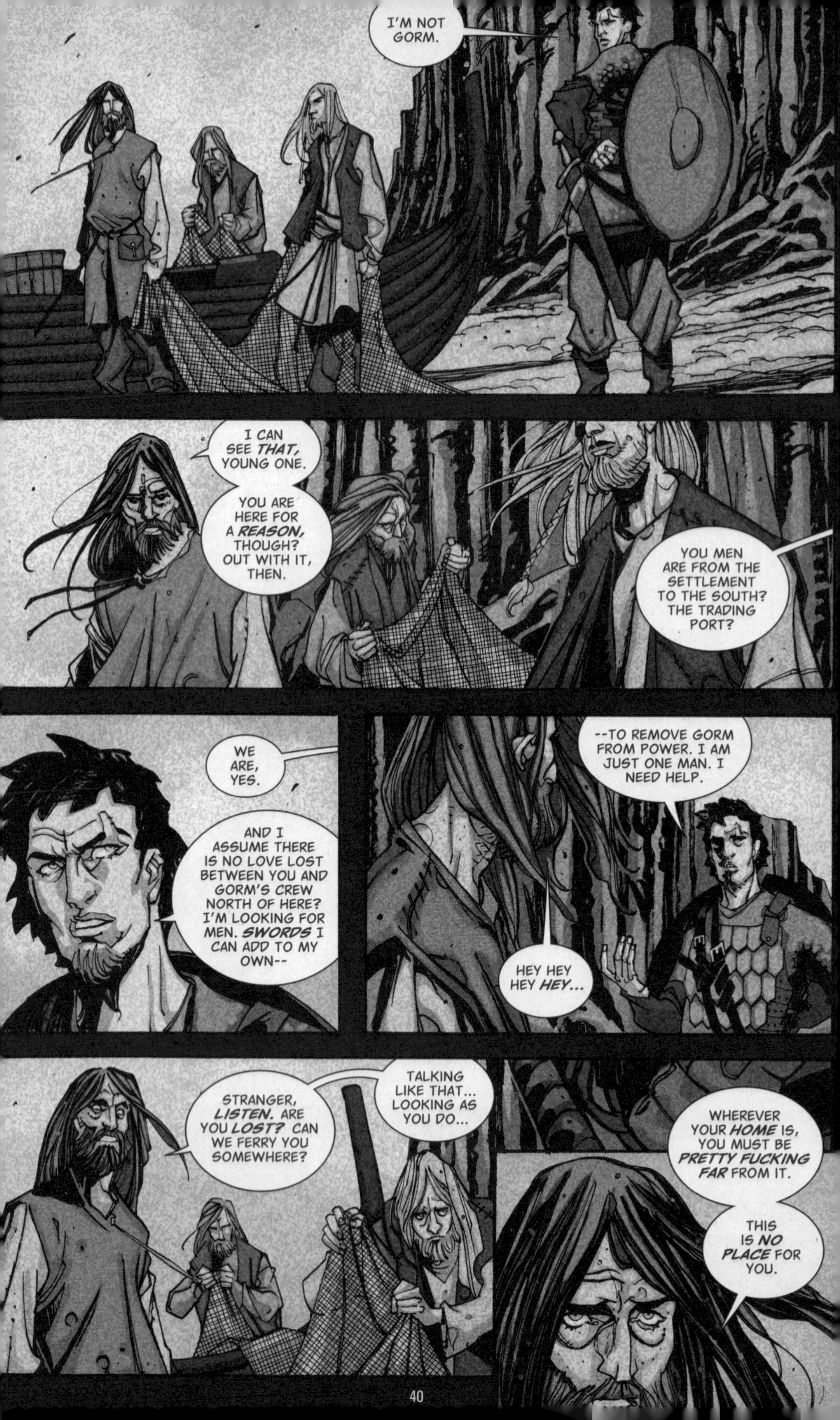
I'M NOT GORM.
I CAN SEE THAT, YOUNG ONE.
YOU ARE HERE FOR A REASON, THOUGH? OUT WITH IT, THEN.
YOU MEN ARE FROM THE SETTLEMENT TO THE SOUTH? THE TRADING PORT?
WE ARE, YES.
AND I ASSUME THERE IS NO LOVE LOST BETWEEN YOU AND GORM'S CREW NORTH OF HERE? I'M LOOKING FOR MEN. SWORDS I CAN ADD TO MY OWN--
--TO REMOVE GORM FROM POWER. I AM JUST ONE MAN. I NEED HELP.
HEY HEY HEY HEY...
STRANGER, LISTEN. ARE YOU LOST? CAN WE FERRY YOU SOMEWHERE?
TALKING LIKE THAT... LOOKING AS YOU DO...
WHEREVER YOUR HOME IS, YOU MUST BE PRETTY FUCKING FAR FROM IT.
THIS IS NO PLACE FOR YOU.

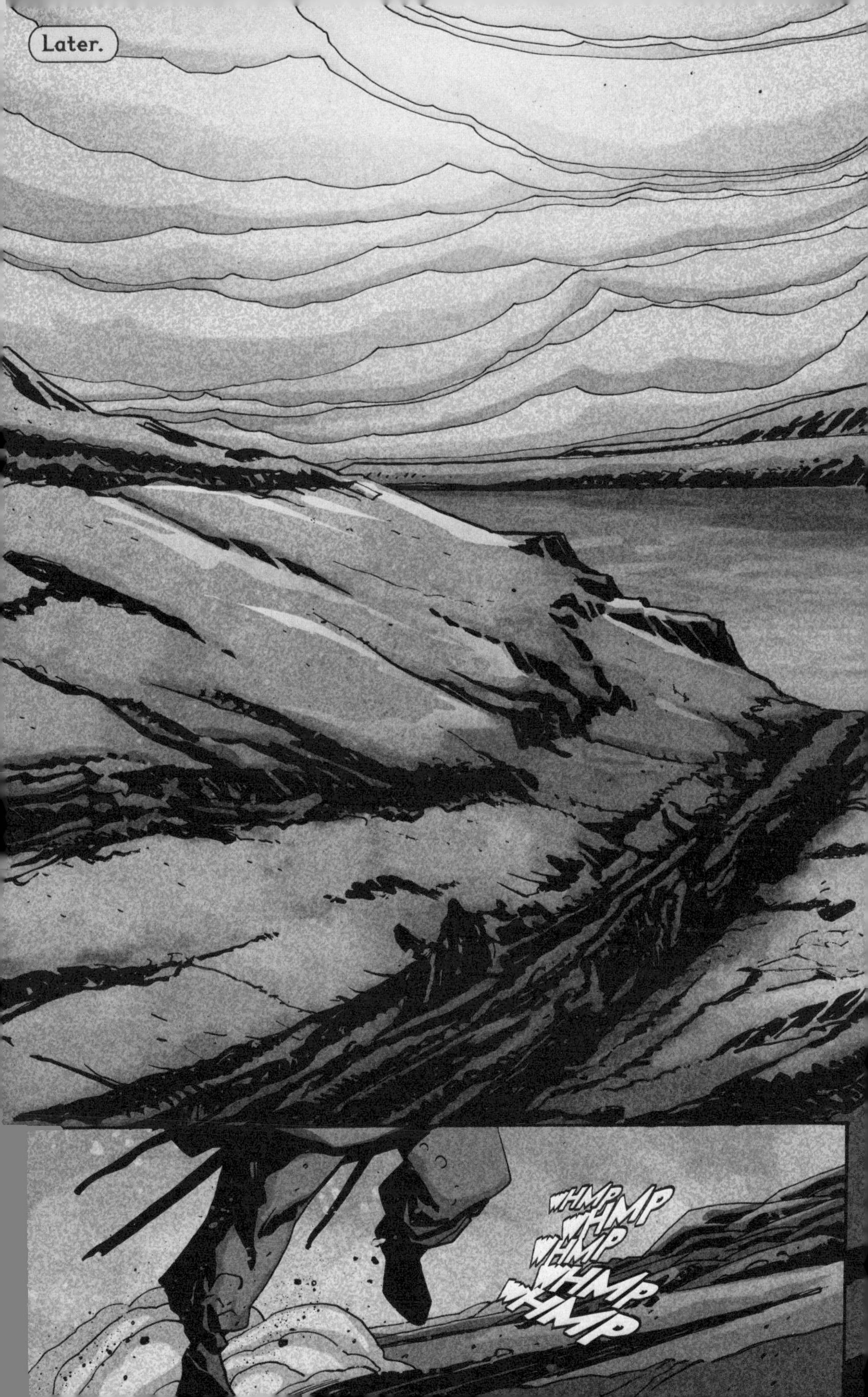
Later.
WHMP
WHMP
WHMP
WHMP
WHMP

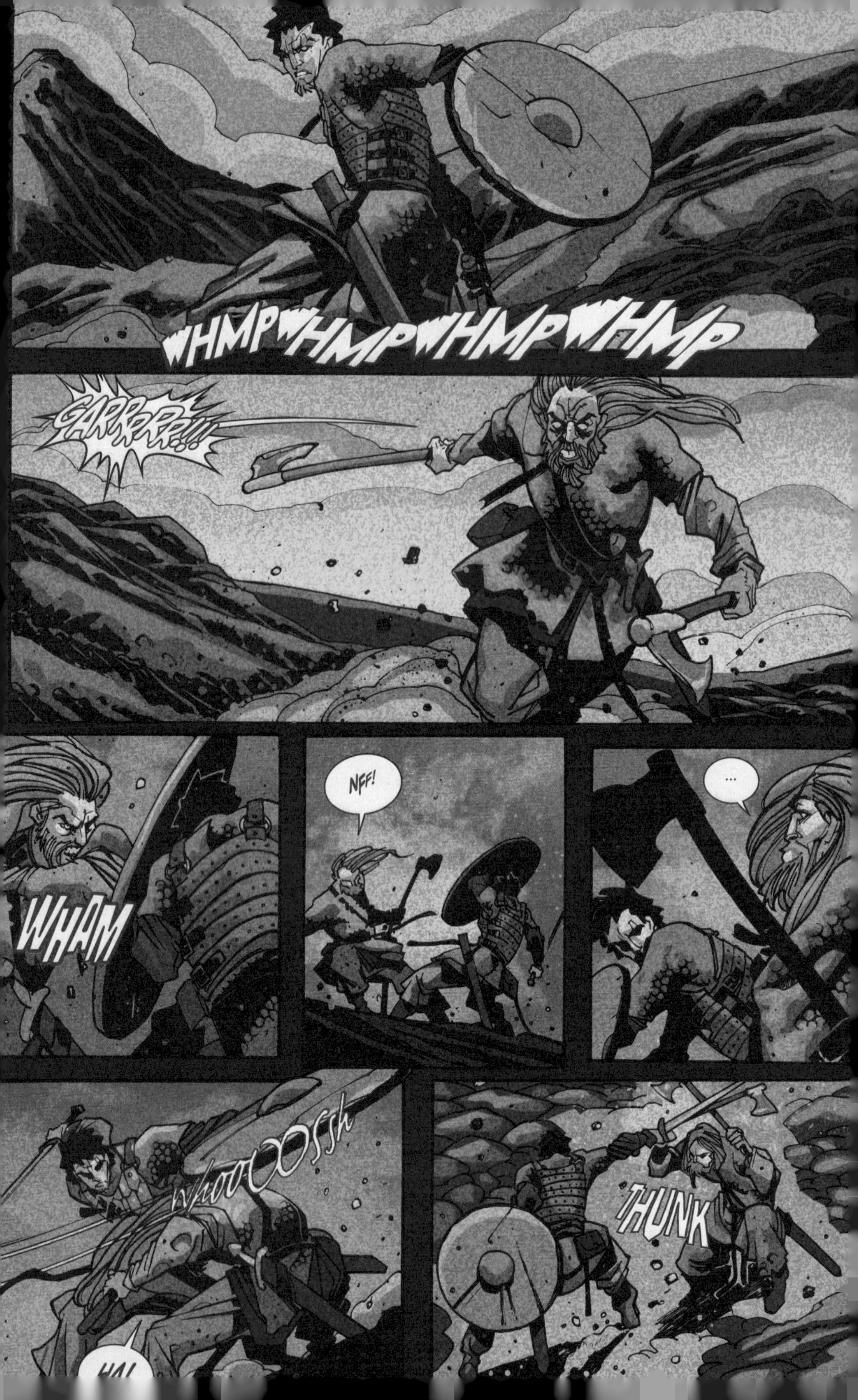
WHMPWHMPWHMPWHMP
GARRRR!!!
WHAM
NFF!
...
whoooOOssh
THUNK
HA!

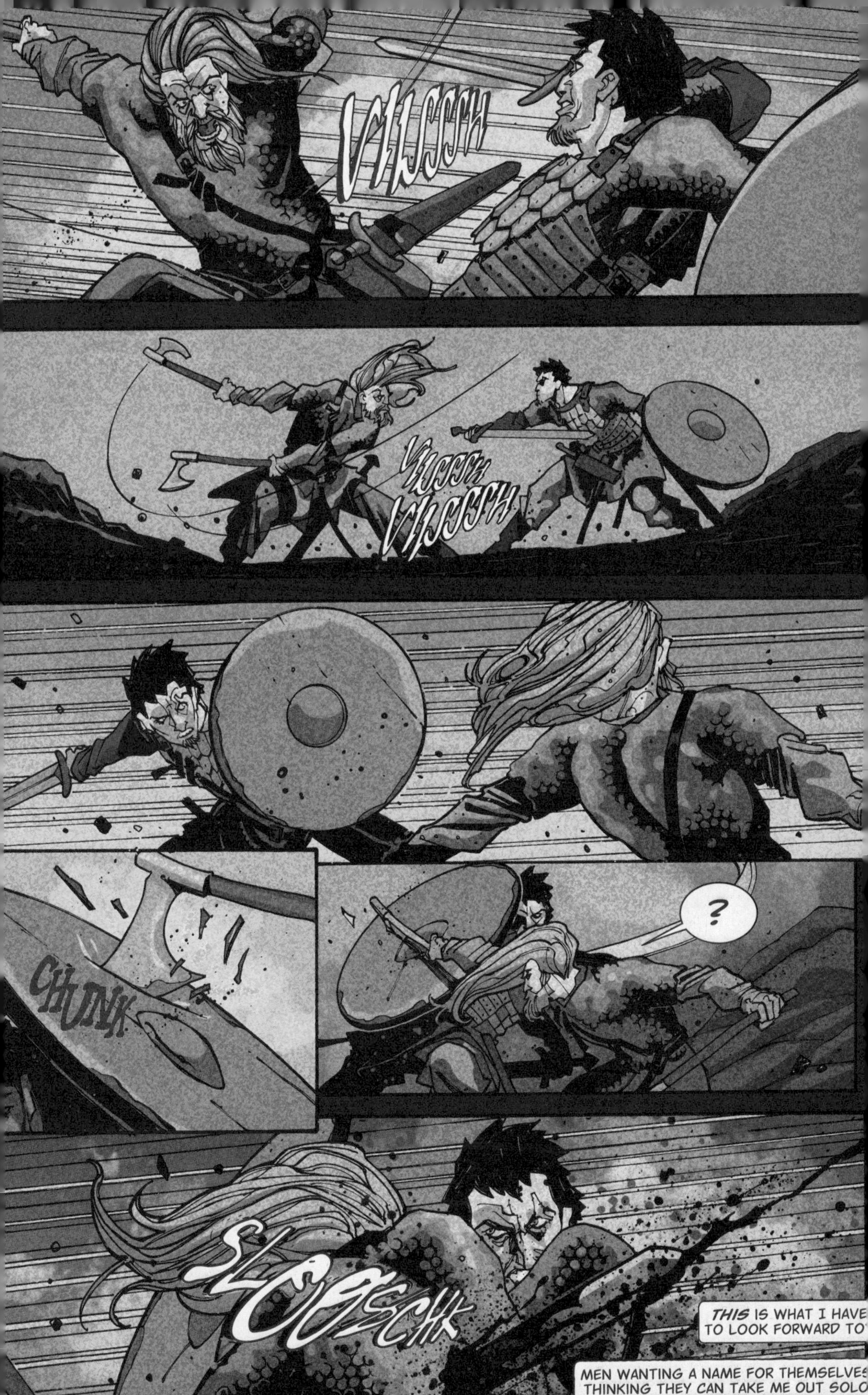
VHUSSH
VHUSSH
VHUSSH
CHUNK
?
SLOOSCHK
THIS IS WHAT I HAVE TO LOOK FORWARD TO.
MEN WANTING A NAME FOR THEMSELVES THINKING THEY CAN TAKE ME OUT SOLO. GORM WOULD NEVER SEND HIS BEST MEN OUT PIECEMEAL LIKE THAT.

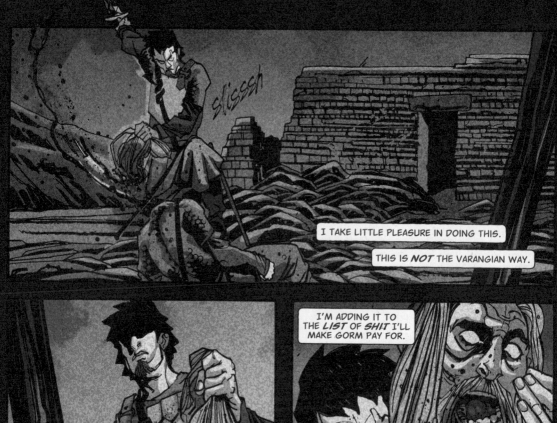

I TAKE LITTLE PLEASURE IN DOING THIS.

THIS IS *NOT* THE VARANGIAN WAY.

I'M ADDING IT TO THE *LIST* OF *SHIT* I'LL MAKE GORM PAY FOR.

BUT IF IT KEEPS JUST *ONE* STUPID FUCK FROM HESITATING BEFORE THROWING AWAY HIS LIFE ON A POINTLESS ASSASSINATION MISSION, I CAN JUSTIFY IT.

snap

THIS HAS BEEN A *REALLY* LONG DAY.

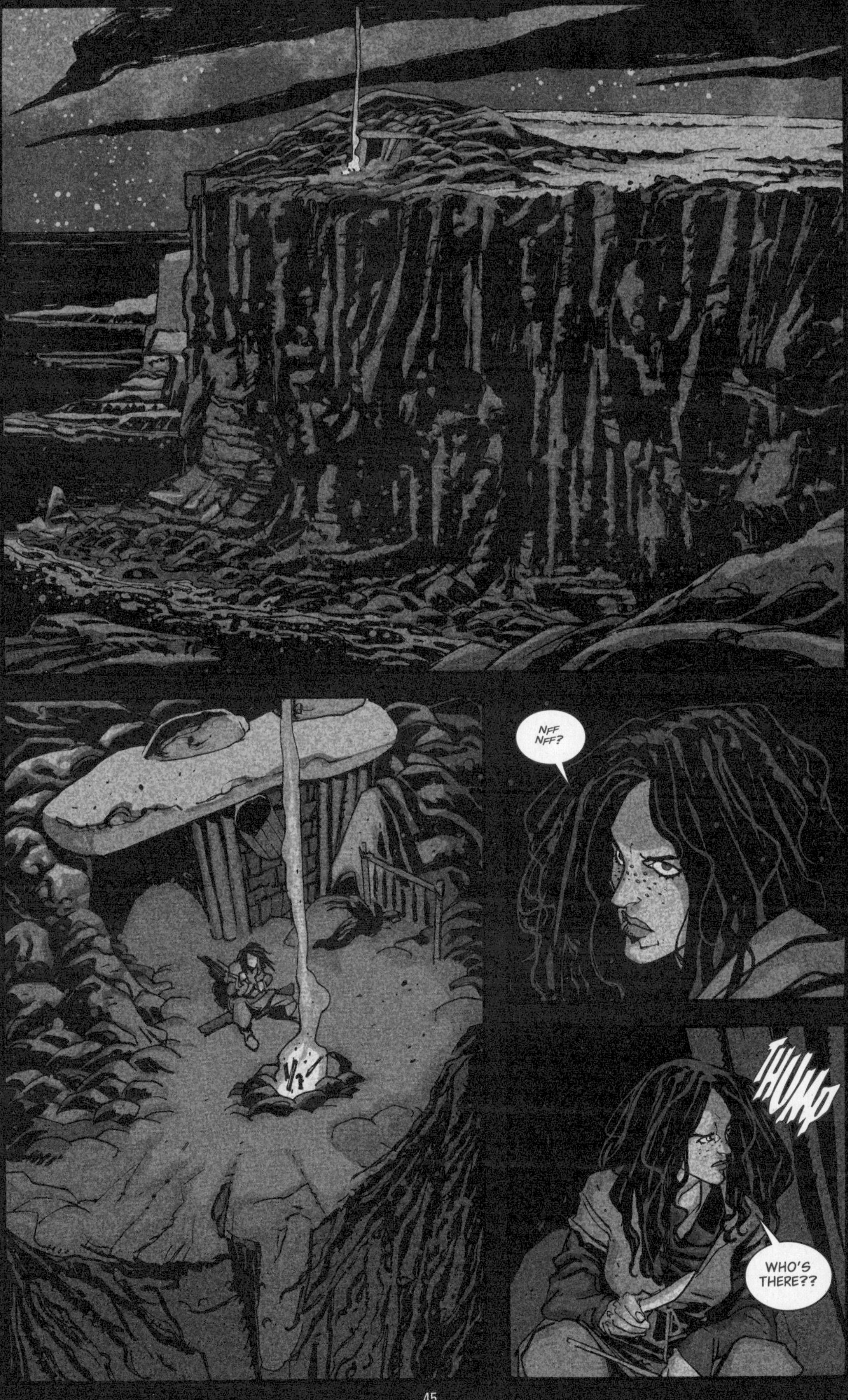
NFF
NFF?
THUMP
WHO'S
THERE??

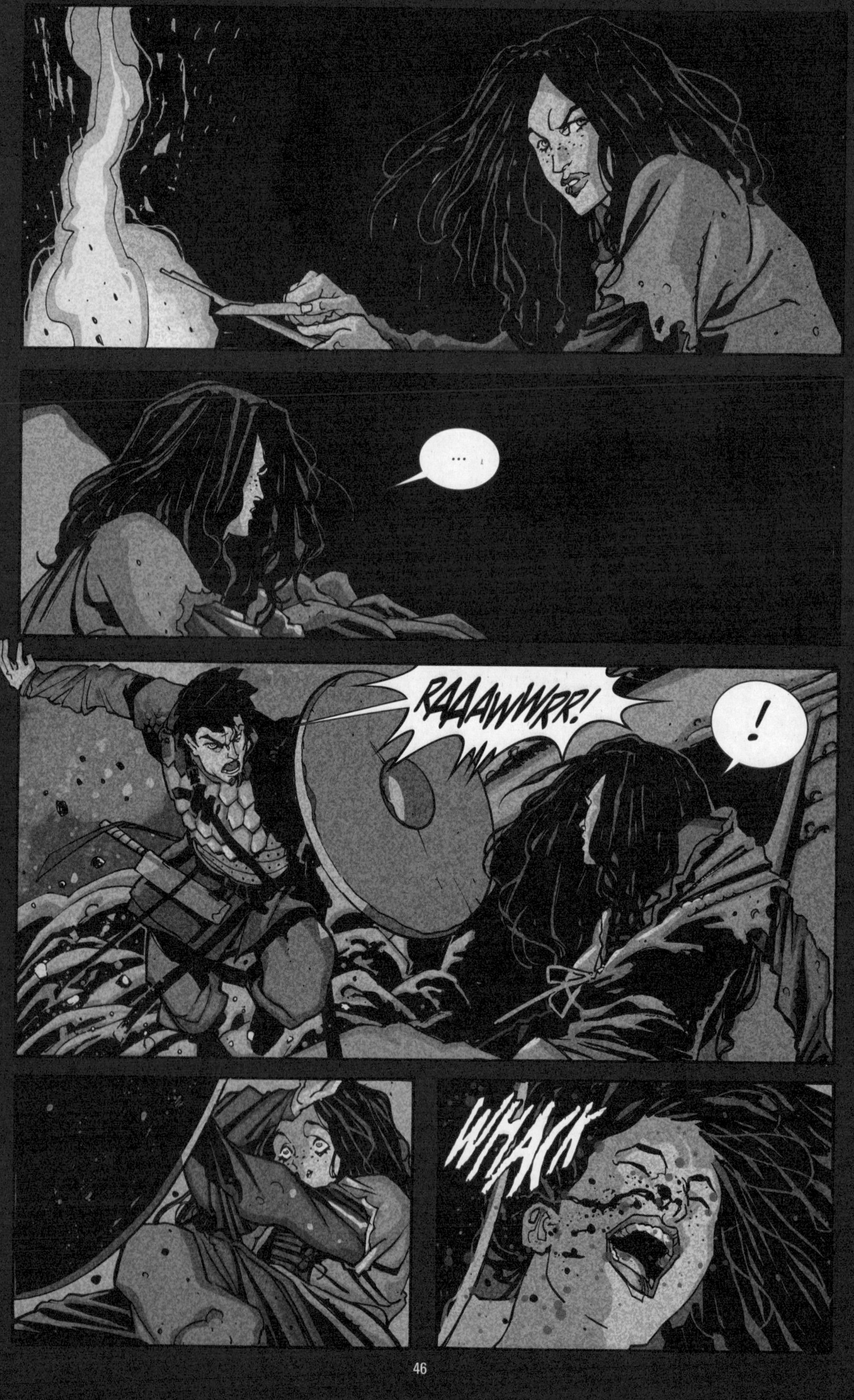
...
RAAAWWRR!
!
WHACK

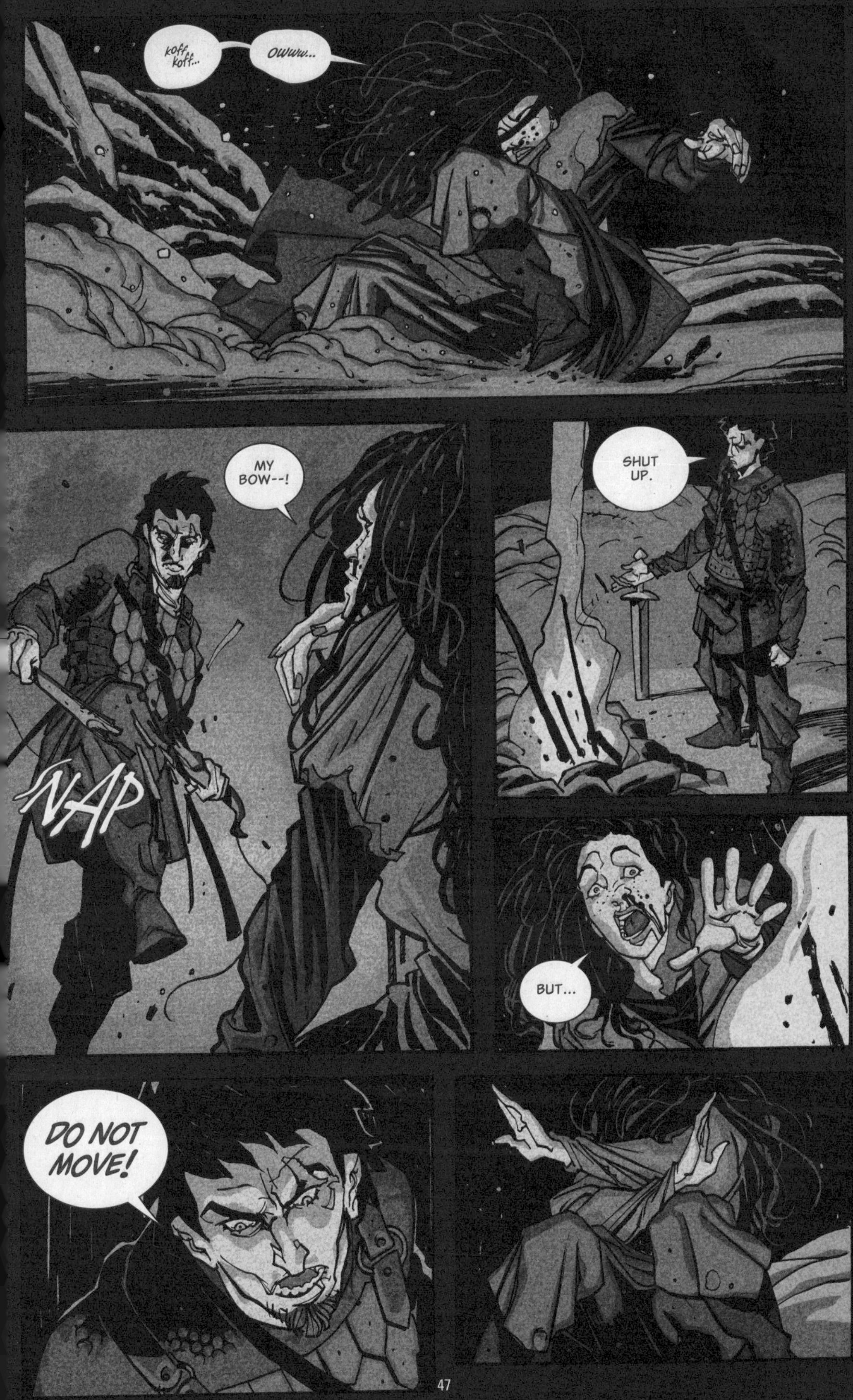
koff koff...
owww...
MY BOW--!
SNAP
SHUT UP.
BUT...
DO NOT MOVE!

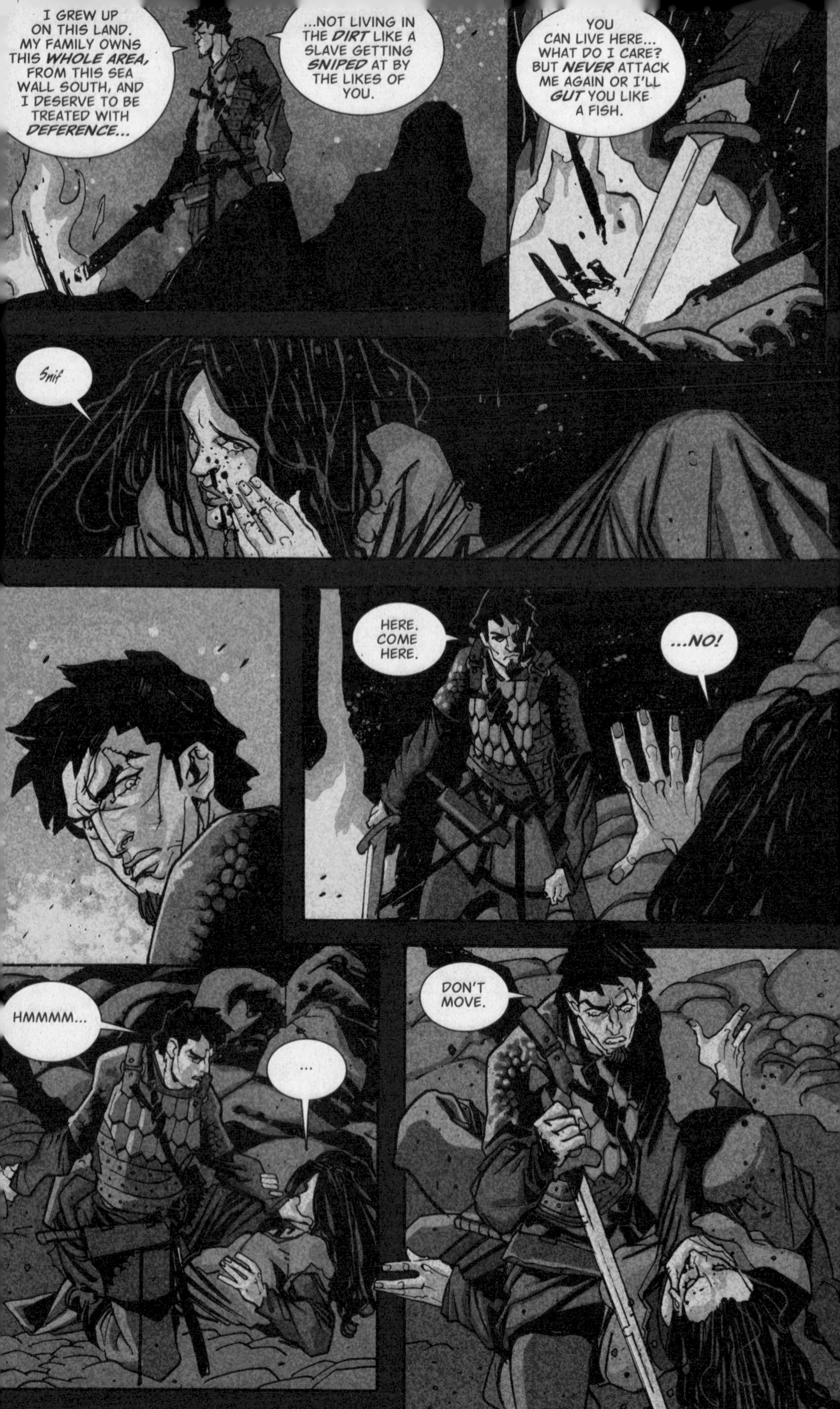
I GREW UP ON THIS LAND. MY FAMILY OWNS THIS WHOLE AREA, FROM THIS SEA WALL SOUTH, AND I DESERVE TO BE TREATED WITH DEFERENCE...
...NOT LIVING IN THE DIRT LIKE A SLAVE GETTING SNIPED AT BY THE LIKES OF YOU.
YOU CAN LIVE HERE... WHAT DO I CARE? BUT NEVER ATTACK ME AGAIN OR I'LL GUT YOU LIKE A FISH.
Snif
HERE. COME HERE.
...NO!
HMMMM...
...
DON'T MOVE.

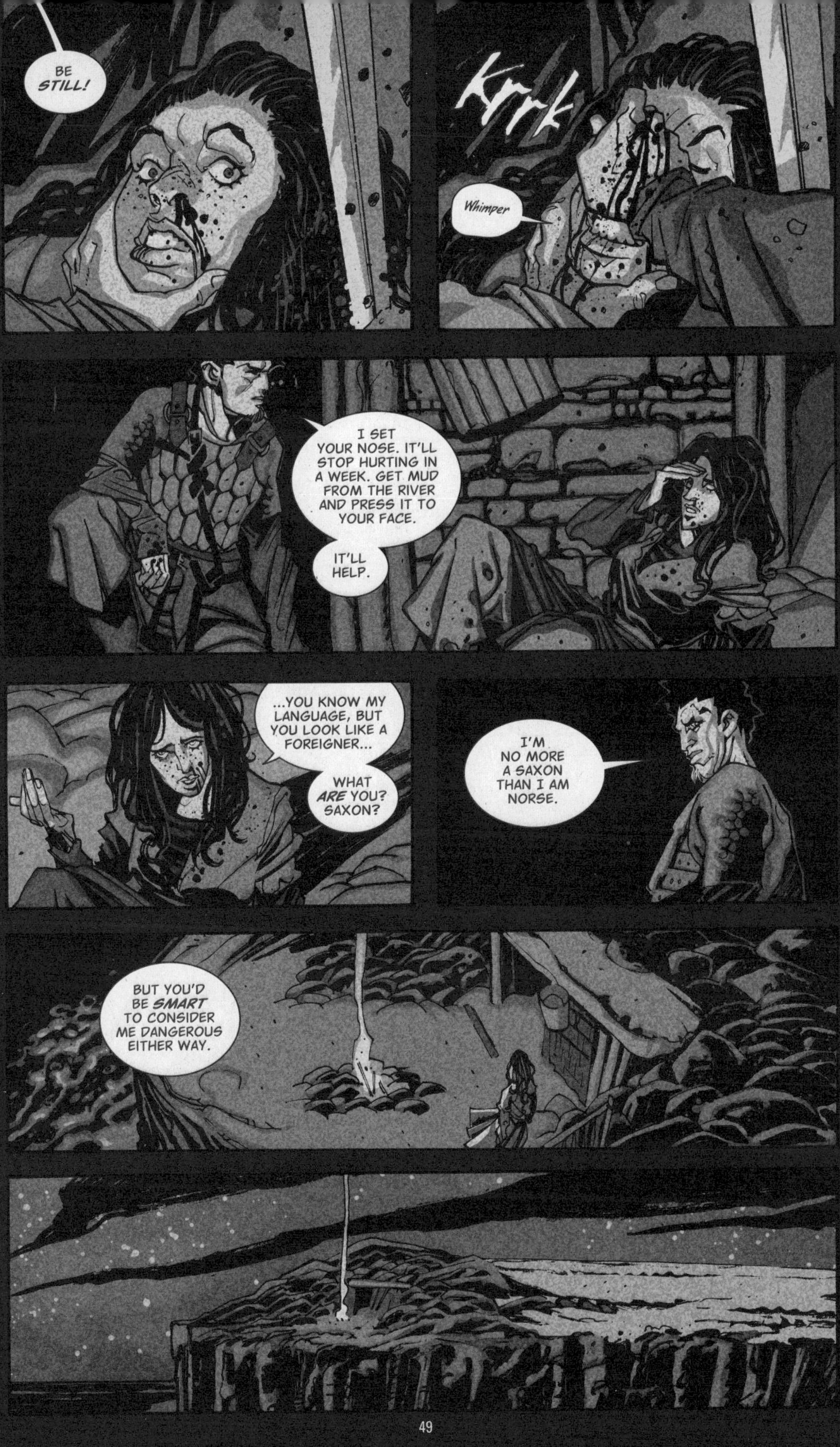

BE STILL!
KRRK
Whimper
I SET YOUR NOSE. IT'LL STOP HURTING IN A WEEK. GET MUD FROM THE RIVER AND PRESS IT TO YOUR FACE.
IT'LL HELP.
...YOU KNOW MY LANGUAGE, BUT YOU LOOK LIKE A FOREIGNER...
WHAT ARE YOU? SAXON?
I'M NO MORE A SAXON THAN I AM NORSE.
BUT YOU'D BE SMART TO CONSIDER ME DANGEROUS EITHER WAY.

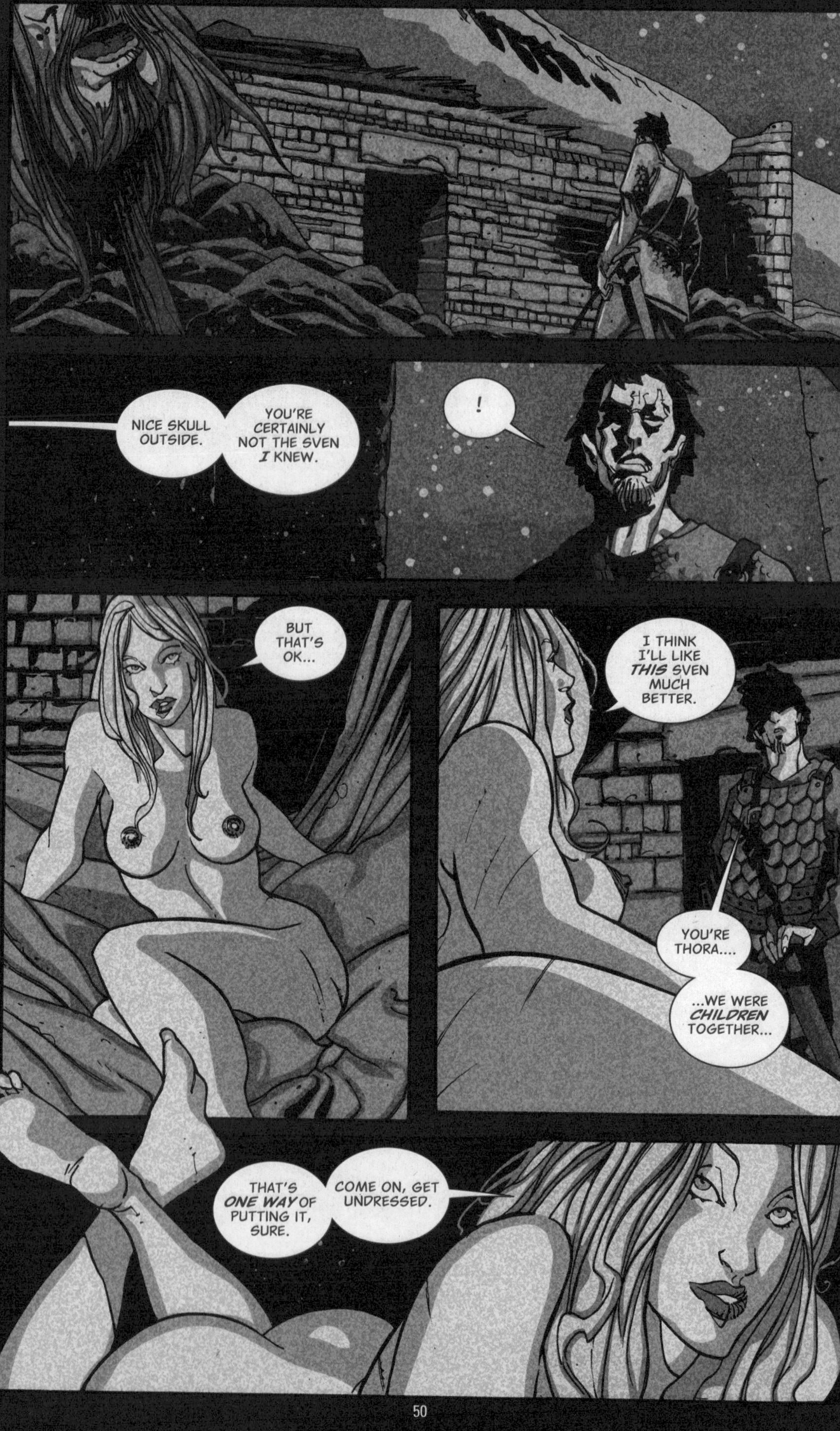
NICE SKULL OUTSIDE.
YOU'RE CERTAINLY NOT THE SVEN *I* KNEW.
!
BUT THAT'S OK...
I THINK I'LL LIKE *THIS* SVEN MUCH BETTER.
YOU'RE THORA....
...WE WERE *CHILDREN* TOGETHER...
THAT'S *ONE WAY* OF PUTTING IT, SURE.
COME ON, GET UNDRESSED.

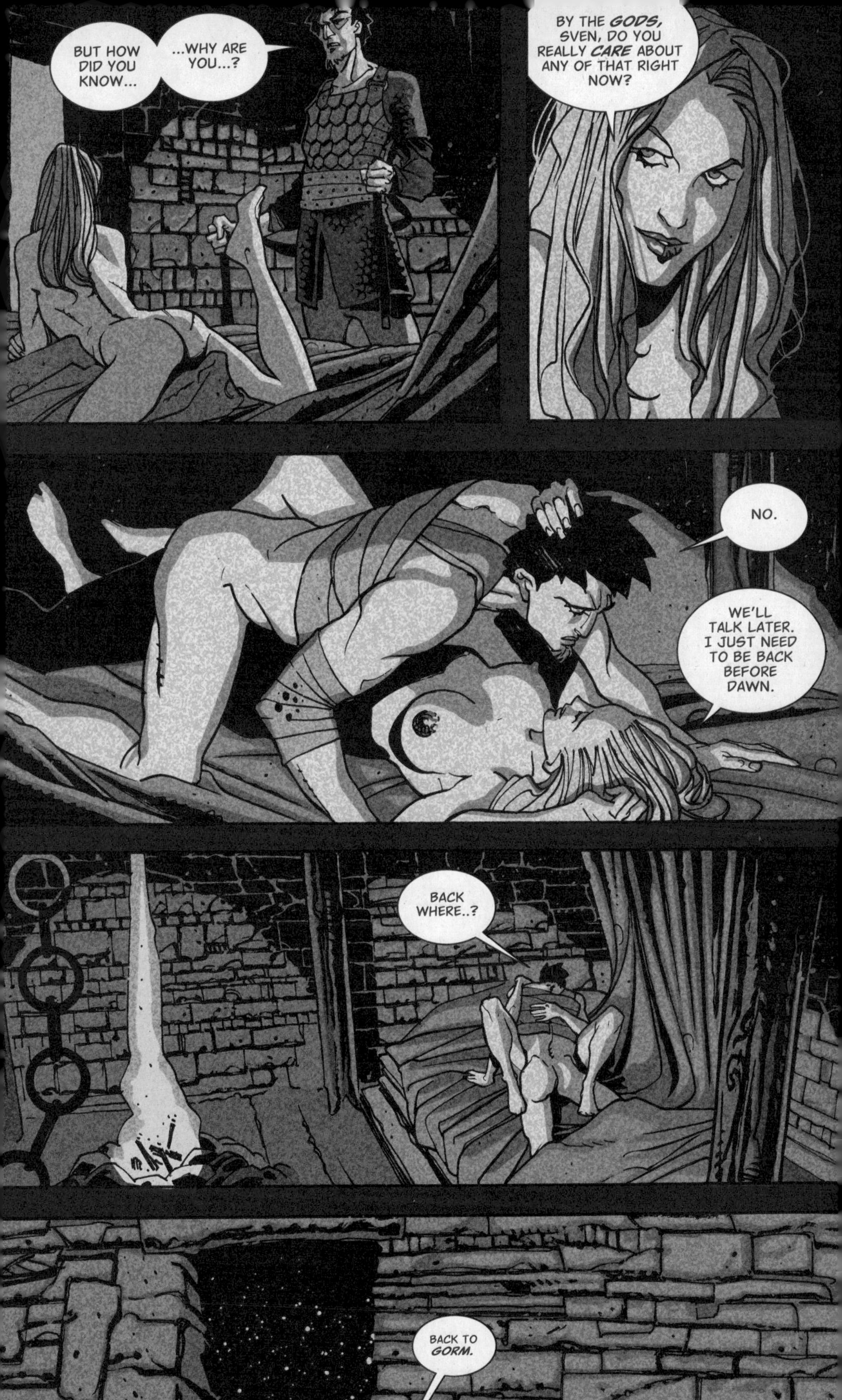
BUT HOW DID YOU KNOW...
...WHY ARE YOU...?
BY THE GODS, SVEN, DO YOU REALLY CARE ABOUT ANY OF THAT RIGHT NOW?
NO.
WE'LL TALK LATER. I JUST NEED TO BE BACK BEFORE DAWN.
BACK WHERE..?
BACK TO GORM.

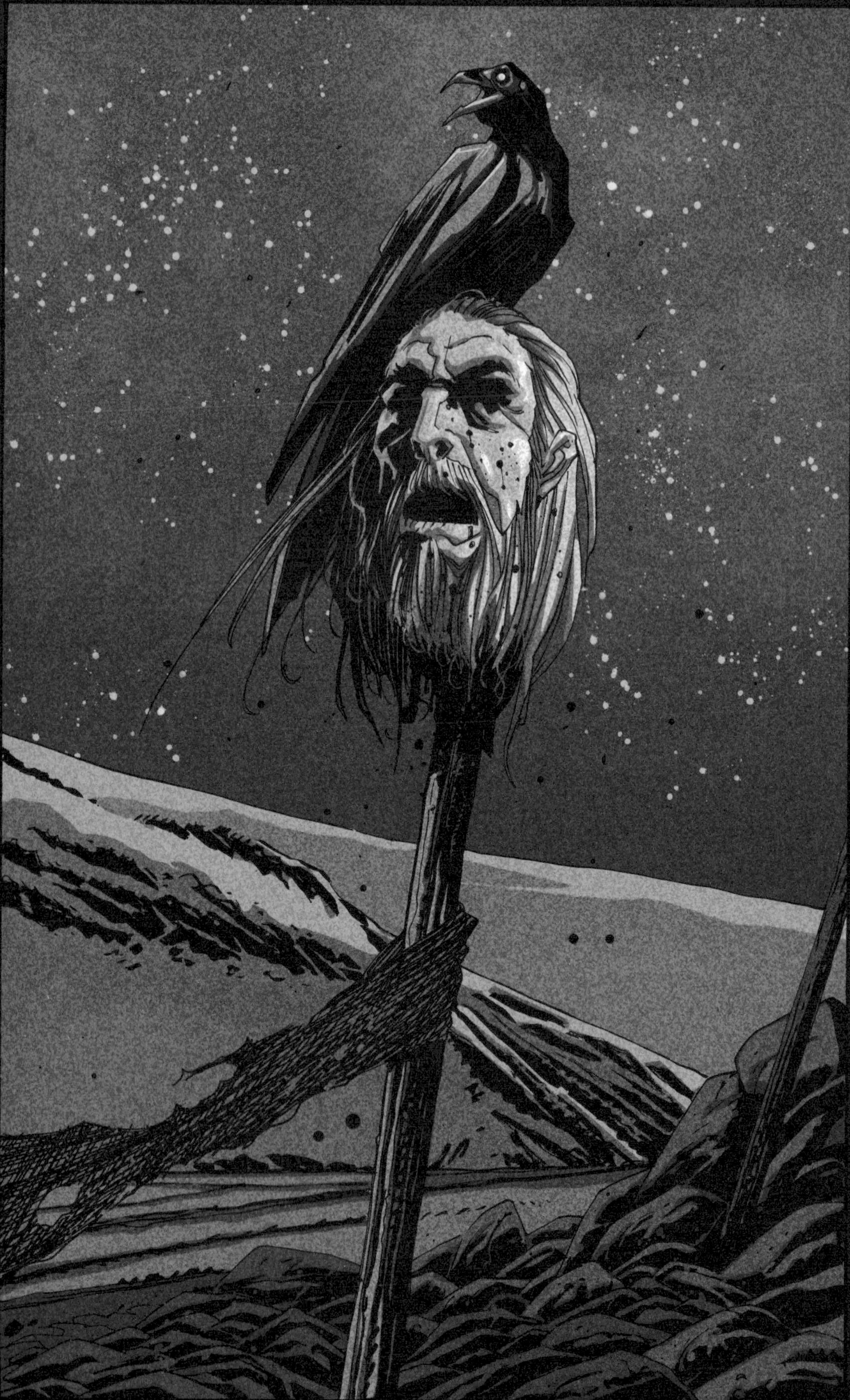

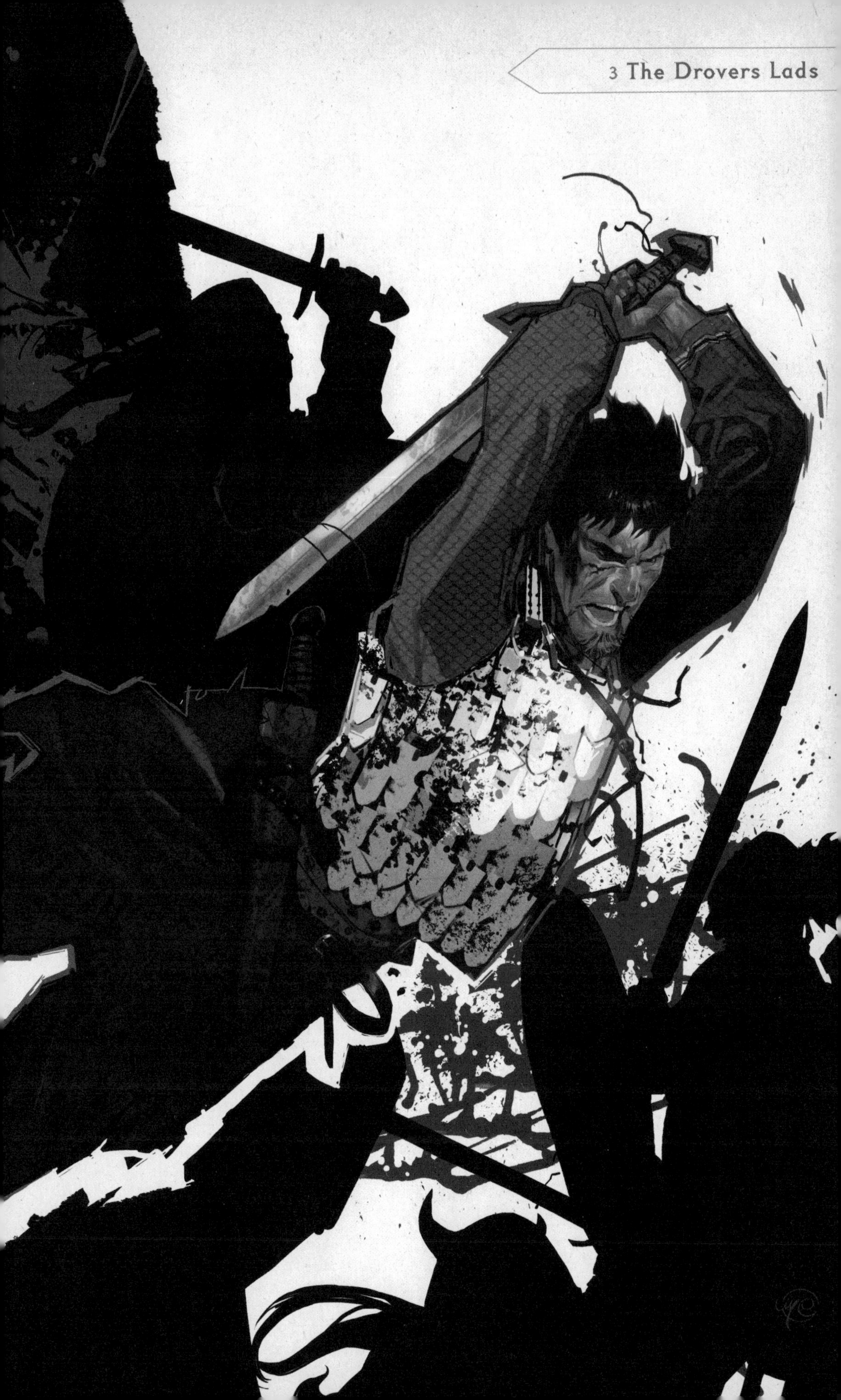

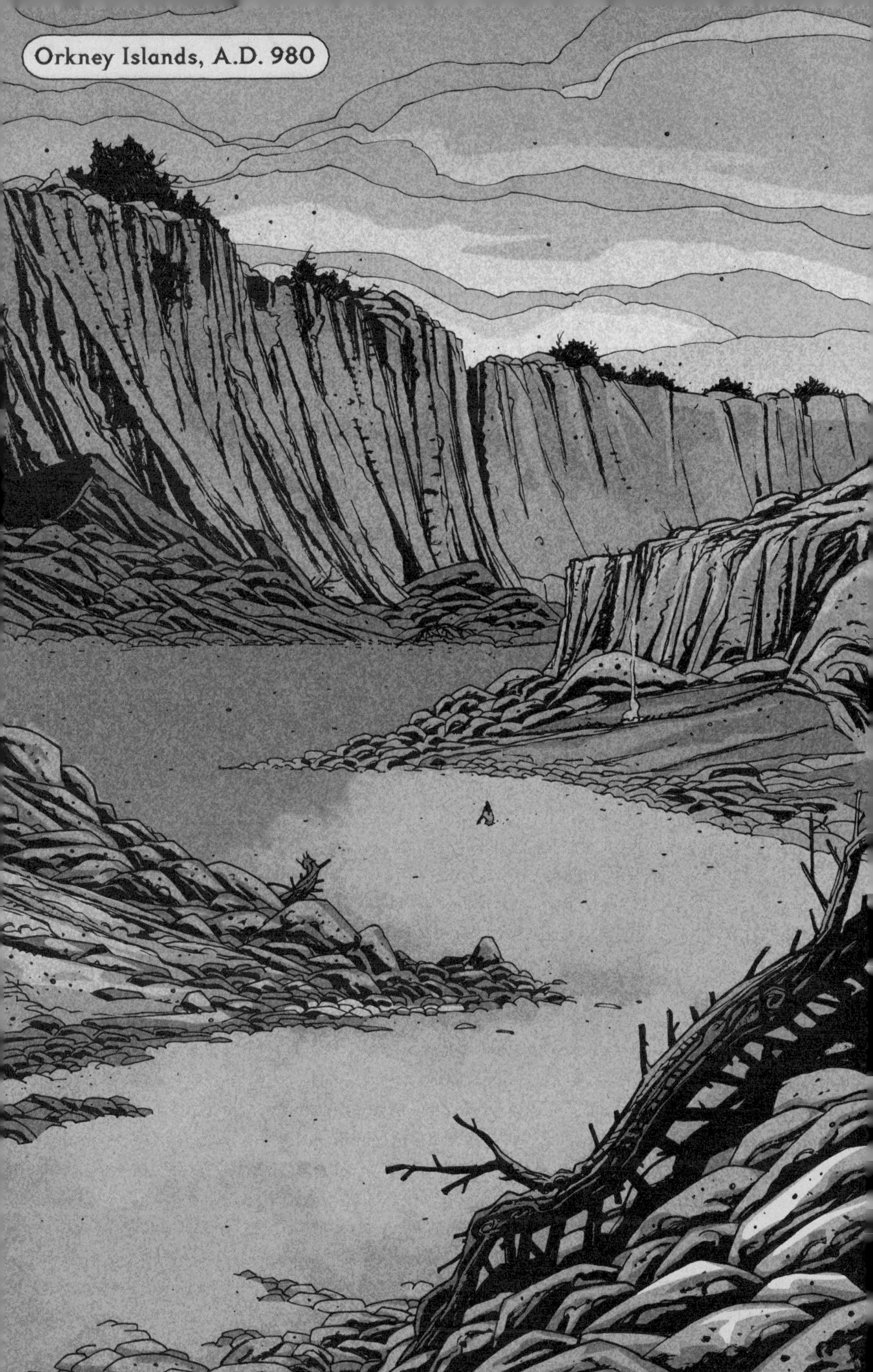
Orkney Islands, A.D. 980

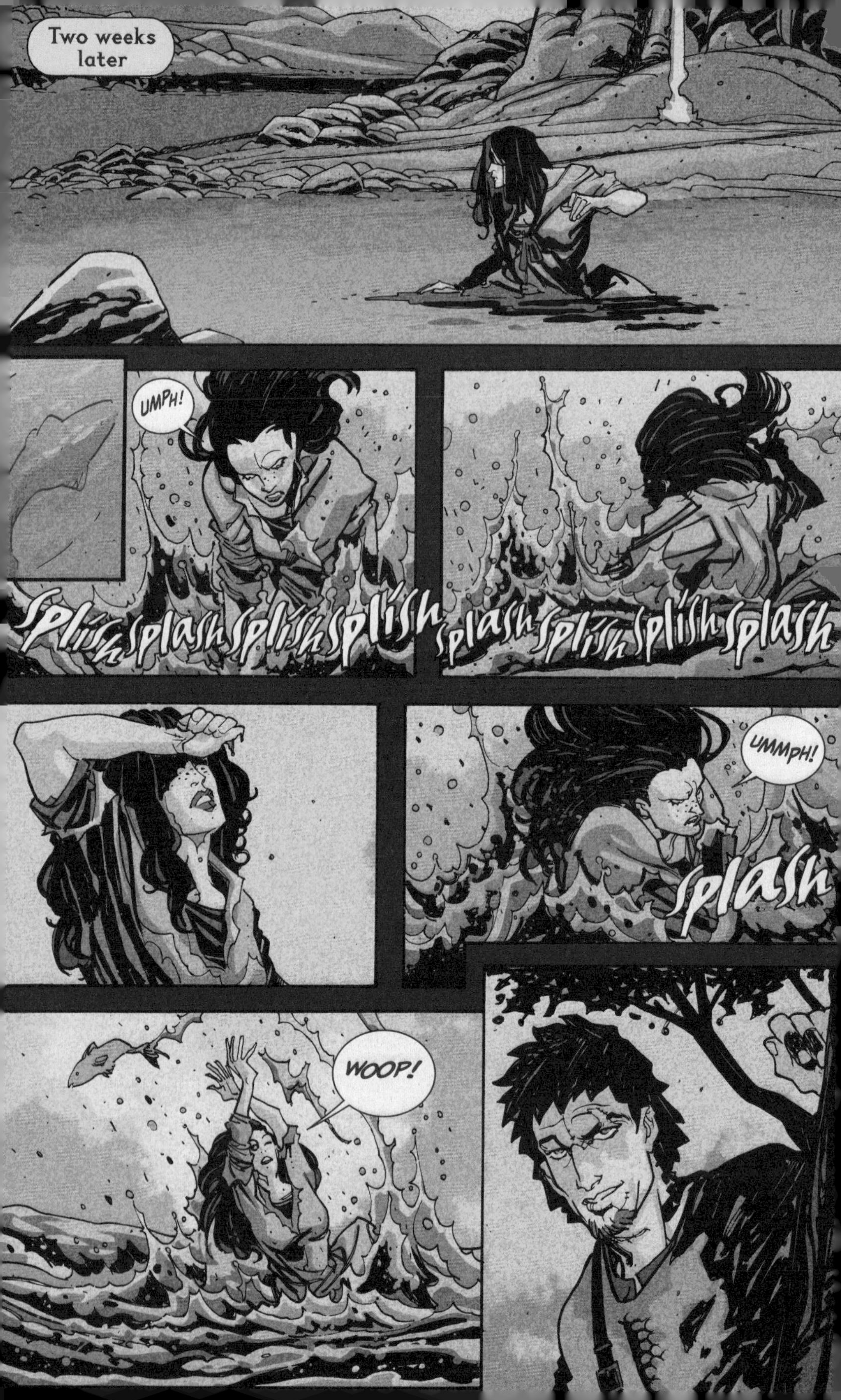
Two weeks later
UMPH!
splish splash splish splish
splash splish splish splash
UMMPH!
SPLASH
WOOP!

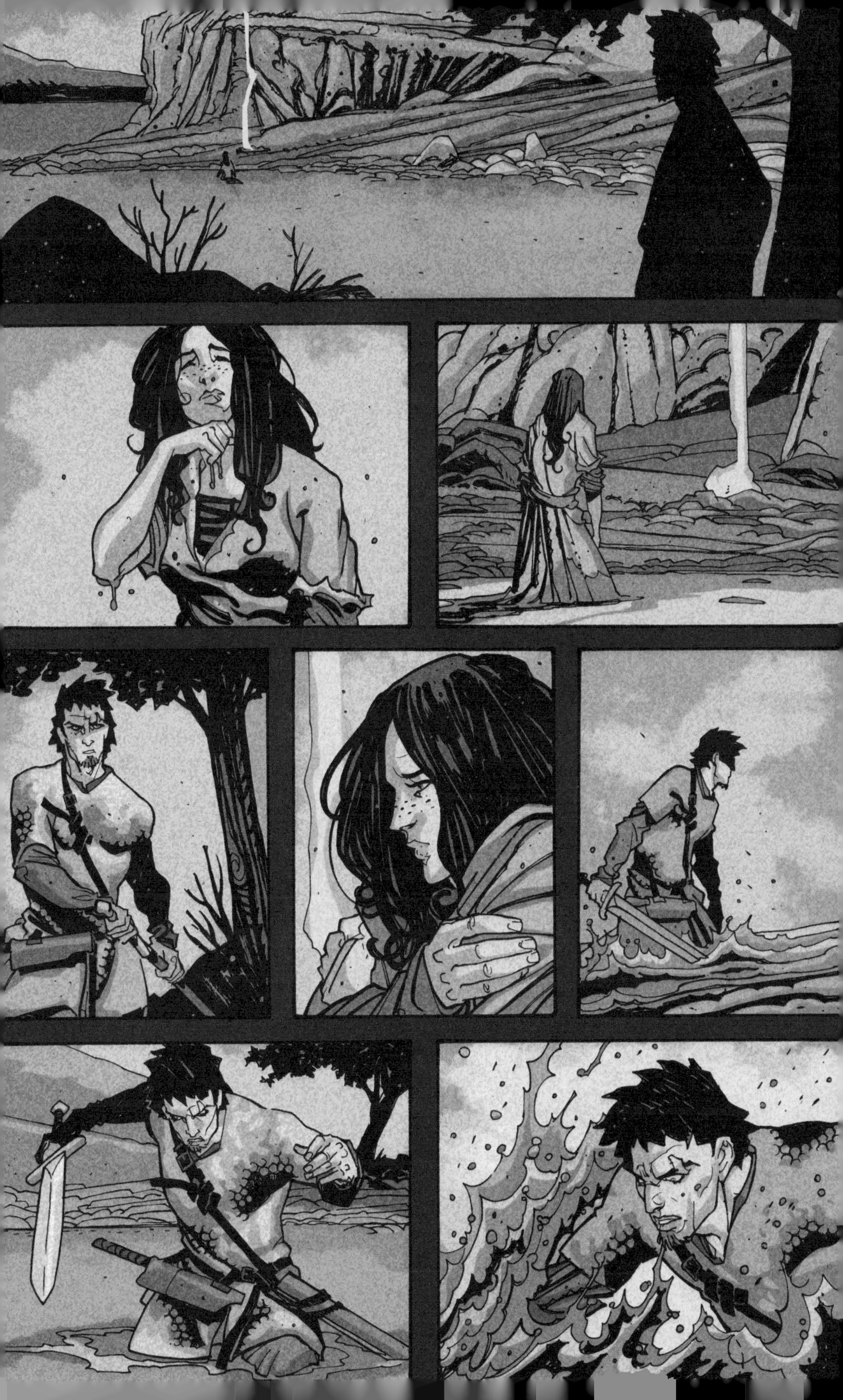

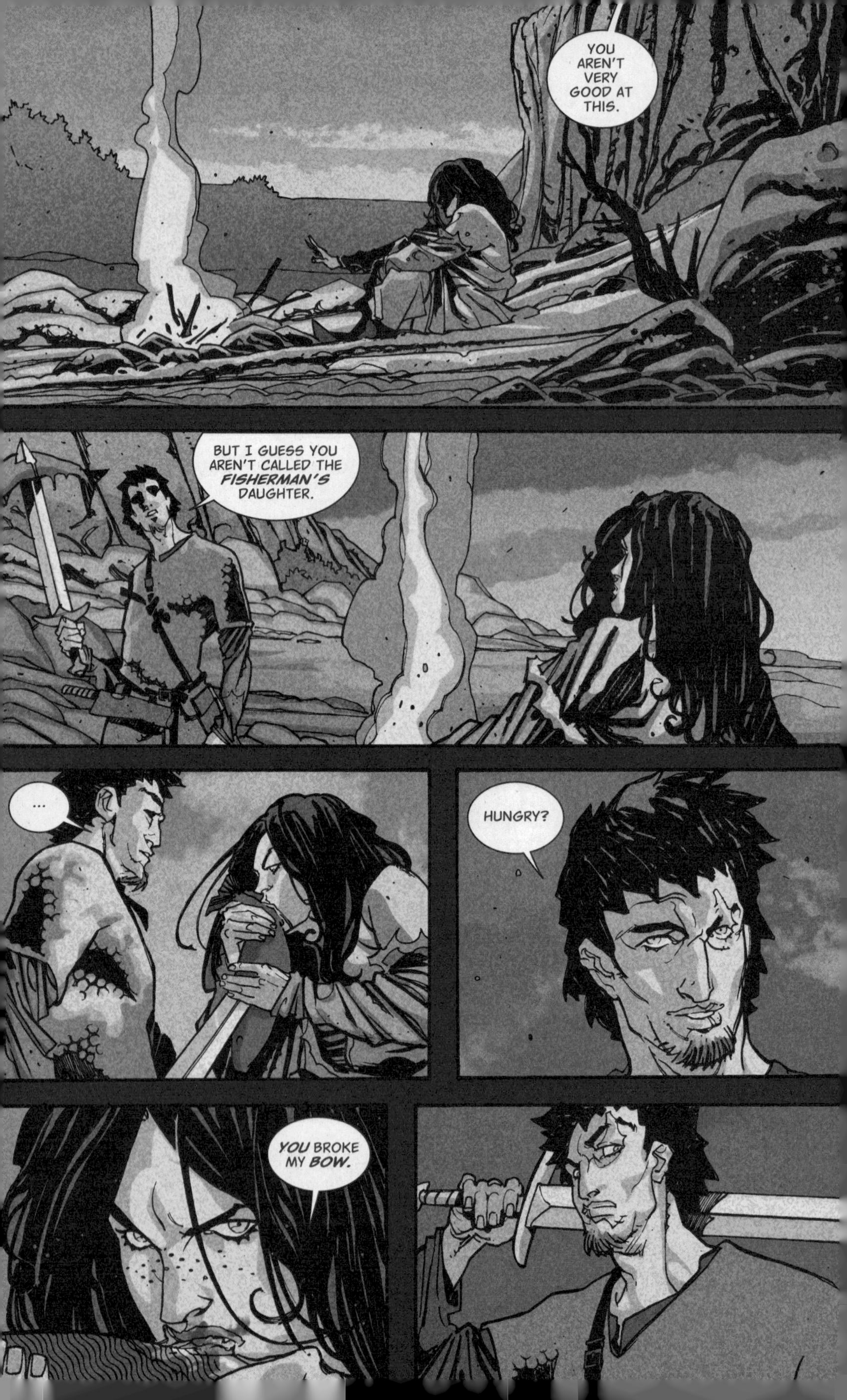
YOU AREN'T VERY GOOD AT THIS.
BUT I GUESS YOU AREN'T CALLED THE *FISHERMAN'S* DAUGHTER.
...
HUNGRY?
YOU BROKE MY *BOW*.

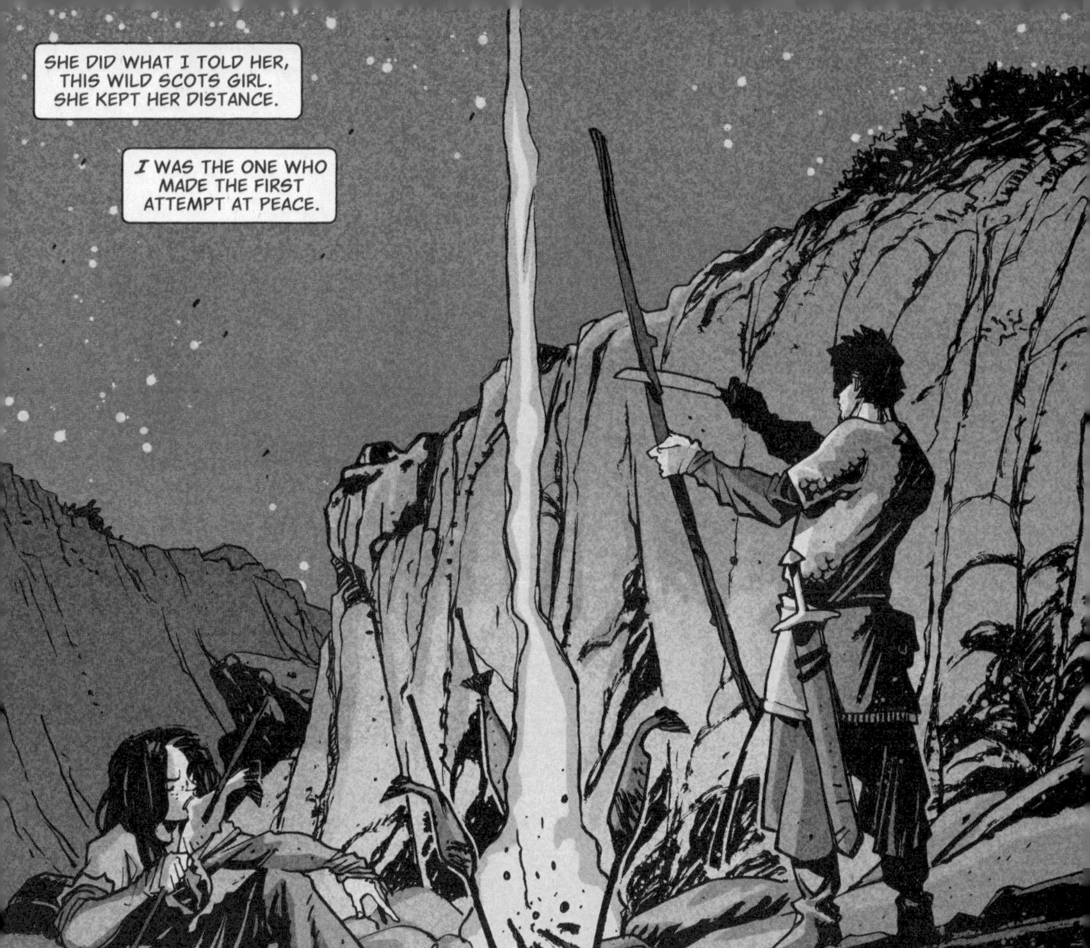
SHE DID WHAT I TOLD HER, THIS WILD SCOTS GIRL. SHE KEPT HER DISTANCE.
I WAS THE ONE WHO MADE THE FIRST ATTEMPT AT PEACE.

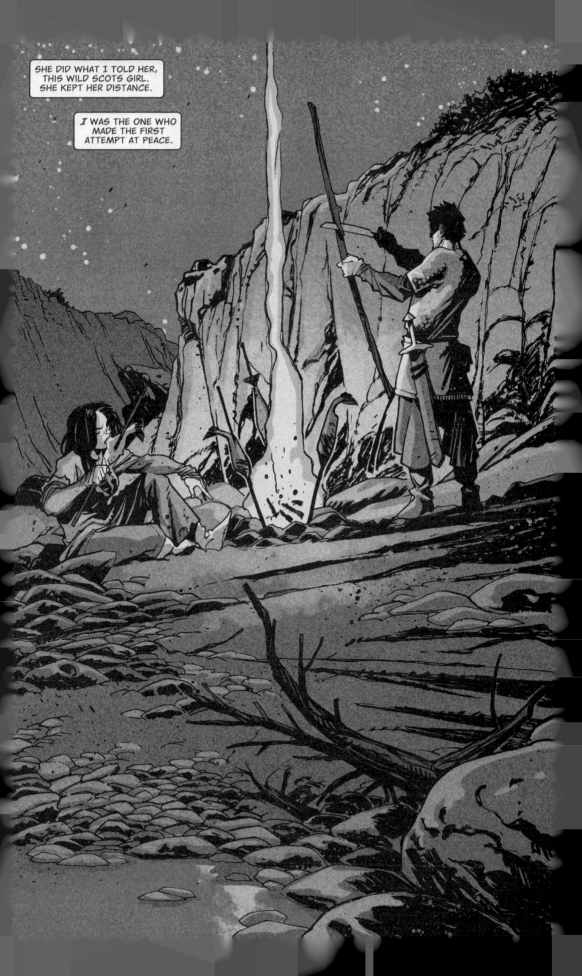

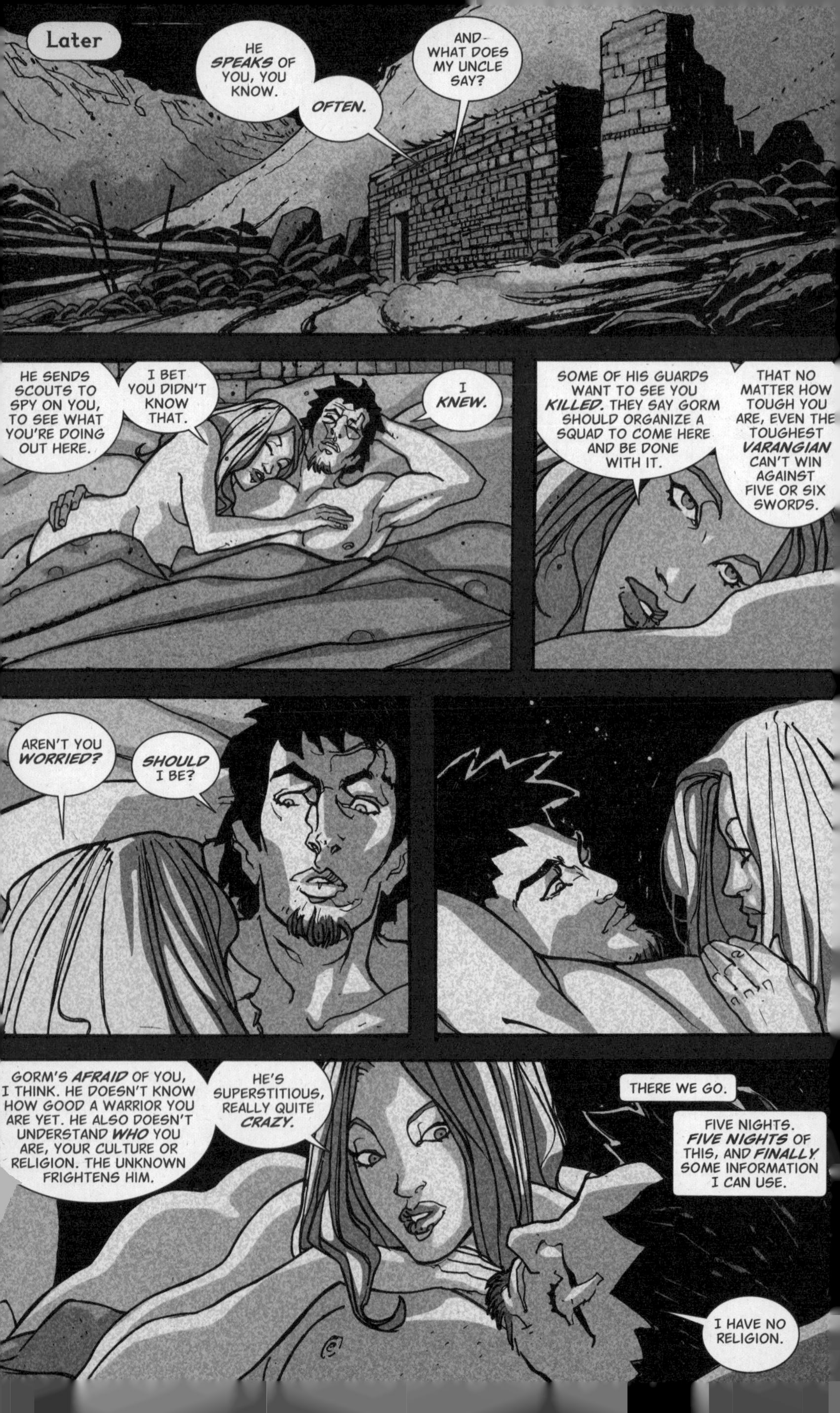
Later
HE SPEAKS OF YOU, YOU KNOW.
OFTEN.
AND WHAT DOES MY UNCLE SAY?
HE SENDS SCOUTS TO SPY ON YOU, TO SEE WHAT YOU'RE DOING OUT HERE.
I BET YOU DIDN'T KNOW THAT.
I KNEW.
SOME OF HIS GUARDS WANT TO SEE YOU KILLED. THEY SAY GORM SHOULD ORGANIZE A SQUAD TO COME HERE AND BE DONE WITH IT.
THAT NO MATTER HOW TOUGH YOU ARE, EVEN THE TOUGHEST VARANGIAN CAN'T WIN AGAINST FIVE OR SIX SWORDS.
AREN'T YOU WORRIED?
SHOULD I BE?
GORM'S AFRAID OF YOU, I THINK. HE DOESN'T KNOW HOW GOOD A WARRIOR YOU ARE YET. HE ALSO DOESN'T UNDERSTAND WHO YOU ARE, YOUR CULTURE OR RELIGION. THE UNKNOWN FRIGHTENS HIM.
HE'S SUPERSTITIOUS, REALLY QUITE CRAZY.
THERE WE GO.
FIVE NIGHTS. FIVE NIGHTS OF THIS, AND FINALLY SOME INFORMATION I CAN USE.
I HAVE NO RELIGION.

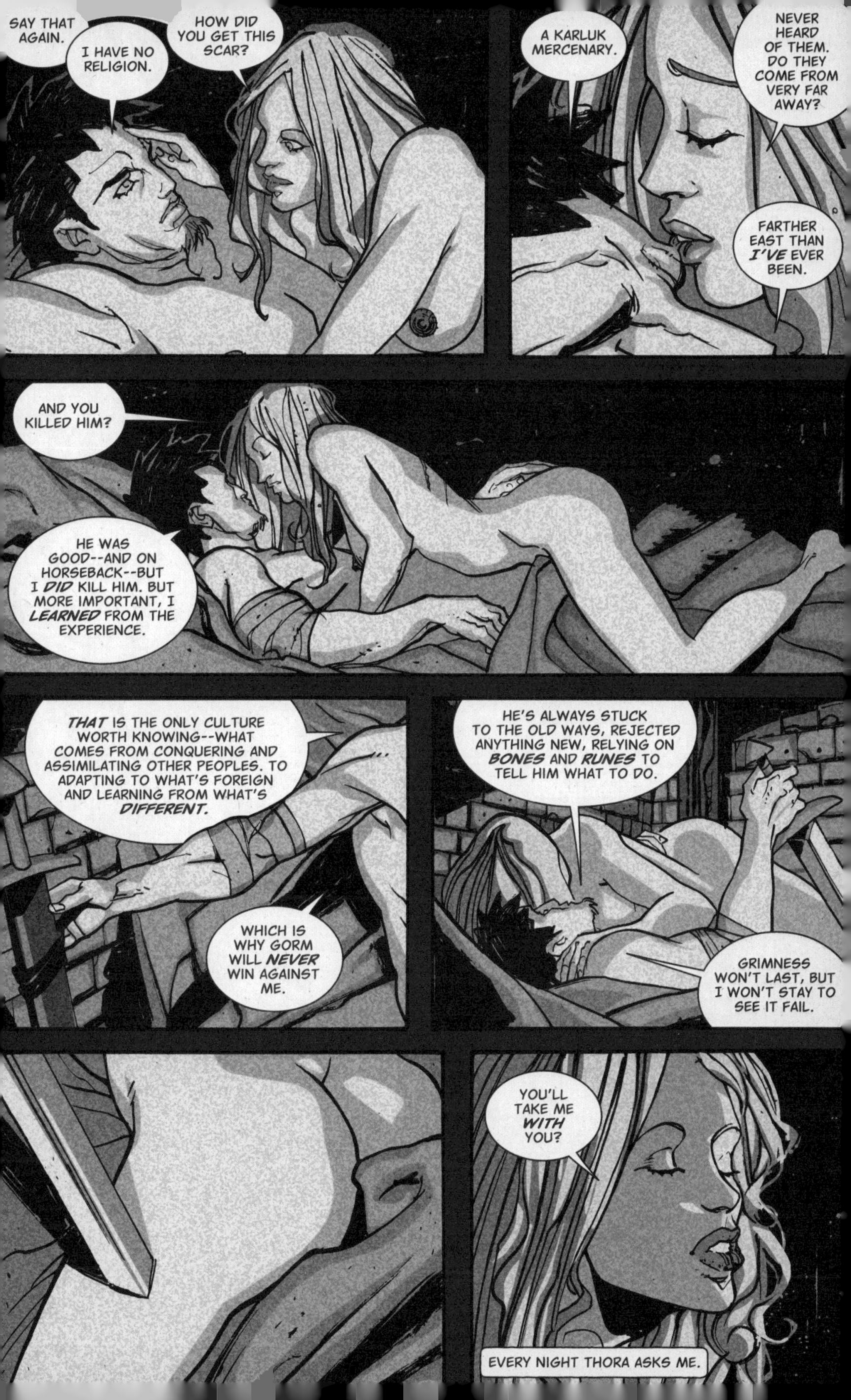

SAY THAT AGAIN.
I HAVE NO RELIGION.
HOW DID YOU GET THIS SCAR?
A KARLUK MERCENARY.
NEVER HEARD OF THEM. DO THEY COME FROM VERY FAR AWAY?
FARTHER EAST THAN *I'VE* EVER BEEN.
AND YOU KILLED HIM?
HE WAS GOOD--AND ON HORSEBACK--BUT I *DID* KILL HIM. BUT MORE IMPORTANT, I *LEARNED* FROM THE EXPERIENCE.
THAT IS THE ONLY CULTURE WORTH KNOWING--WHAT COMES FROM CONQUERING AND ASSIMILATING OTHER PEOPLES. TO ADAPTING TO WHAT'S FOREIGN AND LEARNING FROM WHAT'S *DIFFERENT.*
WHICH IS WHY GORM WILL *NEVER* WIN AGAINST ME.
HE'S ALWAYS STUCK TO THE OLD WAYS, REJECTED ANYTHING NEW, RELYING ON *BONES* AND *RUNES* TO TELL HIM WHAT TO DO.
GRIMNESS WON'T LAST, BUT I WON'T STAY TO SEE IT FAIL.
YOU'LL TAKE ME *WITH* YOU?
EVERY NIGHT THORA ASKS ME.

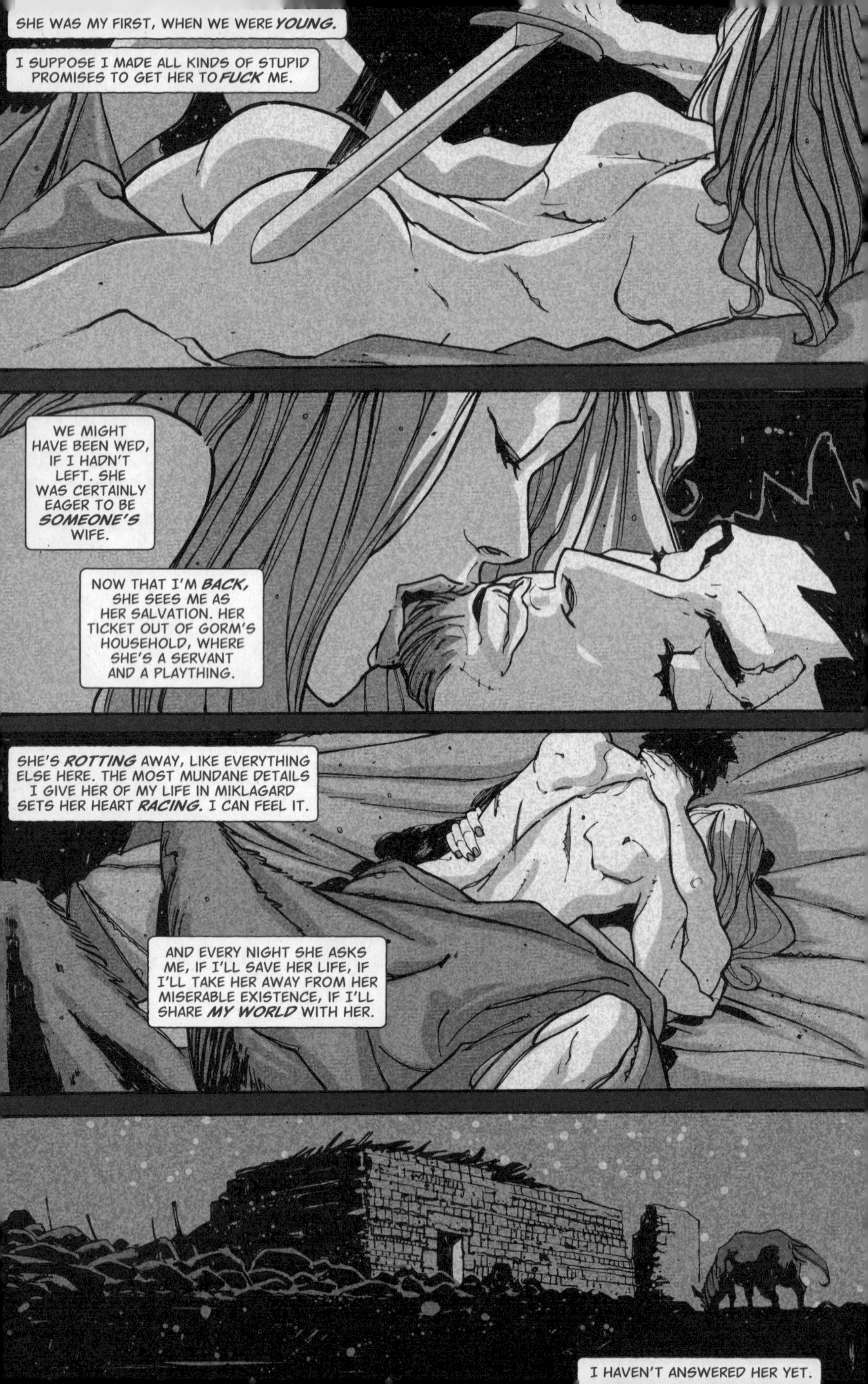
SHE WAS MY FIRST, WHEN WE WERE YOUNG.
I SUPPOSE I MADE ALL KINDS OF STUPID PROMISES TO GET HER TO FUCK ME.
WE MIGHT HAVE BEEN WED, IF I HADN'T LEFT. SHE WAS CERTAINLY EAGER TO BE SOMEONE'S WIFE.
NOW THAT I'M BACK, SHE SEES ME AS HER SALVATION. HER TICKET OUT OF GORM'S HOUSEHOLD, WHERE SHE'S A SERVANT AND A PLAYTHING.
SHE'S ROTTING AWAY, LIKE EVERYTHING ELSE HERE. THE MOST MUNDANE DETAILS I GIVE HER OF MY LIFE IN MIKLAGARD SETS HER HEART RACING. I CAN FEEL IT.
AND EVERY NIGHT SHE ASKS ME, IF I'LL SAVE HER LIFE, IF I'LL TAKE HER AWAY FROM HER MISERABLE EXISTENCE, IF I'LL SHARE MY WORLD WITH HER.
I HAVEN'T ANSWERED HER YET.

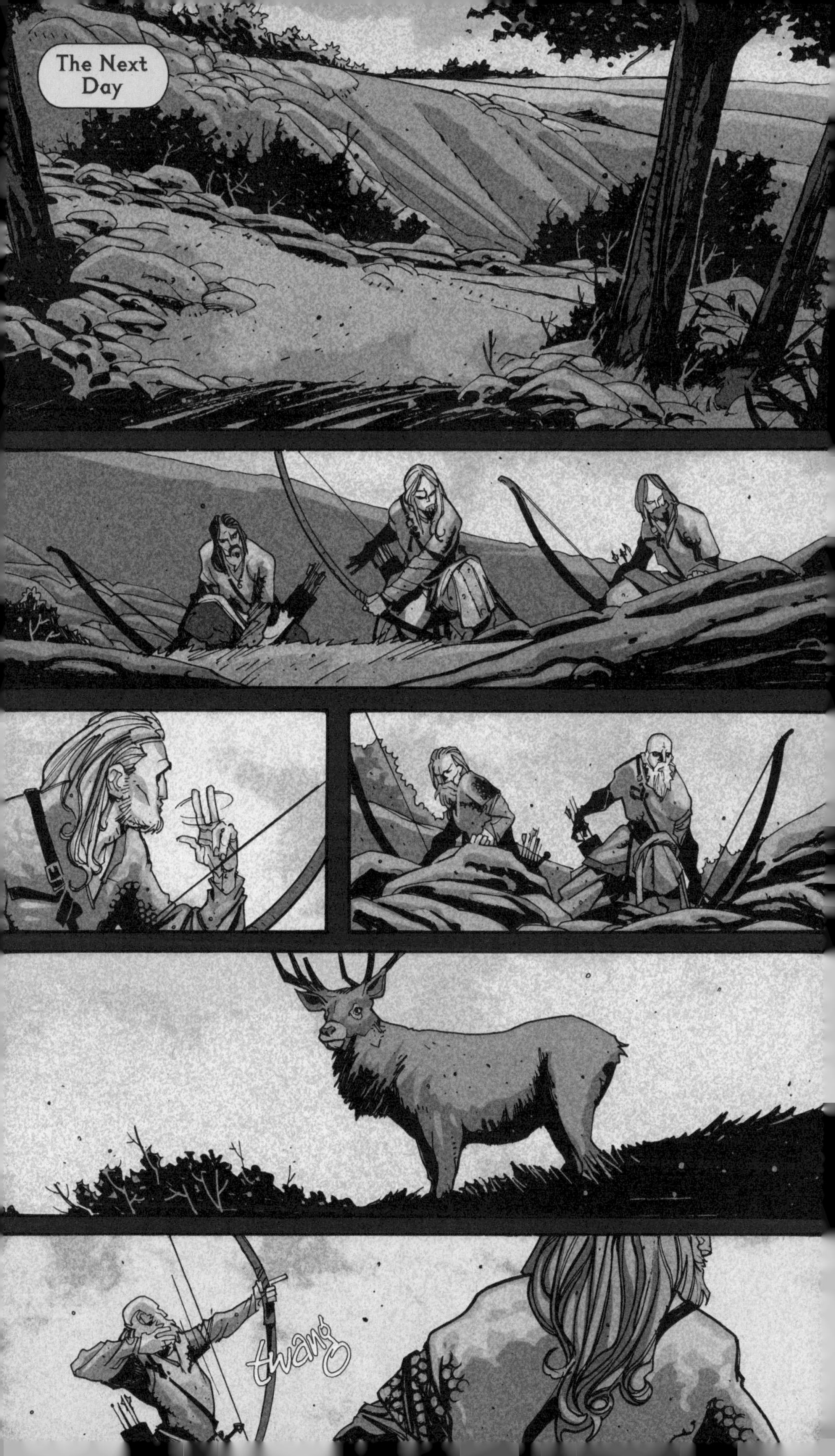
The Next Day
twang

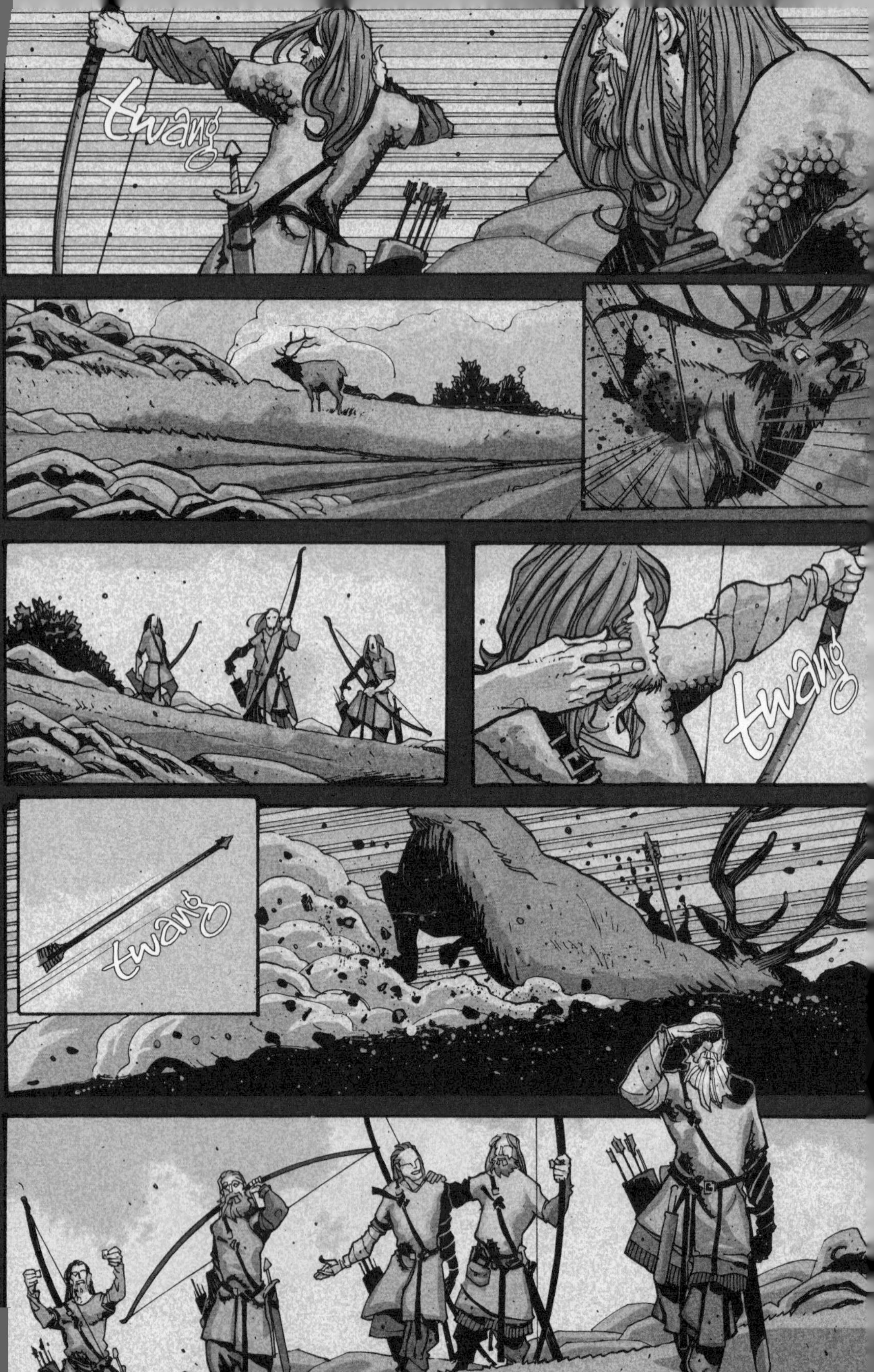
twang
twang
twang

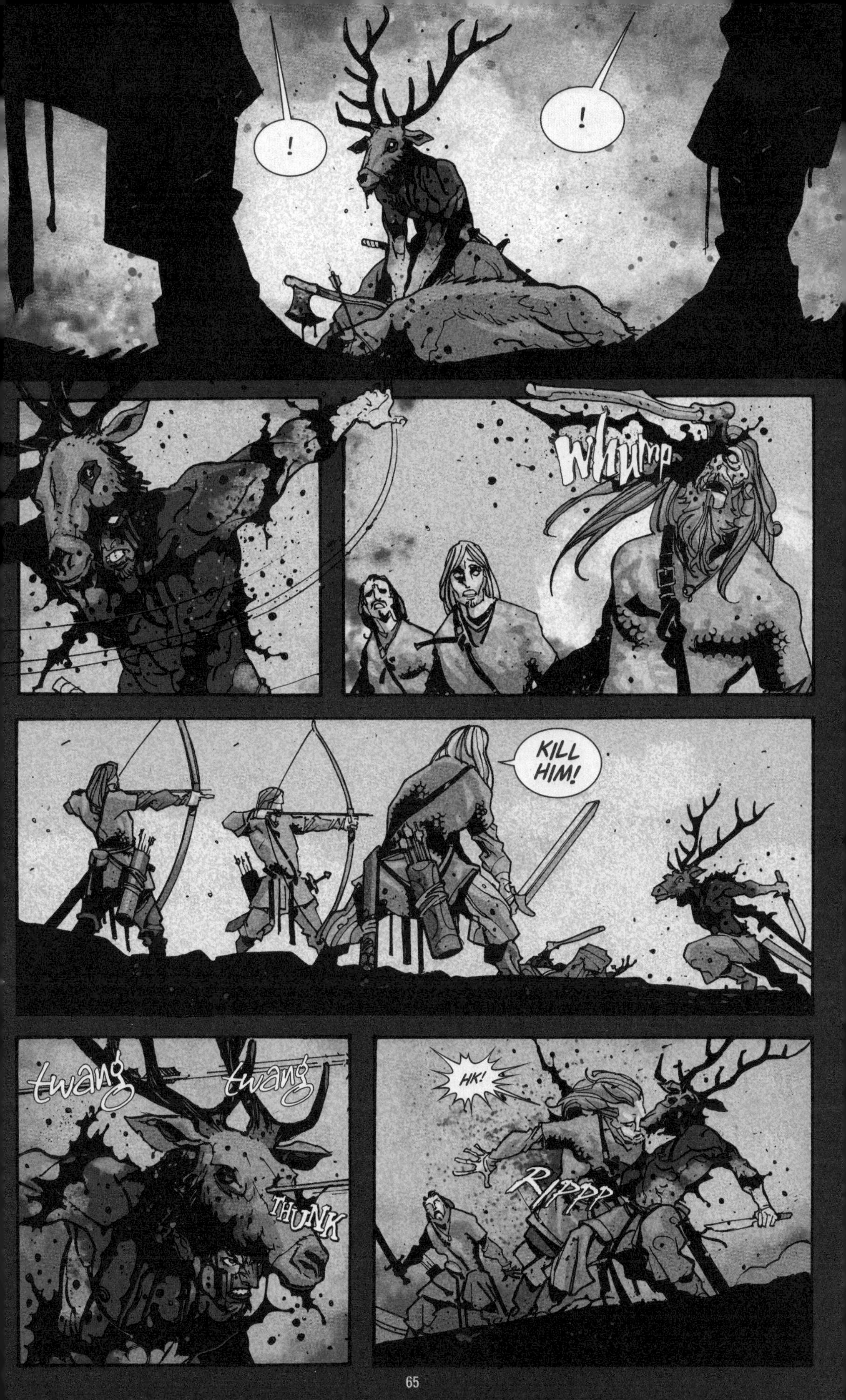
!
!
whump
KILL HIM!
twang
twang
THUNK
HK!
RIPPP

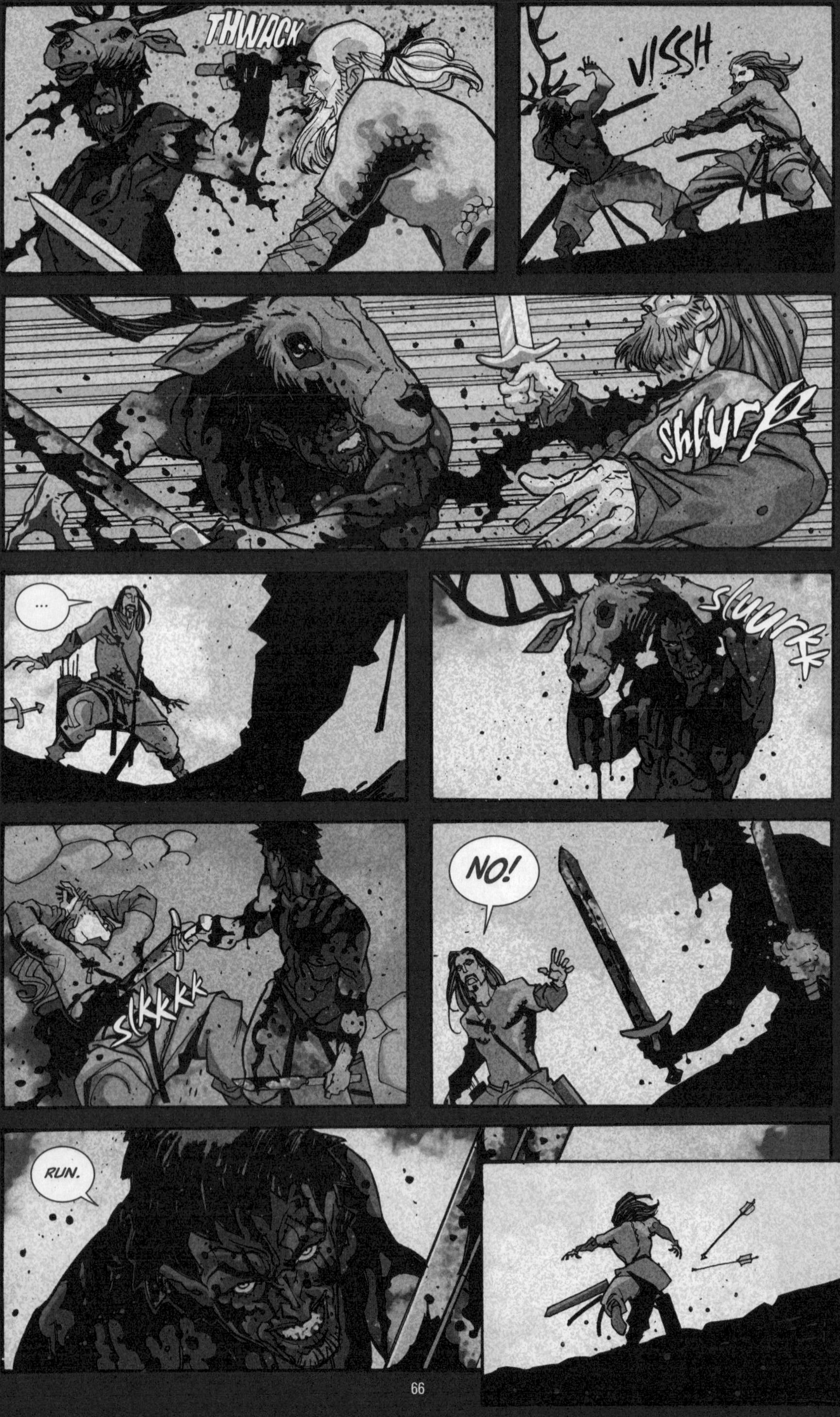
THWACK
VISSH
SHLURP
...
sluurrk
SLKKKK
NO!
RUN.

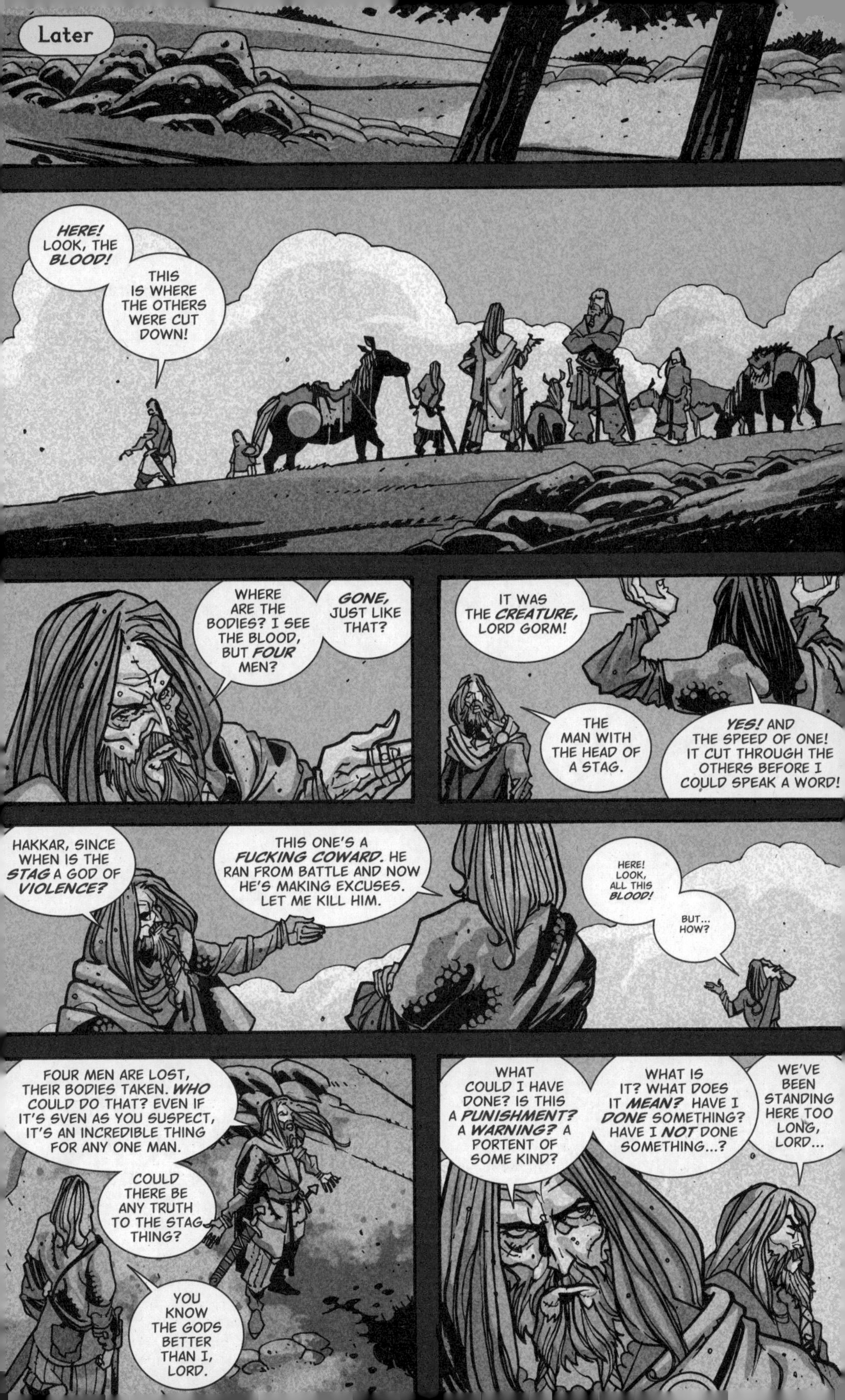
Later
HERE! LOOK, THE BLOOD!
THIS IS WHERE THE OTHERS WERE CUT DOWN!
WHERE ARE THE BODIES? I SEE THE BLOOD, BUT FOUR MEN?
GONE, JUST LIKE THAT?
IT WAS THE CREATURE, LORD GORM!
THE MAN WITH THE HEAD OF A STAG.
YES! AND THE SPEED OF ONE! IT CUT THROUGH THE OTHERS BEFORE I COULD SPEAK A WORD!
HAKKAR, SINCE WHEN IS THE STAG A GOD OF VIOLENCE?
THIS ONE'S A FUCKING COWARD. HE RAN FROM BATTLE AND NOW HE'S MAKING EXCUSES. LET ME KILL HIM.
HERE! LOOK, ALL THIS BLOOD!
BUT... HOW?
FOUR MEN ARE LOST, THEIR BODIES TAKEN. WHO COULD DO THAT? EVEN IF IT'S SVEN AS YOU SUSPECT, IT'S AN INCREDIBLE THING FOR ANY ONE MAN.
COULD THERE BE ANY TRUTH TO THE STAG THING?
YOU KNOW THE GODS BETTER THAN I, LORD.
WHAT COULD I HAVE DONE? IS THIS A PUNISHMENT? A WARNING? A PORTENT OF SOME KIND?
WHAT IS IT? WHAT DOES IT MEAN? HAVE I DONE SOMETHING? HAVE I NOT DONE SOMETHING...?
WE'VE BEEN STANDING HERE TOO LONG, LORD...

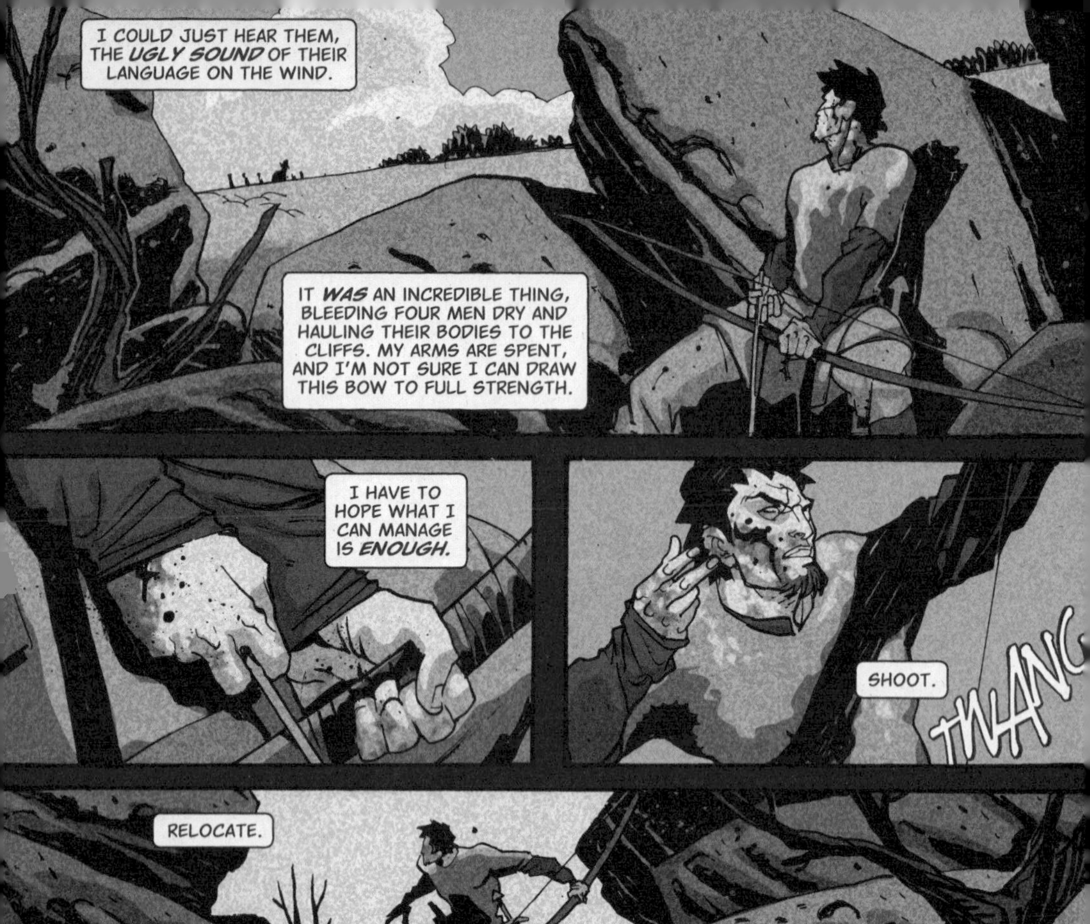
I COULD JUST HEAR THEM, THE UGLY SOUND OF THEIR LANGUAGE ON THE WIND.
IT WAS AN INCREDIBLE THING, BLEEDING FOUR MEN DRY AND HAULING THEIR BODIES TO THE CLIFFS. MY ARMS ARE SPENT, AND I'M NOT SURE I CAN DRAW THIS BOW TO FULL STRENGTH.
I HAVE TO HOPE WHAT I CAN MANAGE IS ENOUGH.
SHOOT.
TWANG
RELOCATE.
PLK
THE HORSES FIRST.
TWANG
SHOOT.
EASY TO HIT A HORSE.
NO!
THE MEN WILL HAVE TO BE TAKEN DOWN BY HAND.

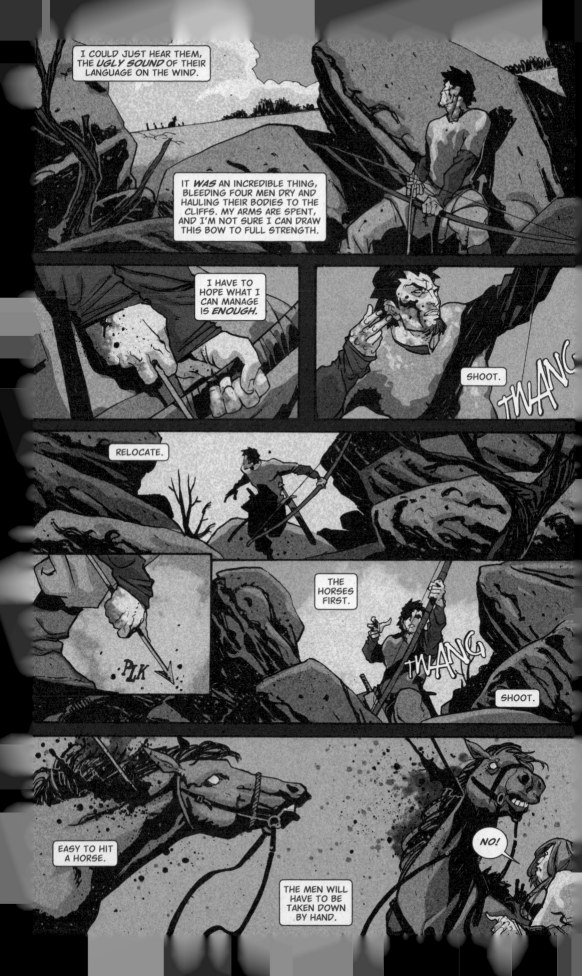

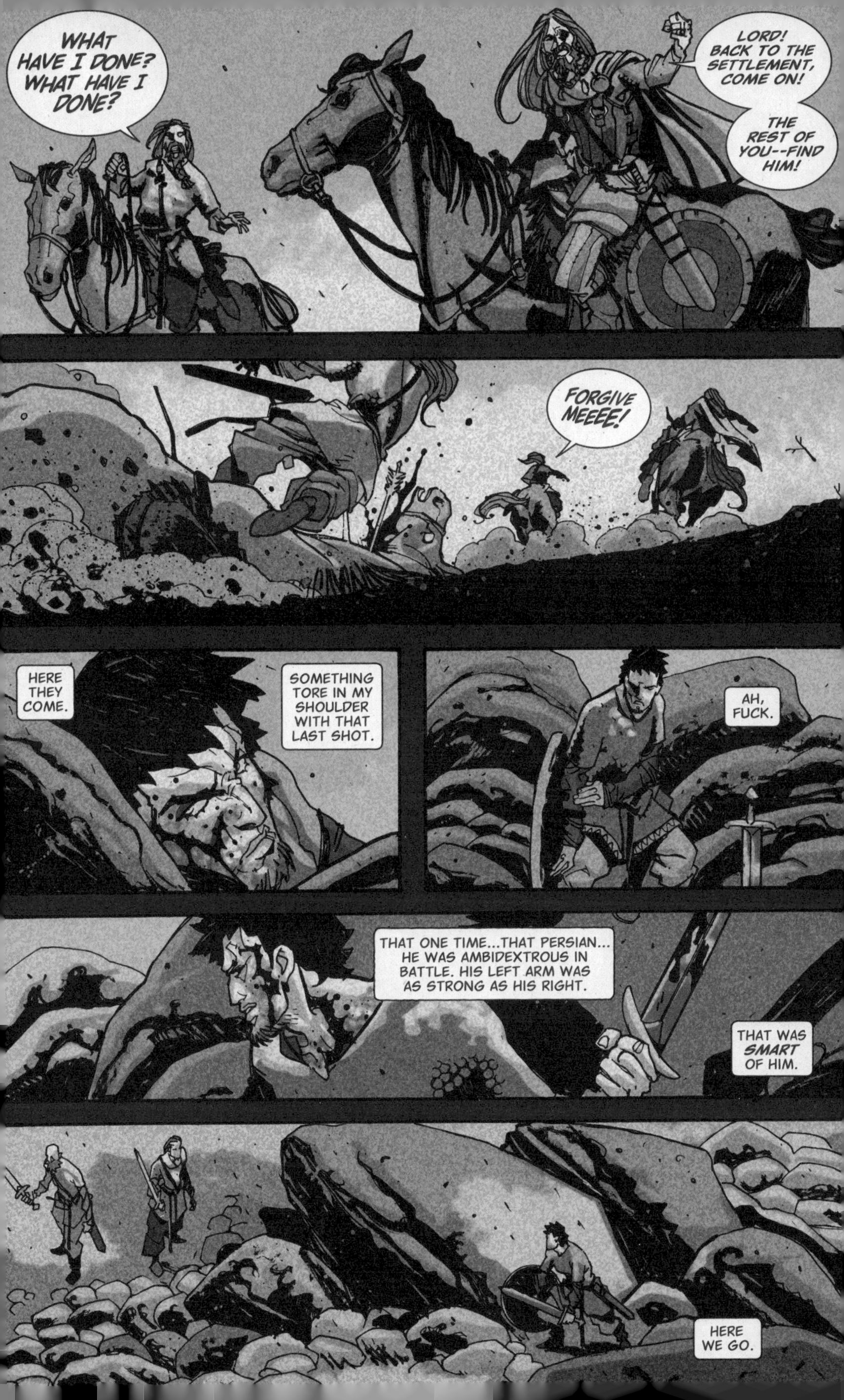
WHAT HAVE I DONE? WHAT HAVE I DONE?
LORD! BACK TO THE SETTLEMENT, COME ON!
THE REST OF YOU--FIND HIM!
FORGIVE MEEEE!
HERE THEY COME.
SOMETHING TORE IN MY SHOULDER WITH THAT LAST SHOT.
AH, FUCK.
THAT ONE TIME...THAT PERSIAN... HE WAS AMBIDEXTROUS IN BATTLE. HIS LEFT ARM WAS AS STRONG AS HIS RIGHT.
THAT WAS SMART OF HIM.
HERE WE GO.

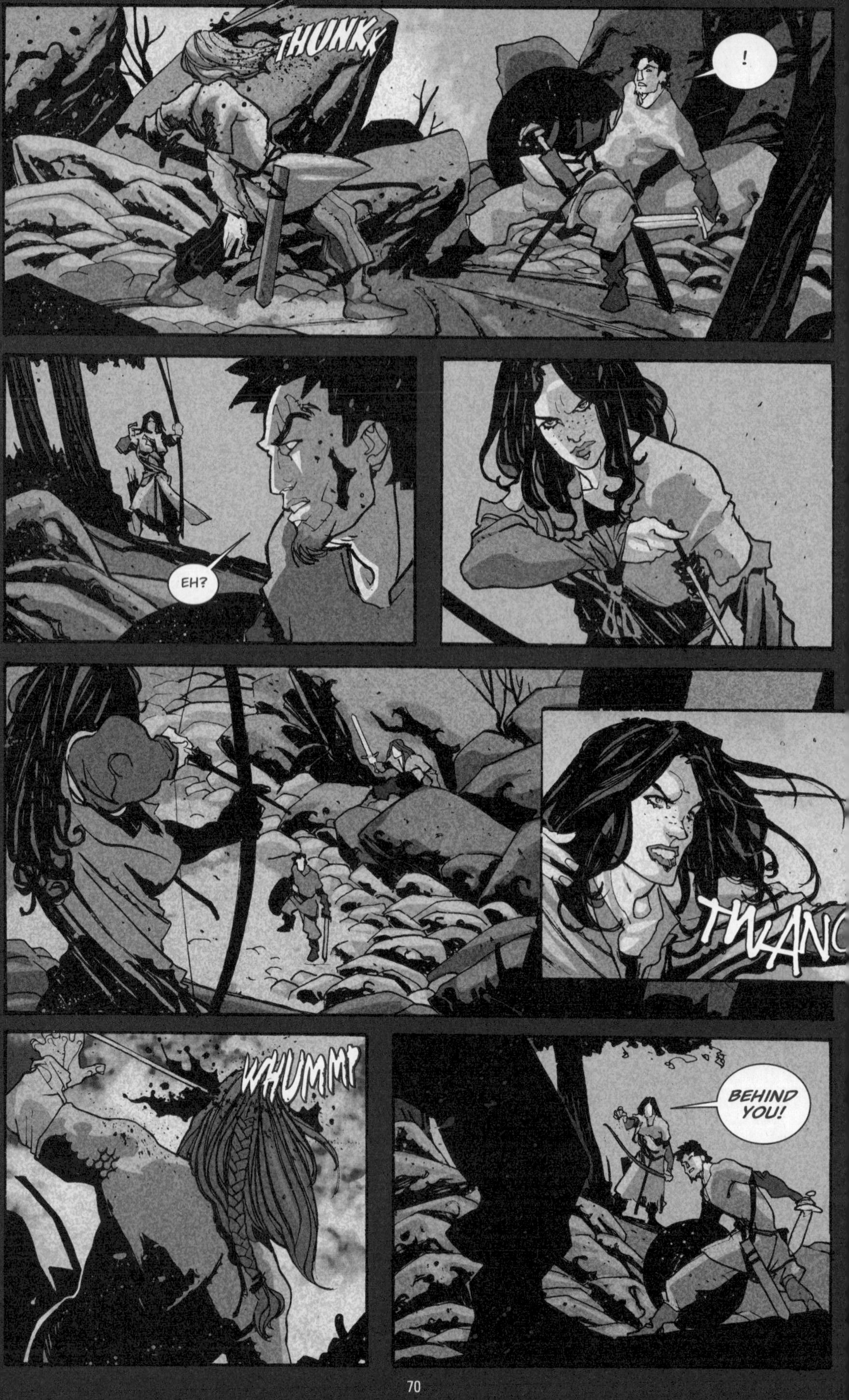
THUNKK
!
EH?
TWANG
WHUMM
BEHIND YOU!

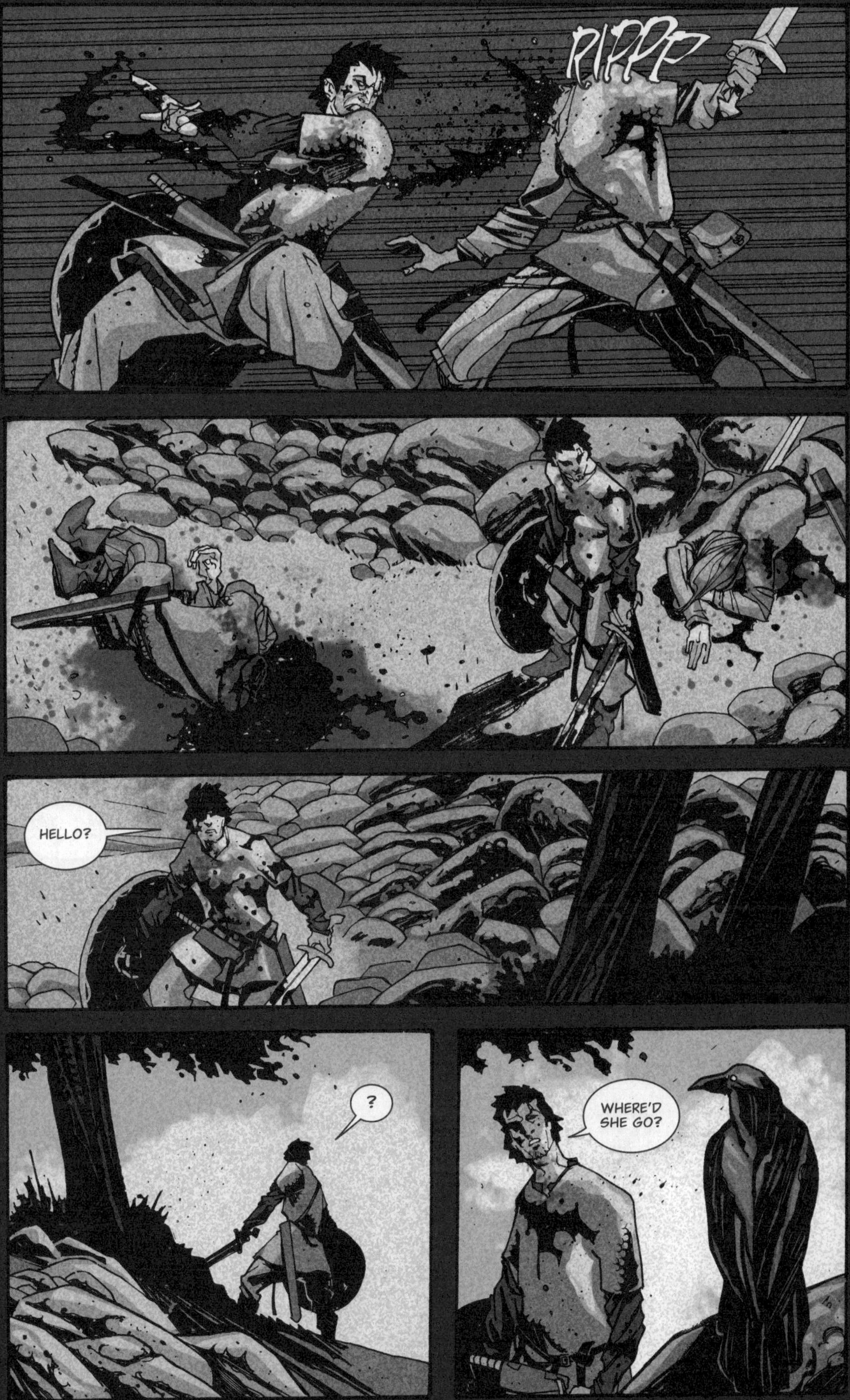
RIPPP
HELLO?
?
WHERE'D SHE GO?

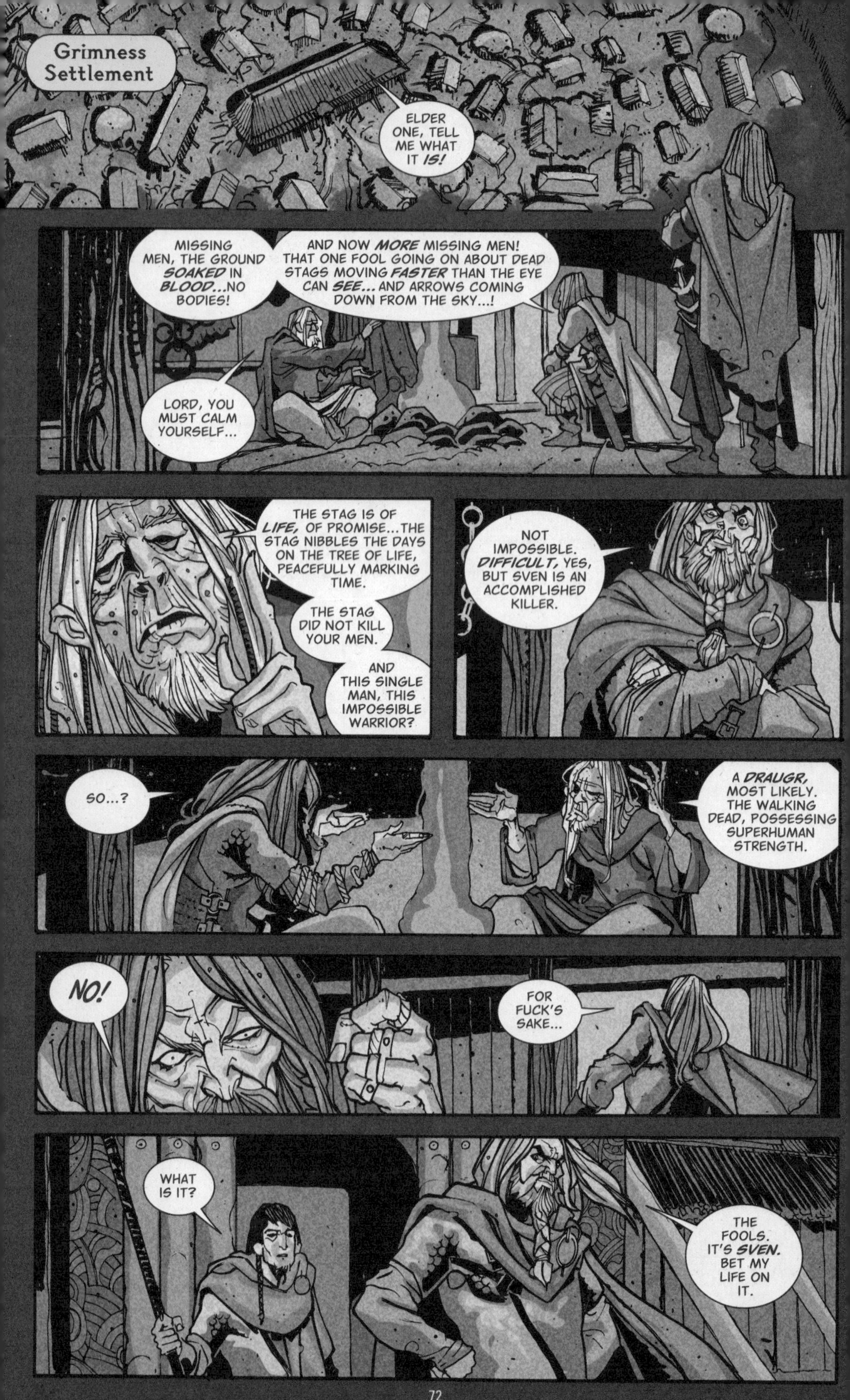
Grimness Settlement
ELDER ONE, TELL ME WHAT IT *IS!*
MISSING MEN, THE GROUND *SOAKED* IN *BLOOD...*NO BODIES!
AND NOW *MORE* MISSING MEN! THAT ONE FOOL GOING ON ABOUT DEAD STAGS MOVING *FASTER* THAN THE EYE CAN *SEE...* AND ARROWS COMING DOWN FROM THE SKY...!
LORD, YOU MUST CALM YOURSELF...
THE STAG IS OF *LIFE,* OF PROMISE...THE STAG NIBBLES THE DAYS ON THE TREE OF LIFE, PEACEFULLY MARKING TIME.
THE STAG DID NOT KILL YOUR MEN.
AND THIS SINGLE MAN, THIS IMPOSSIBLE WARRIOR?
NOT IMPOSSIBLE. *DIFFICULT,* YES, BUT SVEN IS AN ACCOMPLISHED KILLER.
SO...?
A *DRAUGR,* MOST LIKELY. THE WALKING DEAD, POSSESSING SUPERHUMAN STRENGTH.
NO!
FOR FUCK'S SAKE...
WHAT IS IT?
THE FOOLS. IT'S *SVEN.* BET MY LIFE ON IT.

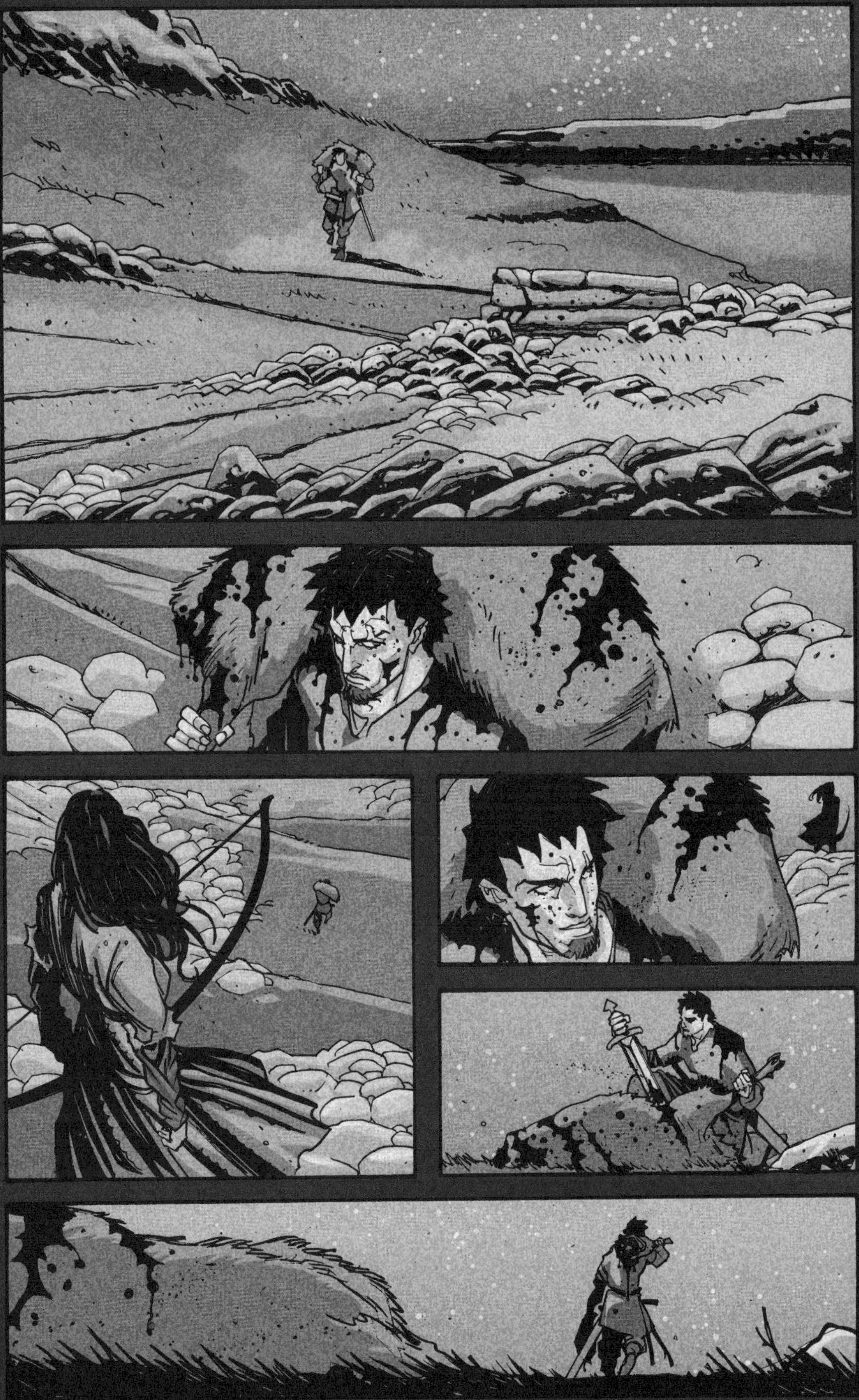

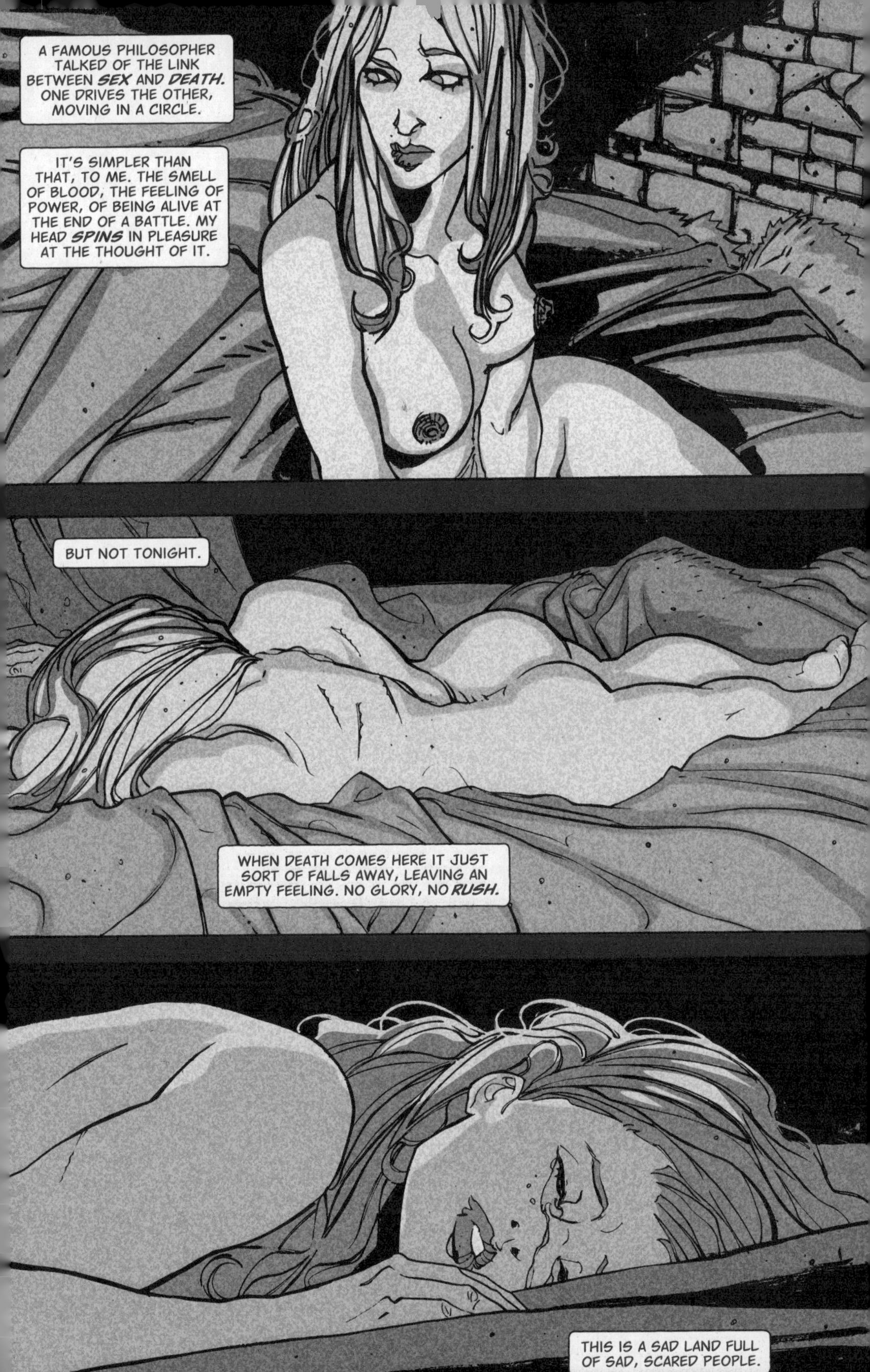
A FAMOUS PHILOSOPHER TALKED OF THE LINK BETWEEN SEX AND DEATH. ONE DRIVES THE OTHER, MOVING IN A CIRCLE.
IT'S SIMPLER THAN THAT, TO ME. THE SMELL OF BLOOD, THE FEELING OF POWER, OF BEING ALIVE AT THE END OF A BATTLE. MY HEAD SPINS IN PLEASURE AT THE THOUGHT OF IT.
BUT NOT TONIGHT.
WHEN DEATH COMES HERE IT JUST SORT OF FALLS AWAY, LEAVING AN EMPTY FEELING. NO GLORY, NO RUSH.
THIS IS A SAD LAND FULL OF SAD, SCARED PEOPLE.

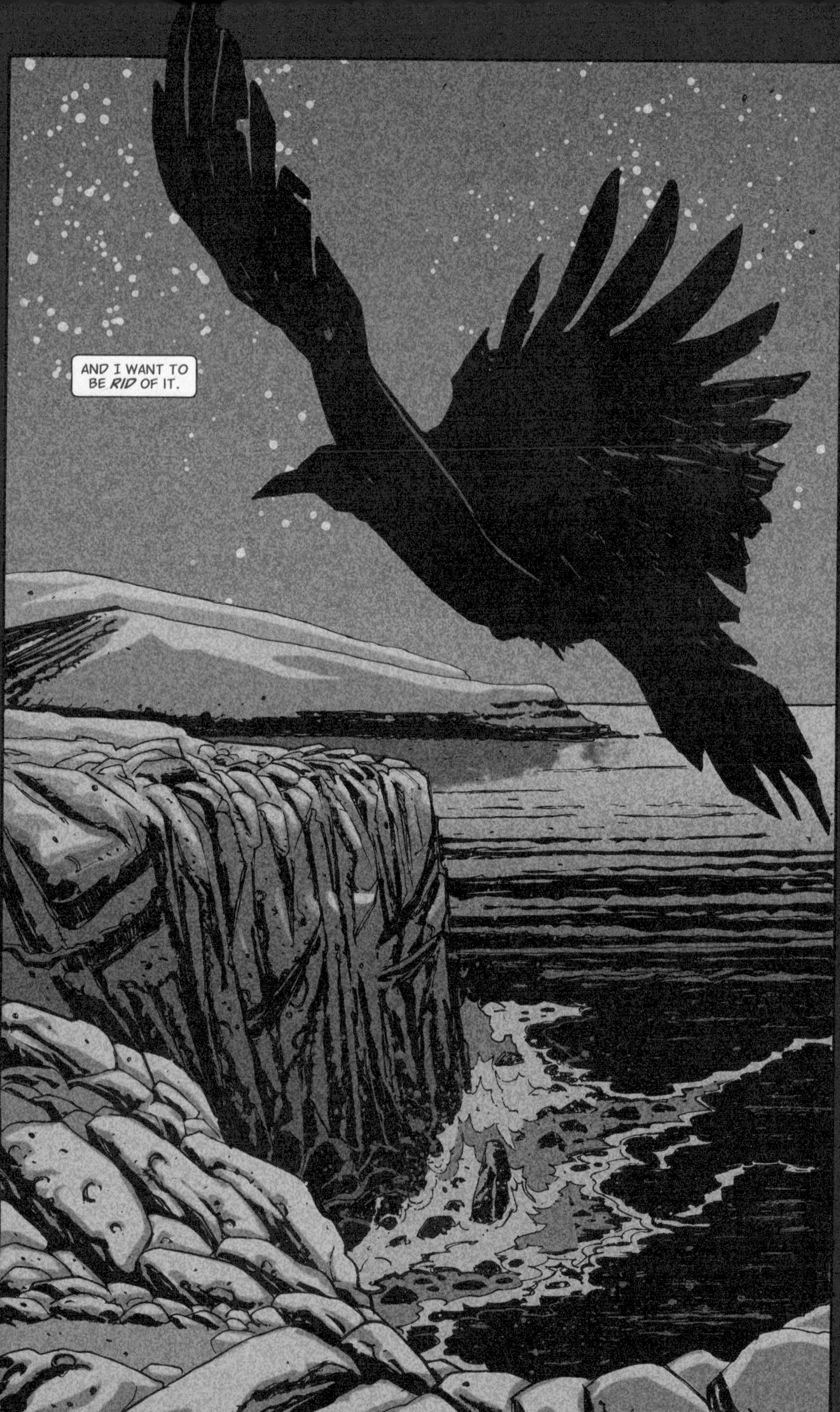
AND I WANT TO BE RID OF IT.

4 The Chill Eastern Wind

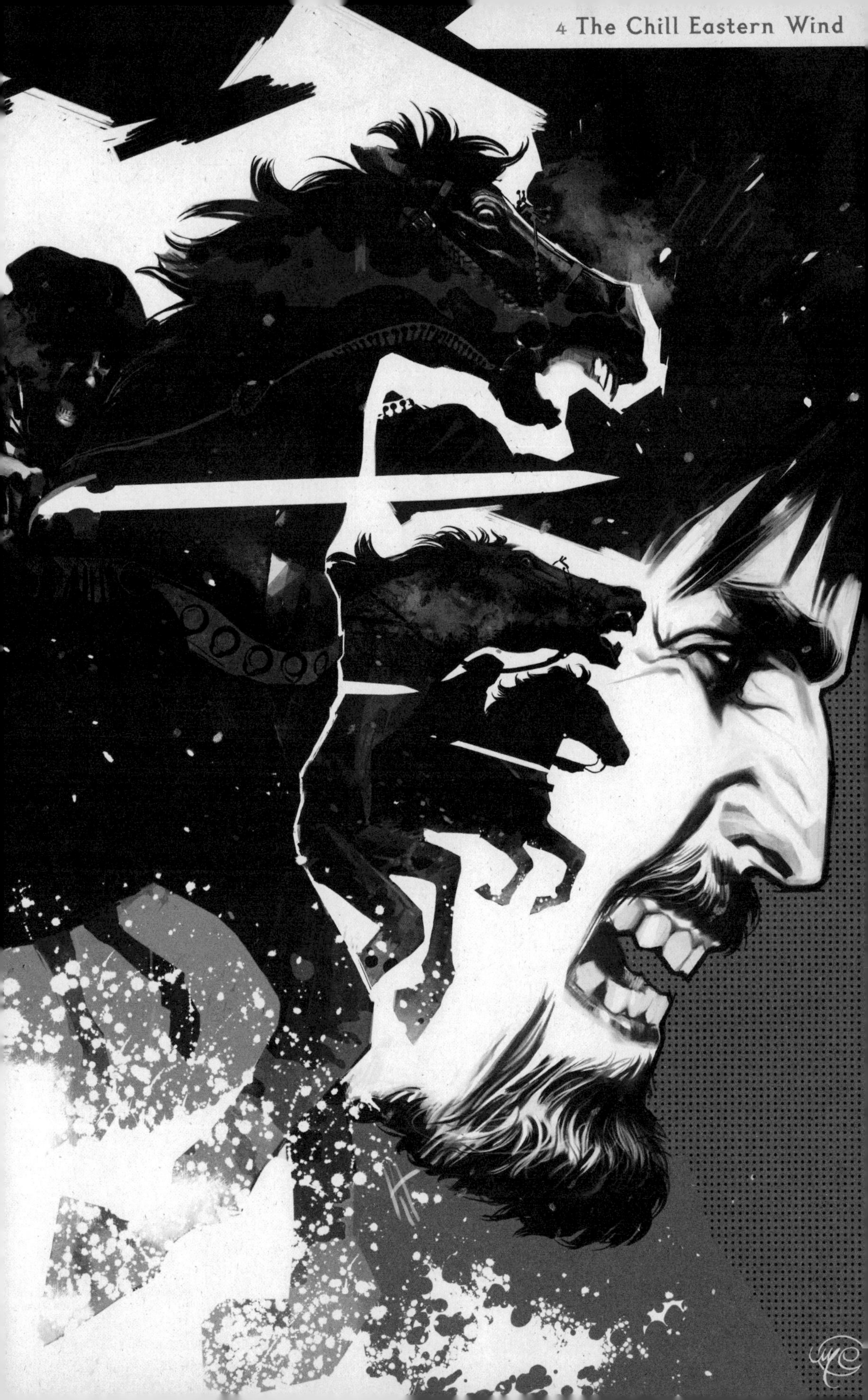

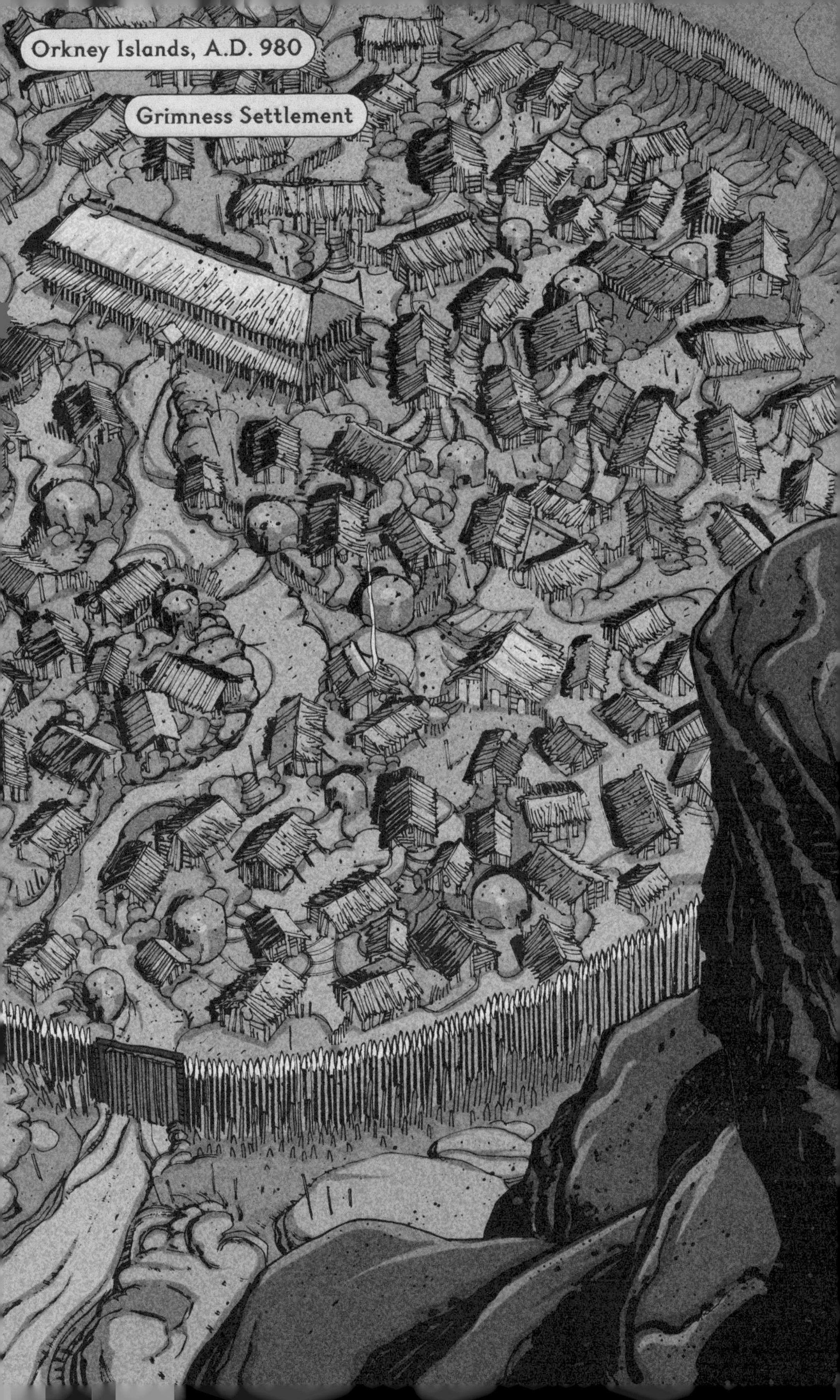
Orkney Islands, A.D. 980
Grimness Settlement

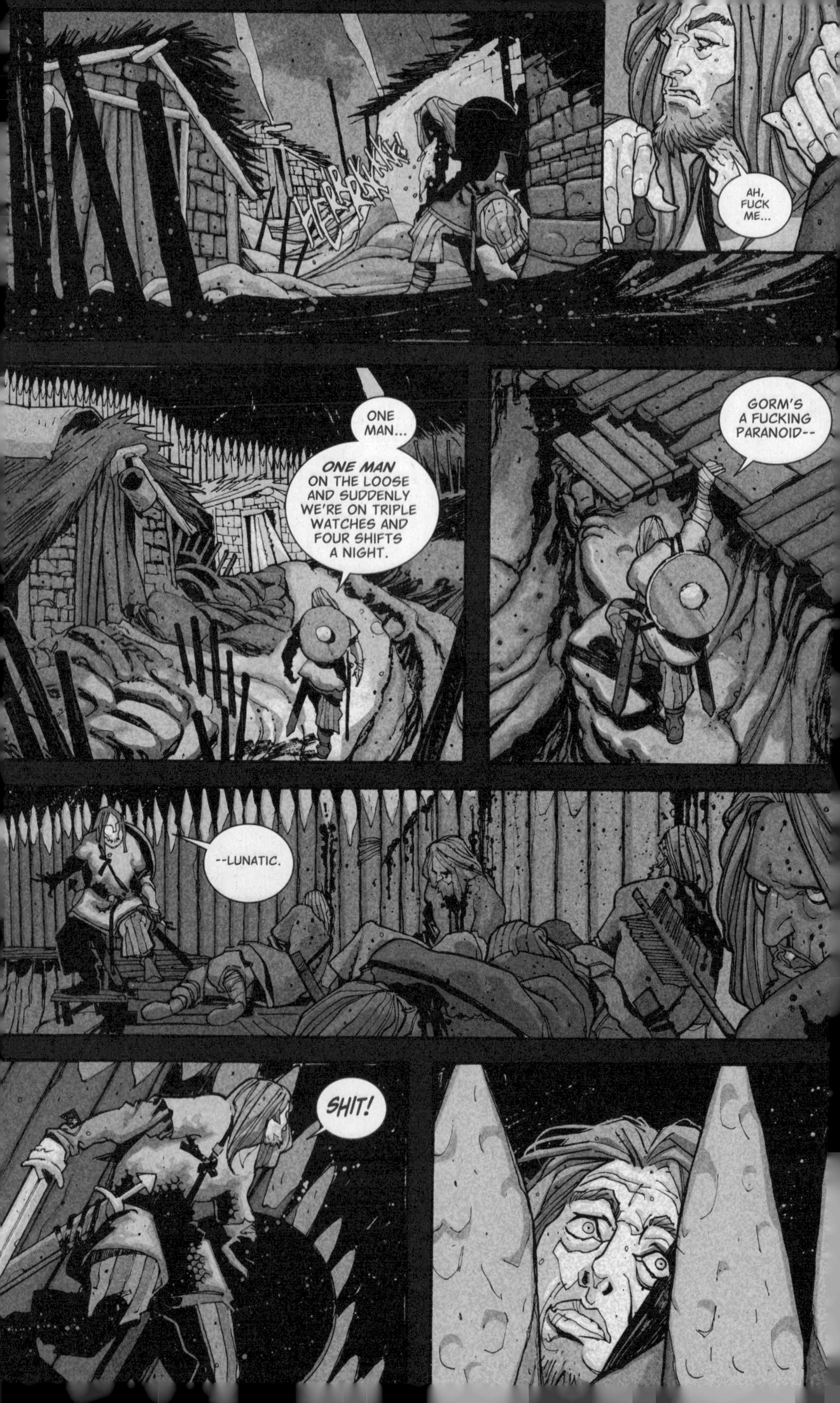
AH, FUCK ME...
ONE MAN...
ONE MAN ON THE LOOSE AND SUDDENLY WE'RE ON TRIPLE WATCHES AND FOUR SHIFTS A NIGHT.
GORM'S A FUCKING PARANOID--
--LUNATIC.
SHIT!

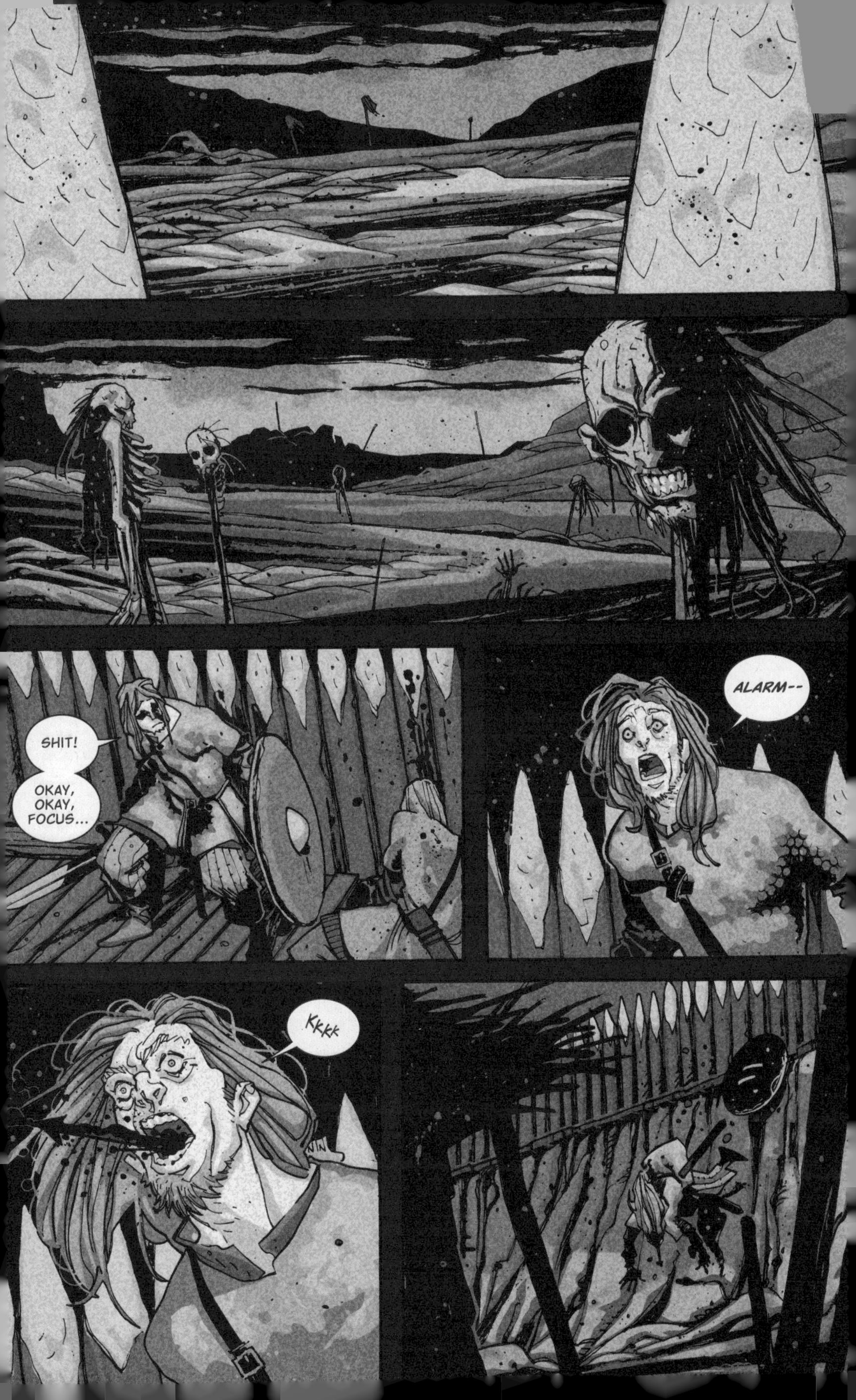
SHIT!
OKAY, OKAY, FOCUS...
ALARM--
KKKK

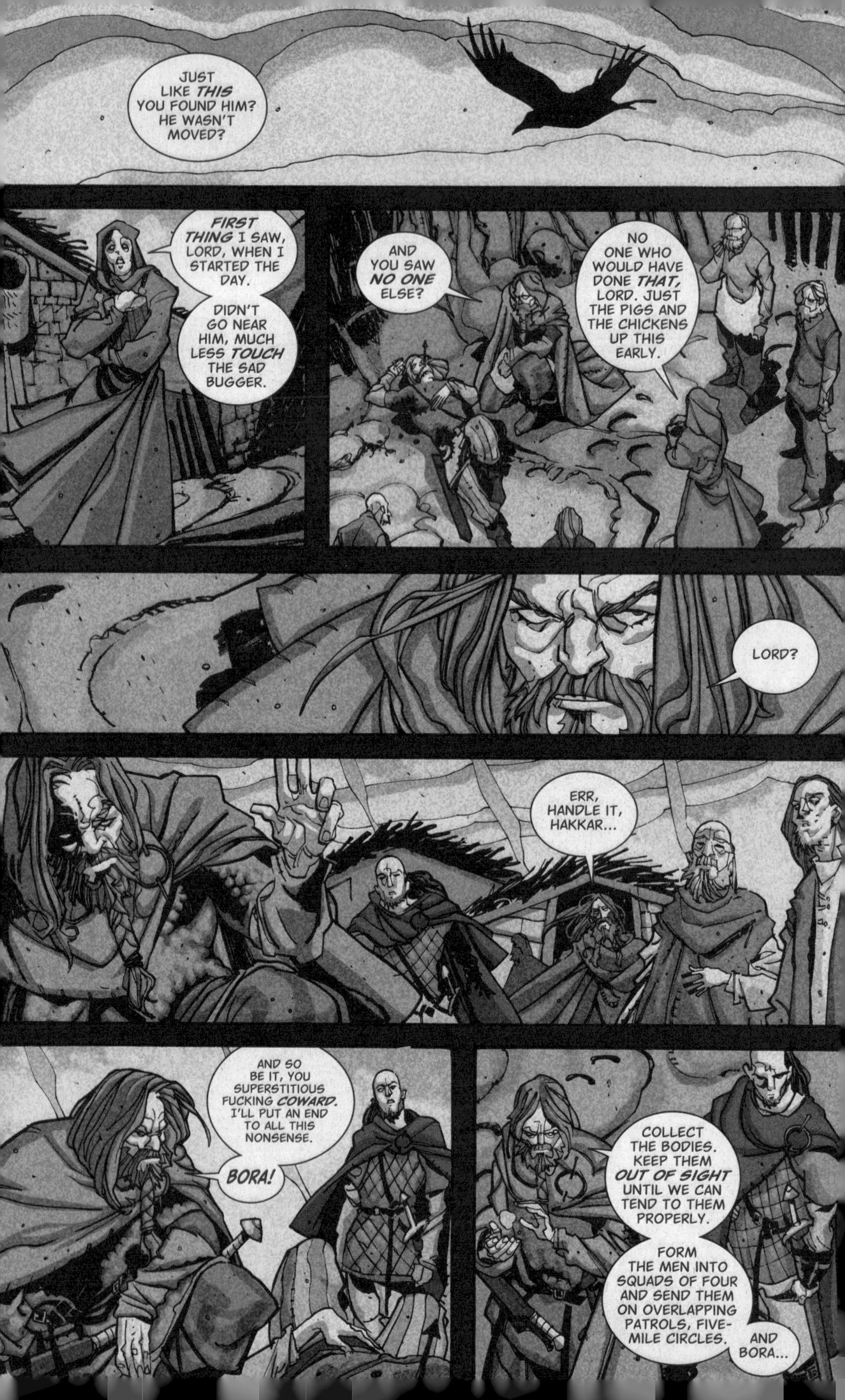
JUST LIKE *THIS* YOU FOUND HIM? HE WASN'T MOVED?
FIRST THING I SAW, LORD, WHEN I STARTED THE DAY.
DIDN'T GO NEAR HIM, MUCH LESS *TOUCH* THE SAD BUGGER.
AND YOU SAW *NO ONE* ELSE?
NO ONE WHO WOULD HAVE DONE *THAT,* LORD. JUST THE PIGS AND THE CHICKENS UP THIS EARLY.
LORD?
ERR, HANDLE IT, HAKKAR...
AND SO BE IT, YOU SUPERSTITIOUS FUCKING *COWARD.* I'LL PUT AN END TO ALL THIS NONSENSE.
BORA!
COLLECT THE BODIES. KEEP THEM *OUT OF SIGHT* UNTIL WE CAN TEND TO THEM PROPERLY.
FORM THE MEN INTO SQUADS OF FOUR AND SEND THEM ON OVERLAPPING PATROLS, FIVE-MILE CIRCLES.
AND BORA...

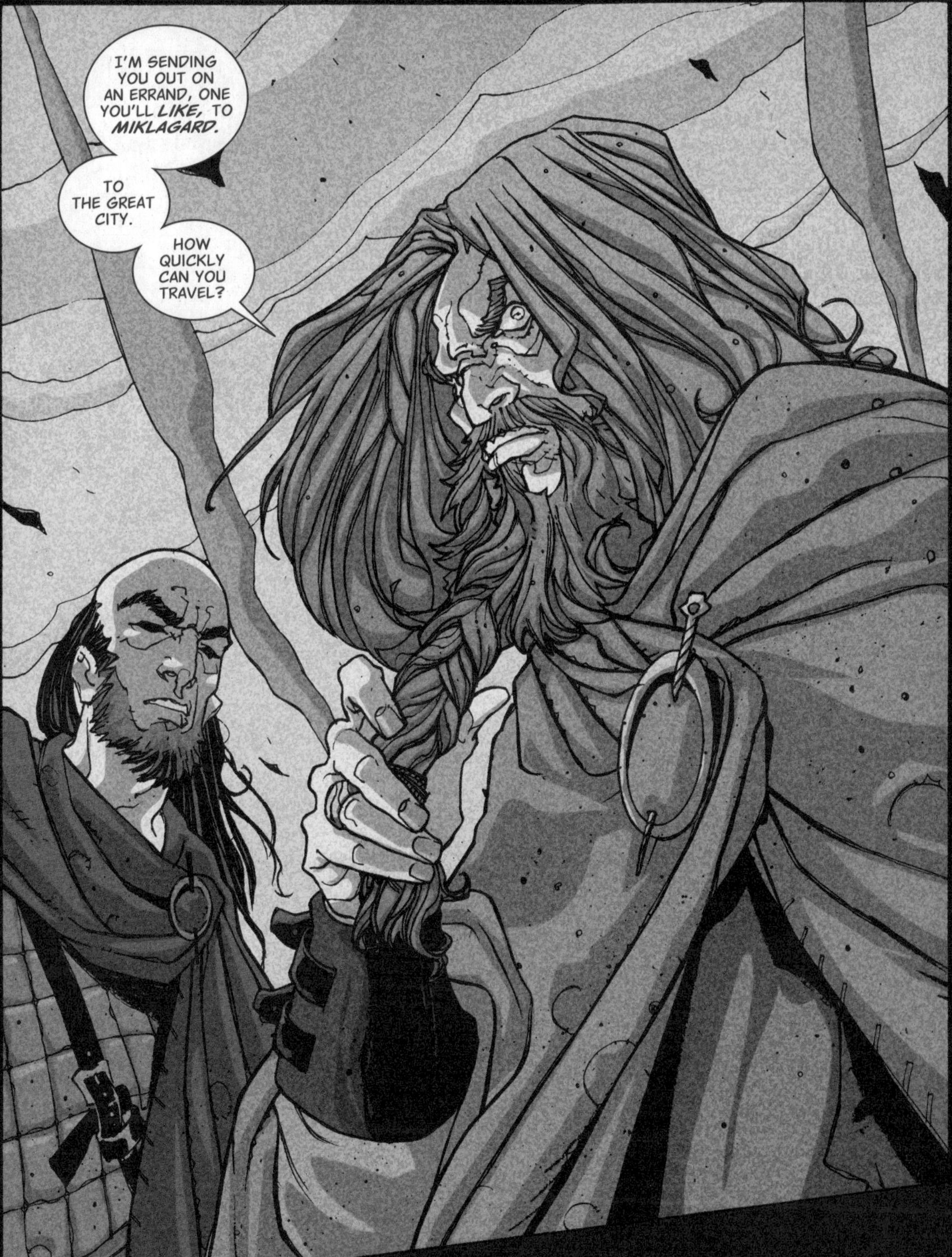

I'M SENDING YOU OUT ON AN ERRAND, ONE YOU'LL *LIKE*, TO *MIKLAGARD*.
TO THE GREAT CITY.
HOW QUICKLY CAN YOU TRAVEL?

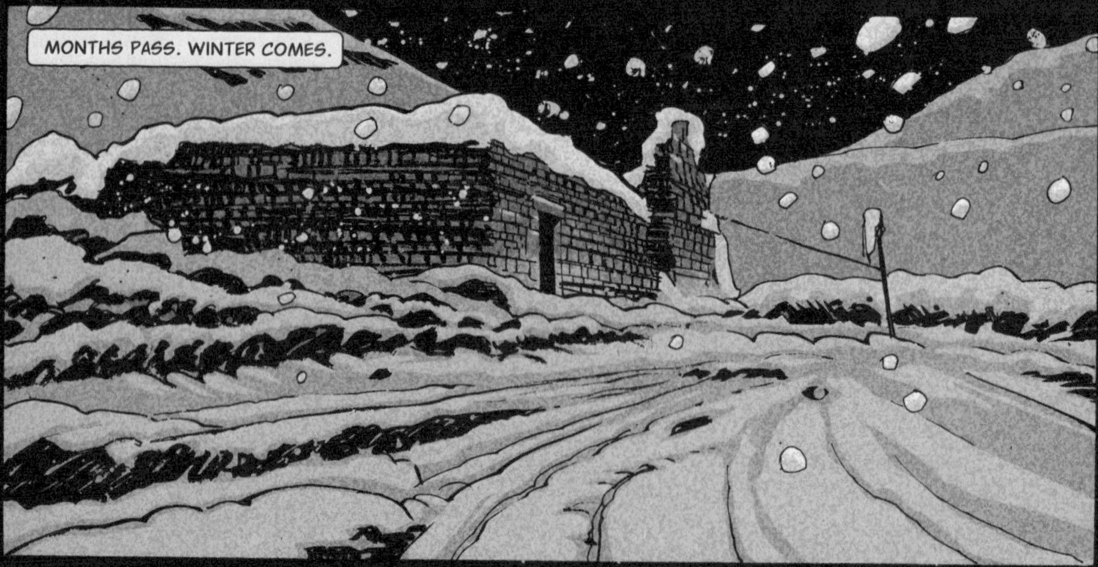
MONTHS PASS. WINTER COMES.

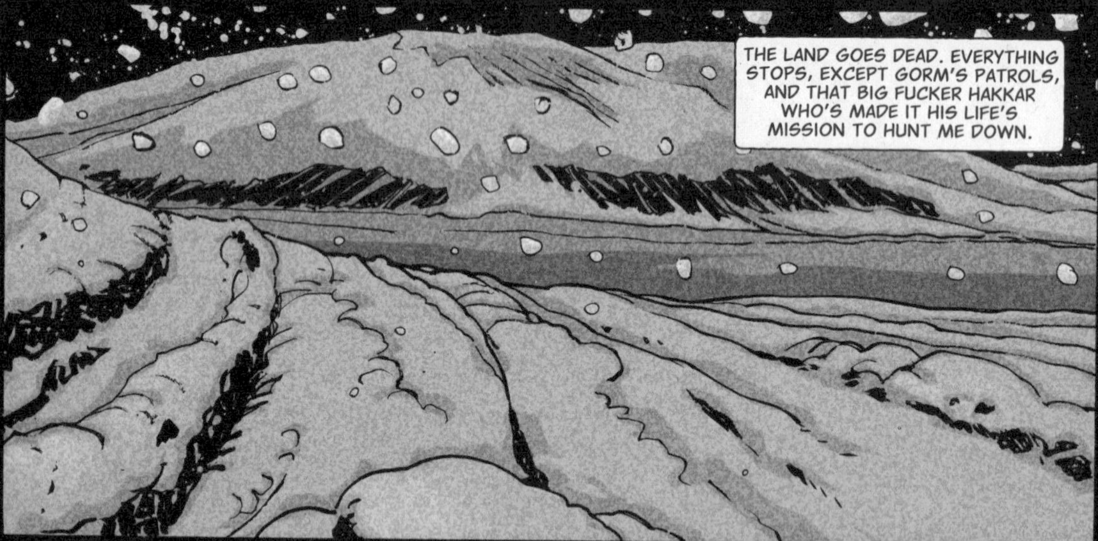
THE LAND GOES DEAD. EVERYTHING STOPS, EXCEPT GORM'S PATROLS, AND THAT BIG FUCKER HAKKAR WHO'S MADE IT HIS LIFE'S MISSION TO HUNT ME DOWN.

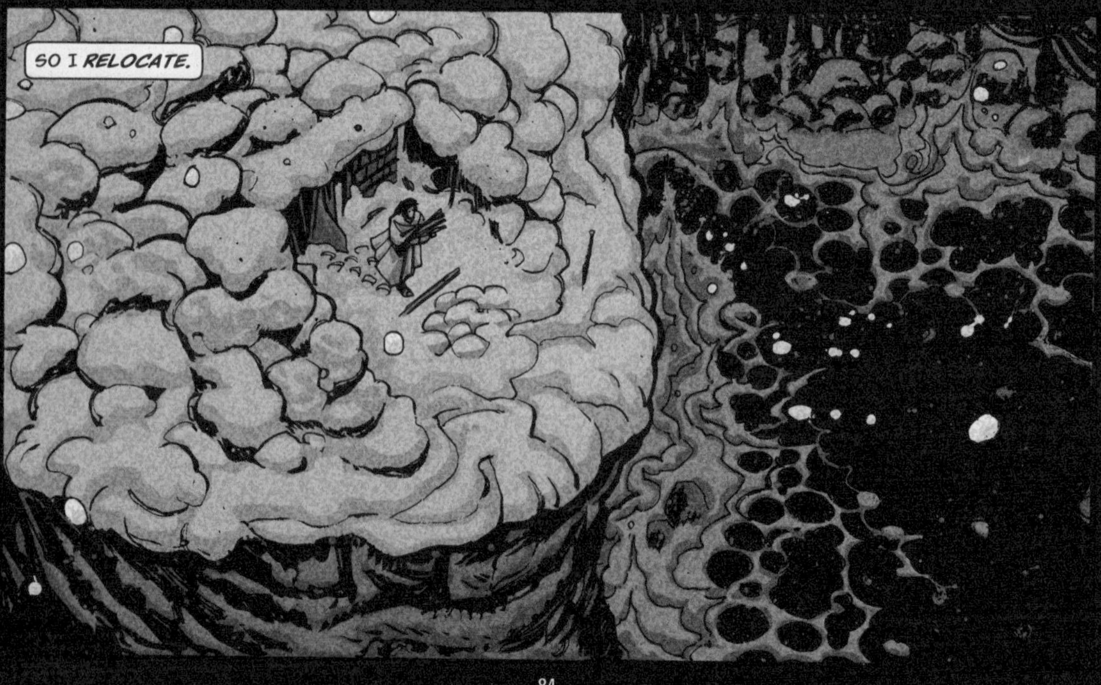
SO I *RELOCATE.*

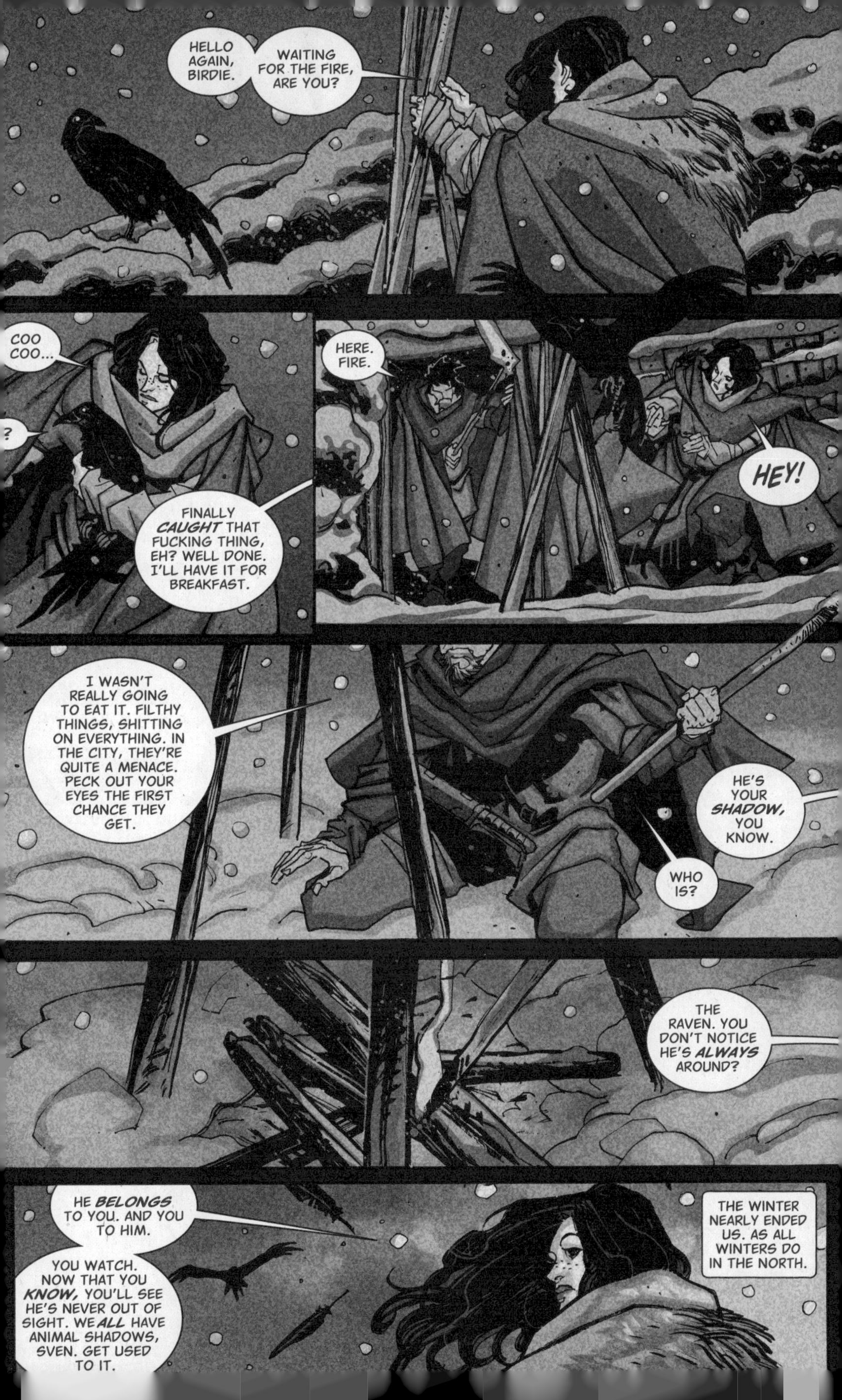
HELLO AGAIN, BIRDIE.
WAITING FOR THE FIRE, ARE YOU?
COO COO...
?
FINALLY *CAUGHT* THAT FUCKING THING, EH? WELL DONE. I'LL HAVE IT FOR BREAKFAST.
HERE. FIRE.
HEY!
I WASN'T REALLY GOING TO EAT IT. FILTHY THINGS, SHITTING ON EVERYTHING. IN THE CITY, THEY'RE QUITE A MENACE. PECK OUT YOUR EYES THE FIRST CHANCE THEY GET.
HE'S YOUR *SHADOW,* YOU KNOW.
WHO IS?
THE RAVEN. YOU DON'T NOTICE HE'S *ALWAYS* AROUND?
HE *BELONGS* TO YOU. AND YOU TO HIM.
YOU WATCH. NOW THAT YOU *KNOW,* YOU'LL SEE HE'S NEVER OUT OF SIGHT. WE *ALL* HAVE ANIMAL SHADOWS, SVEN. GET USED TO IT.
THE WINTER NEARLY ENDED US. AS ALL WINTERS DO IN THE NORTH.

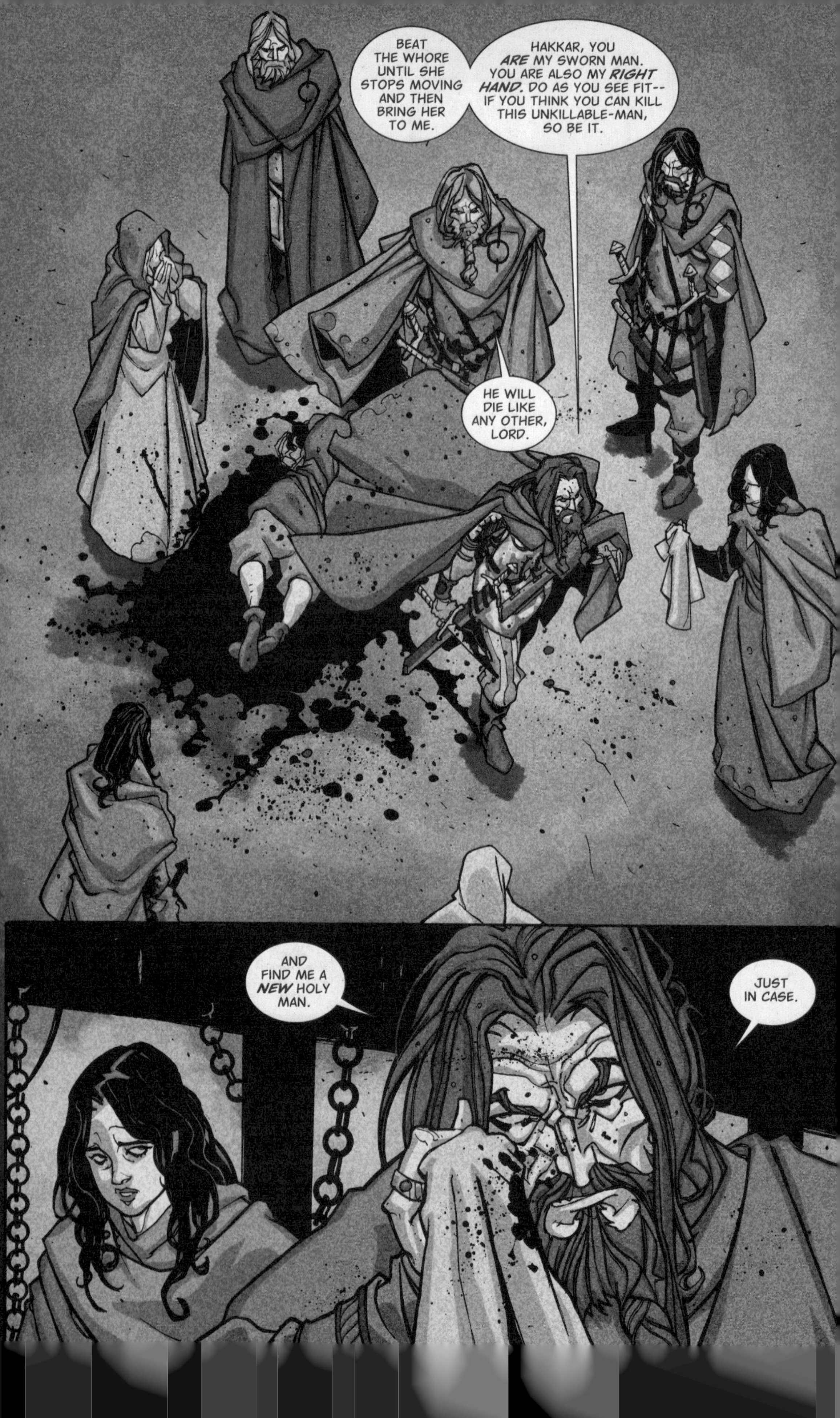
BEAT THE WHORE UNTIL SHE STOPS MOVING AND THEN BRING HER TO ME.
HAKKAR, YOU *ARE* MY SWORN MAN. YOU ARE ALSO MY *RIGHT HAND.* DO AS YOU SEE FIT-- IF YOU THINK YOU CAN KILL THIS UNKILLABLE-MAN, SO BE IT.
HE WILL DIE LIKE ANY OTHER, LORD.
AND FIND ME A *NEW* HOLY MAN.
JUST IN CASE.

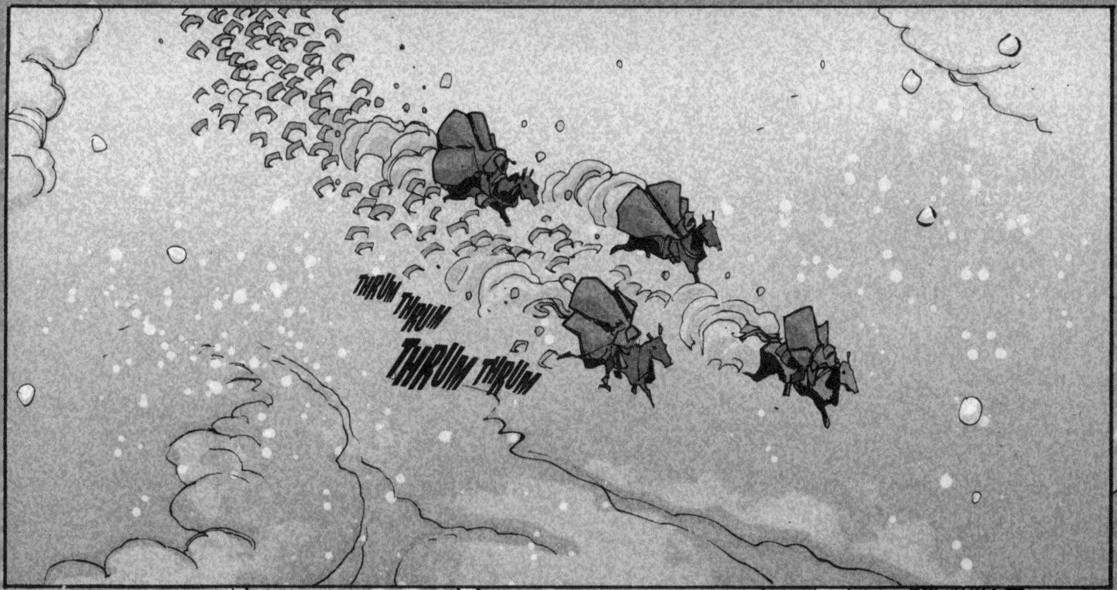
THRUM THRUM
THRUM THRUM

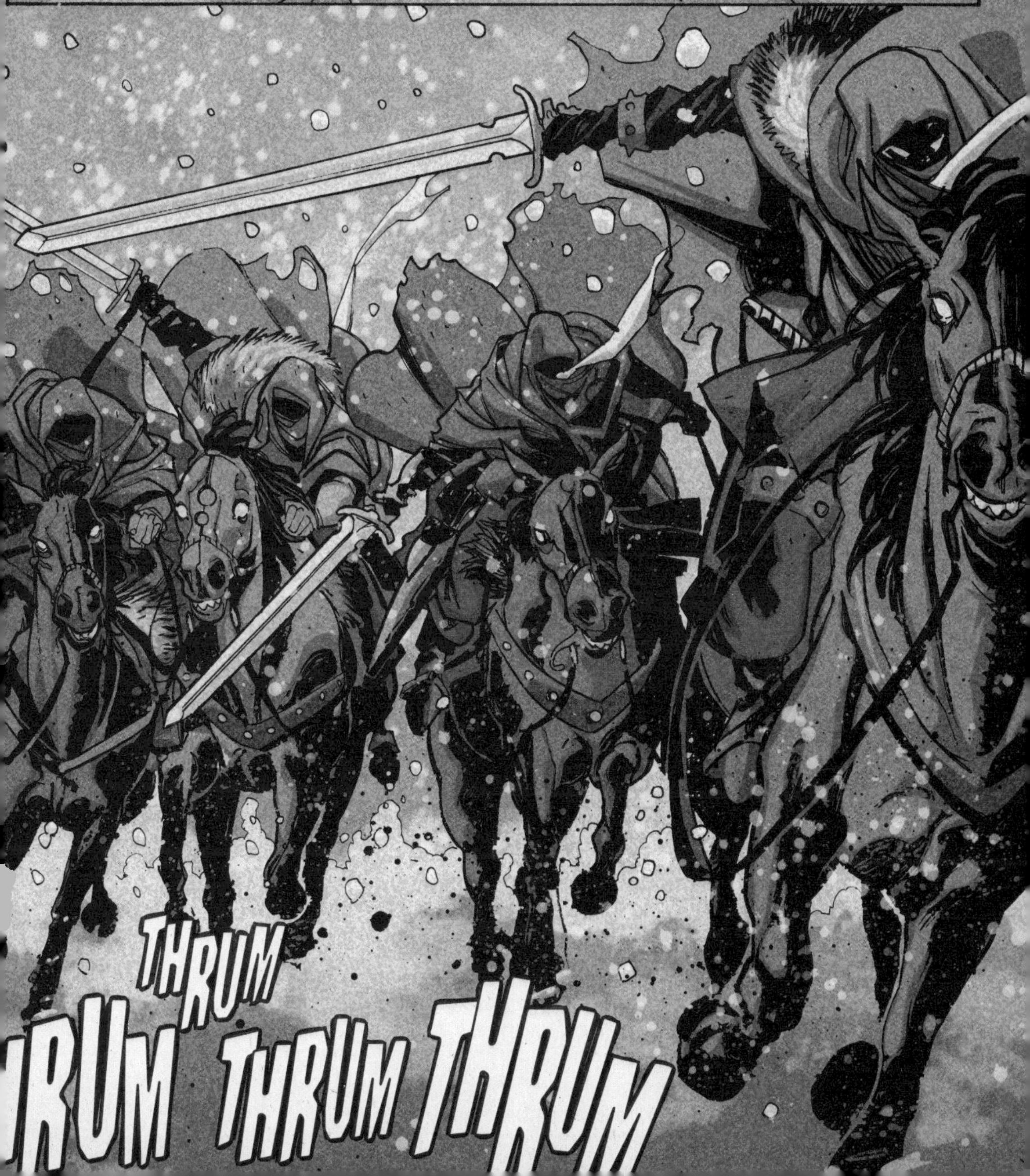
THRUM
RUM THRUM THRUM

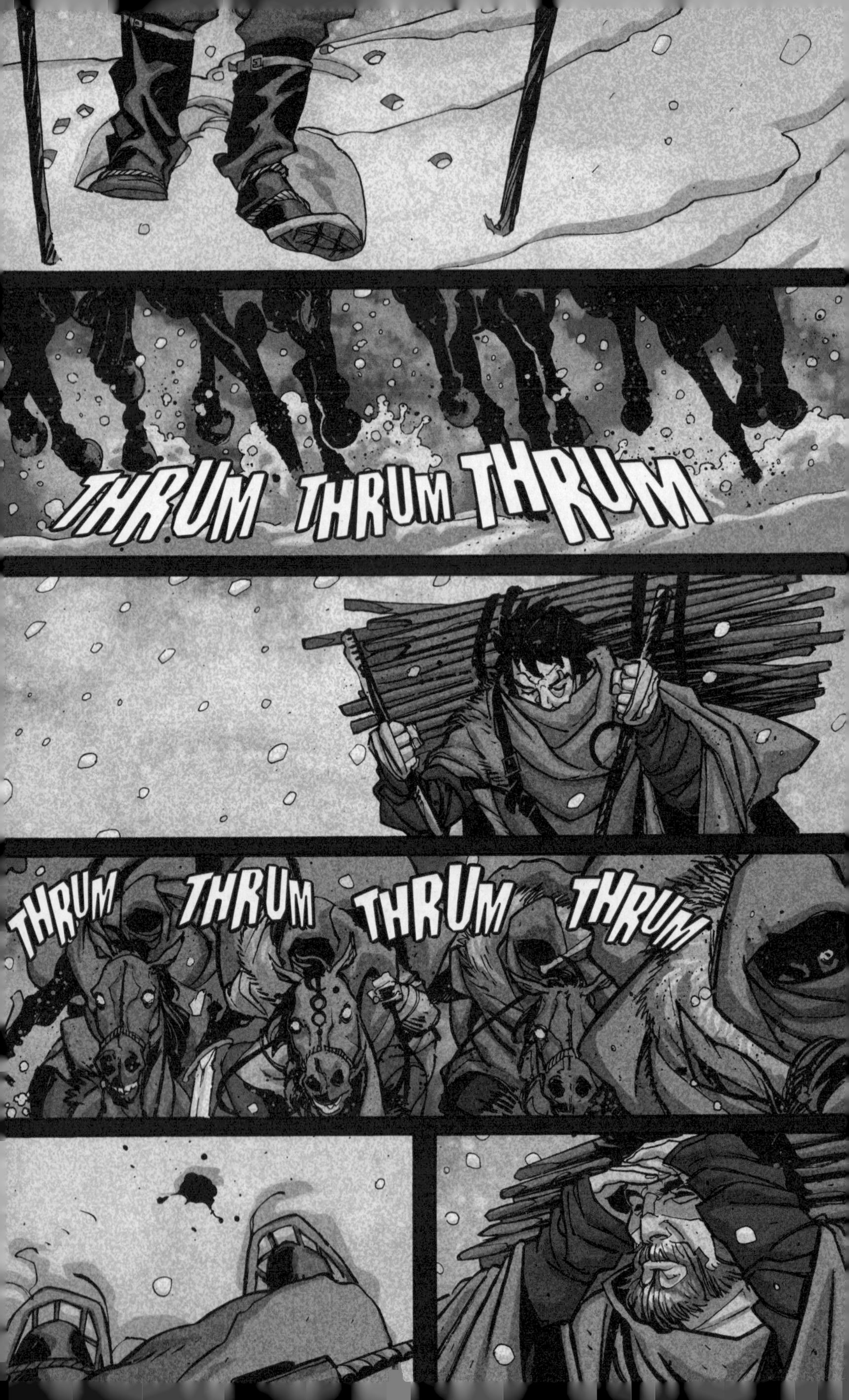
THRUM THRUM THRUM
THRUM THRUM THRUM THRUM

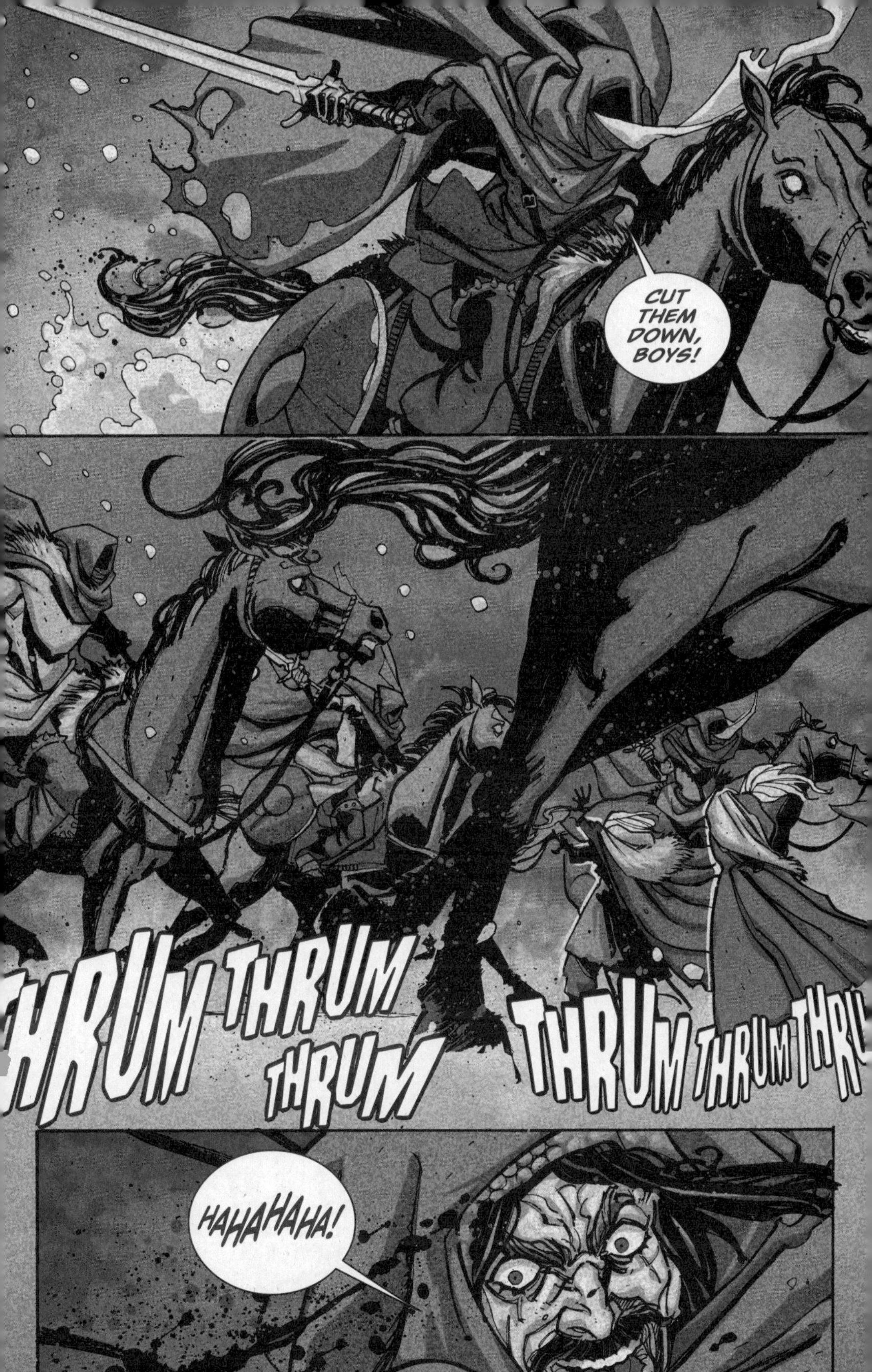
CUT THEM DOWN, BOYS!
THRUM THRUM THRUM
THRUM THRUM THRU
HAHAHAHA!

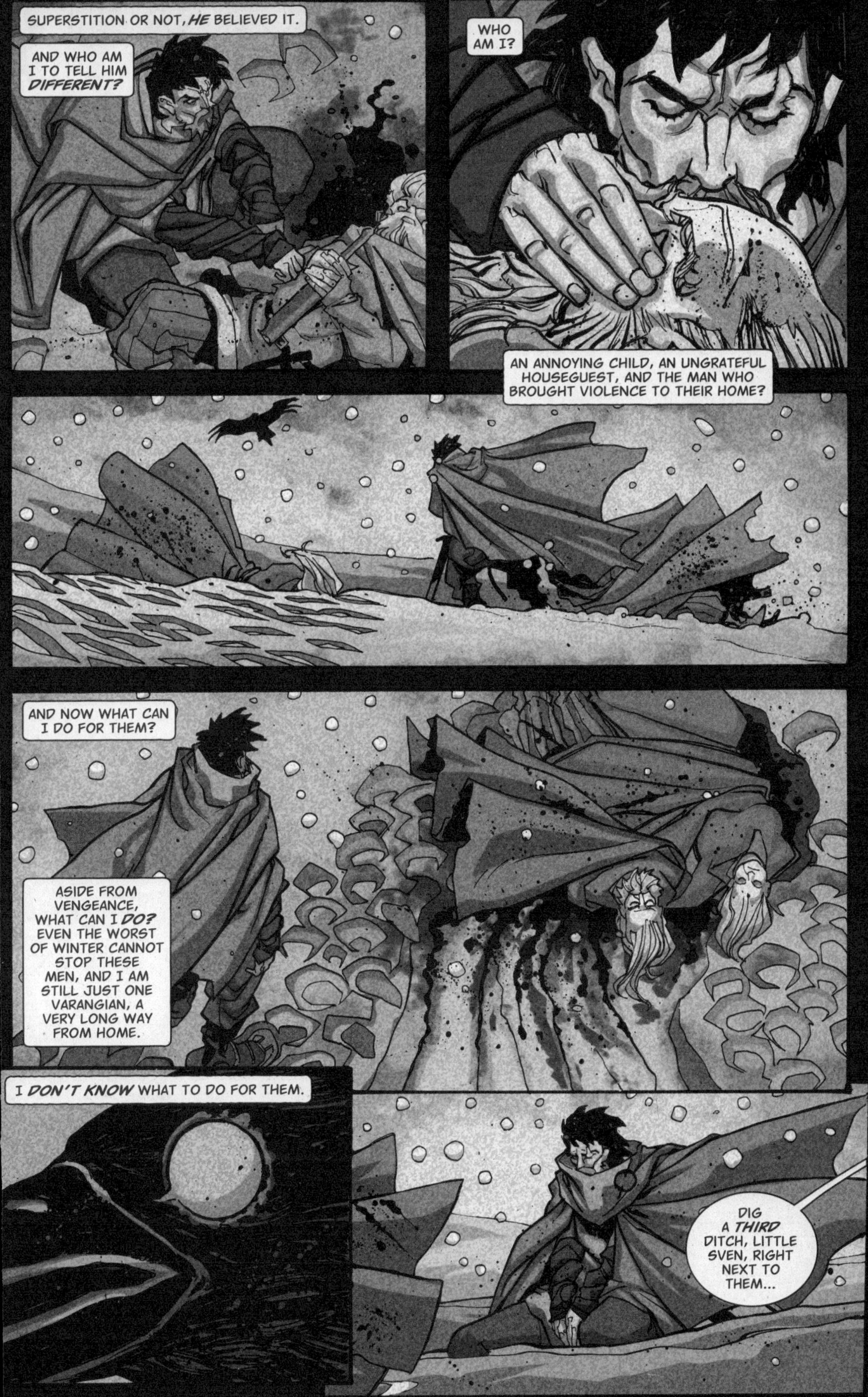
SUPERSTITION OR NOT, *HE* BELIEVED IT.
AND WHO AM I TO TELL HIM *DIFFERENT?*
WHO AM I?
AN ANNOYING CHILD, AN UNGRATEFUL HOUSEGUEST, AND THE MAN WHO BROUGHT VIOLENCE TO THEIR HOME?
AND NOW WHAT CAN I DO FOR THEM?
ASIDE FROM VENGEANCE, WHAT CAN I *DO?* EVEN THE WORST OF WINTER CANNOT STOP THESE MEN, AND I AM STILL JUST ONE VARANGIAN, A VERY LONG WAY FROM HOME.
I *DON'T KNOW* WHAT TO DO FOR THEM.
DIG A *THIRD* DITCH, LITTLE SVEN, RIGHT NEXT TO THEM...

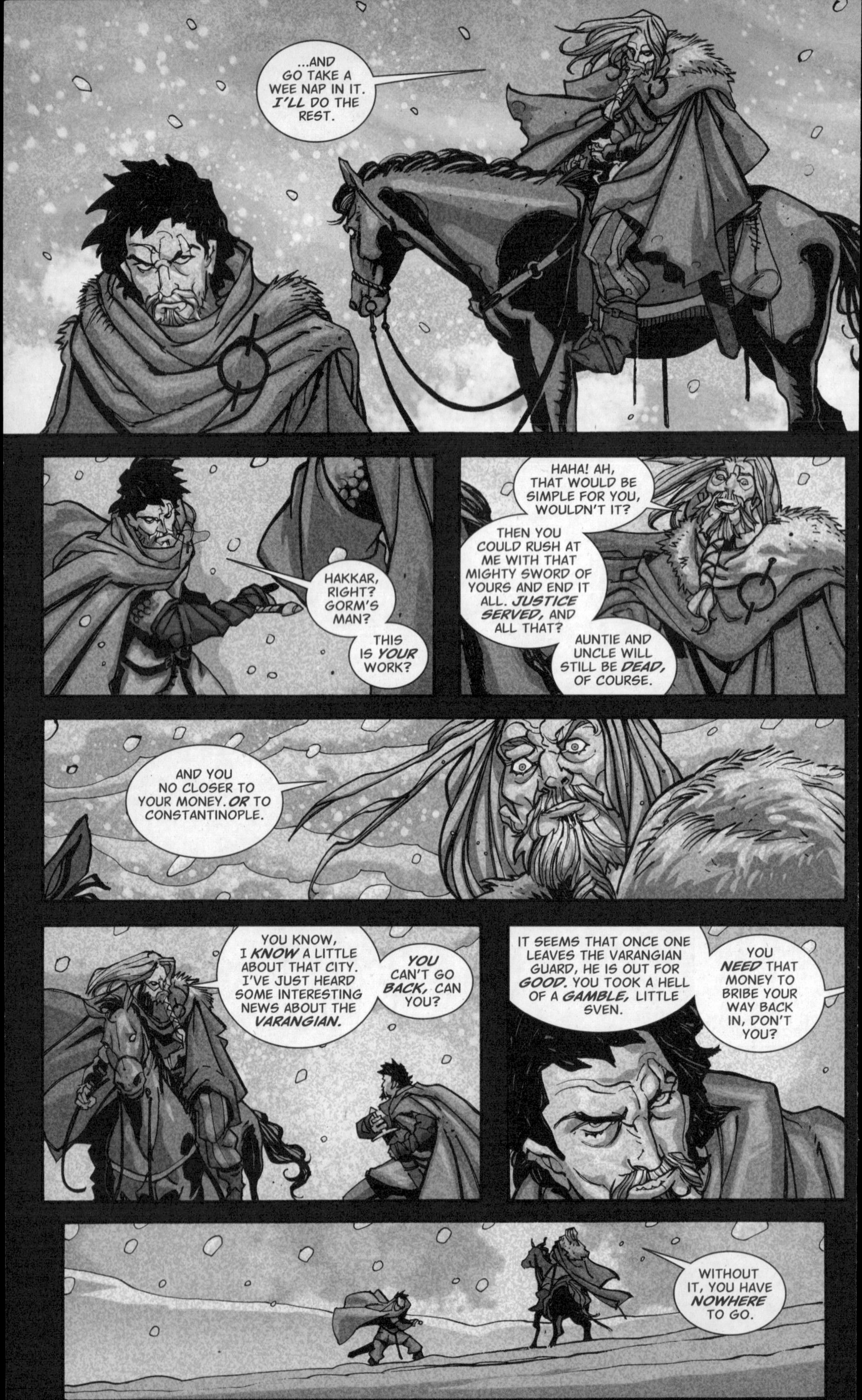
...AND GO TAKE A WEE NAP IN IT. *I'LL* DO THE REST.
HAKKAR, RIGHT? GORM'S MAN?
THIS IS *YOUR* WORK?
HAHA! AH, THAT WOULD BE SIMPLE FOR YOU, WOULDN'T IT?
THEN YOU COULD RUSH AT ME WITH THAT MIGHTY SWORD OF YOURS AND END IT ALL. *JUSTICE SERVED,* AND ALL THAT?
AUNTIE AND UNCLE WILL STILL BE *DEAD,* OF COURSE.
AND YOU NO CLOSER TO YOUR MONEY. *OR* TO CONSTANTINOPLE.
YOU KNOW, I *KNOW* A LITTLE ABOUT THAT CITY. I'VE JUST HEARD SOME INTERESTING NEWS ABOUT THE *VARANGIAN.*
YOU CAN'T GO *BACK,* CAN YOU?
IT SEEMS THAT ONCE ONE LEAVES THE VARANGIAN GUARD, HE IS OUT FOR *GOOD.* YOU TOOK A HELL OF A *GAMBLE,* LITTLE SVEN.
YOU *NEED* THAT MONEY TO BRIBE YOUR WAY BACK IN, DON'T YOU?
WITHOUT IT, YOU HAVE *NOWHERE* TO GO.

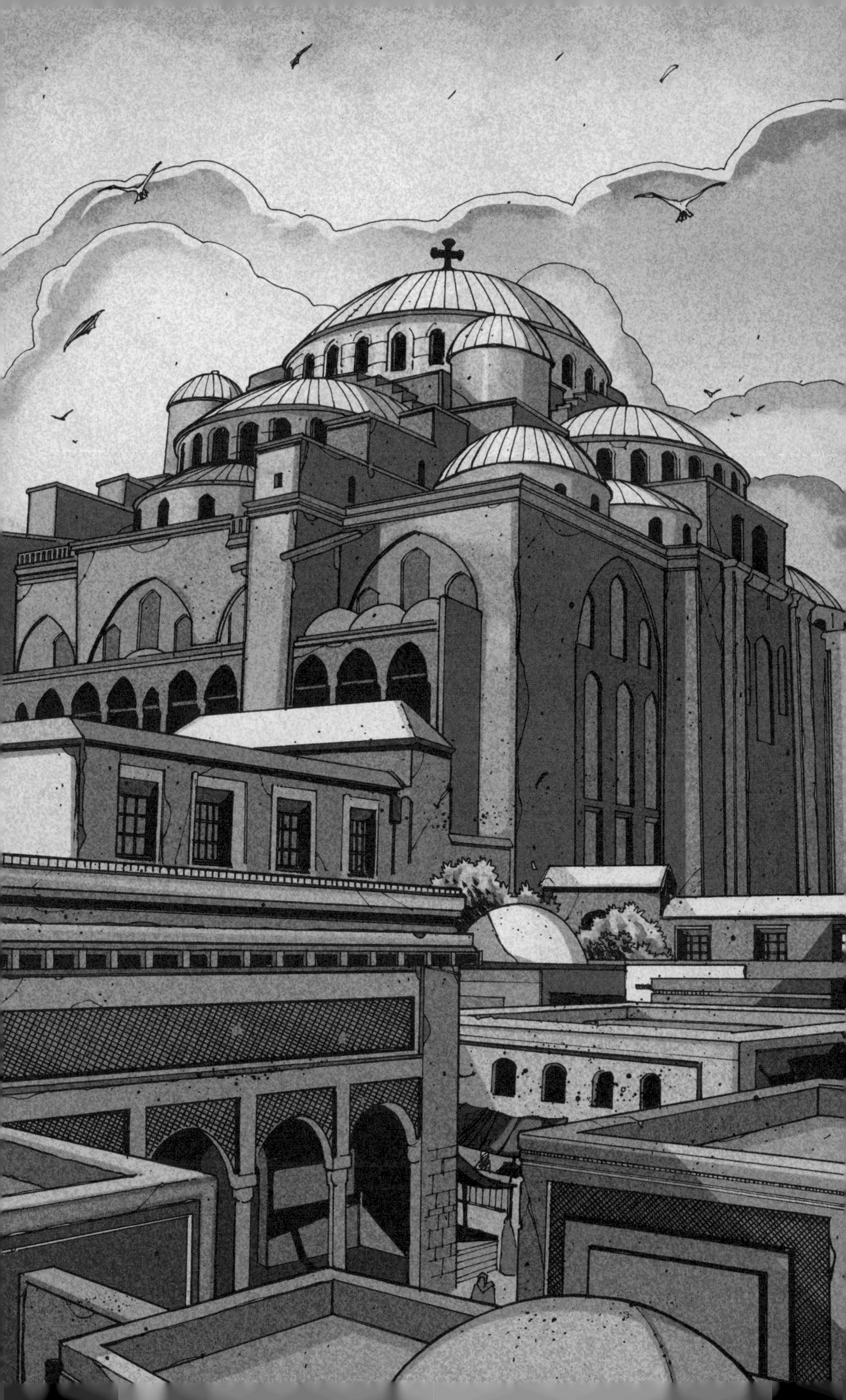

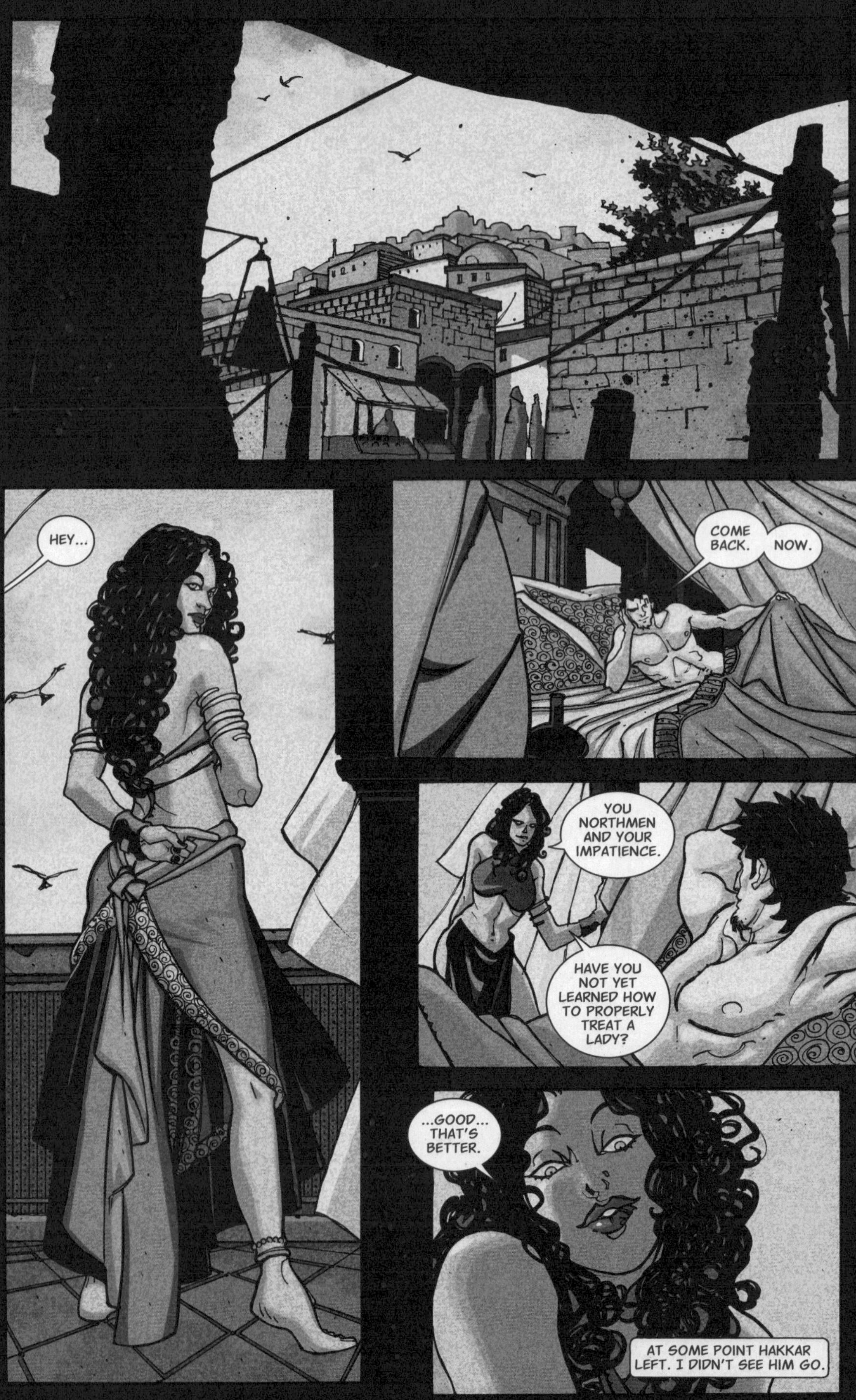
HEY...
COME BACK.
NOW.
YOU NORTHMEN AND YOUR IMPATIENCE.
HAVE YOU NOT YET LEARNED HOW TO PROPERLY TREAT A LADY?
...GOOD... THAT'S BETTER.
AT SOME POINT HAKKAR LEFT. I DIDN'T SEE HIM GO.

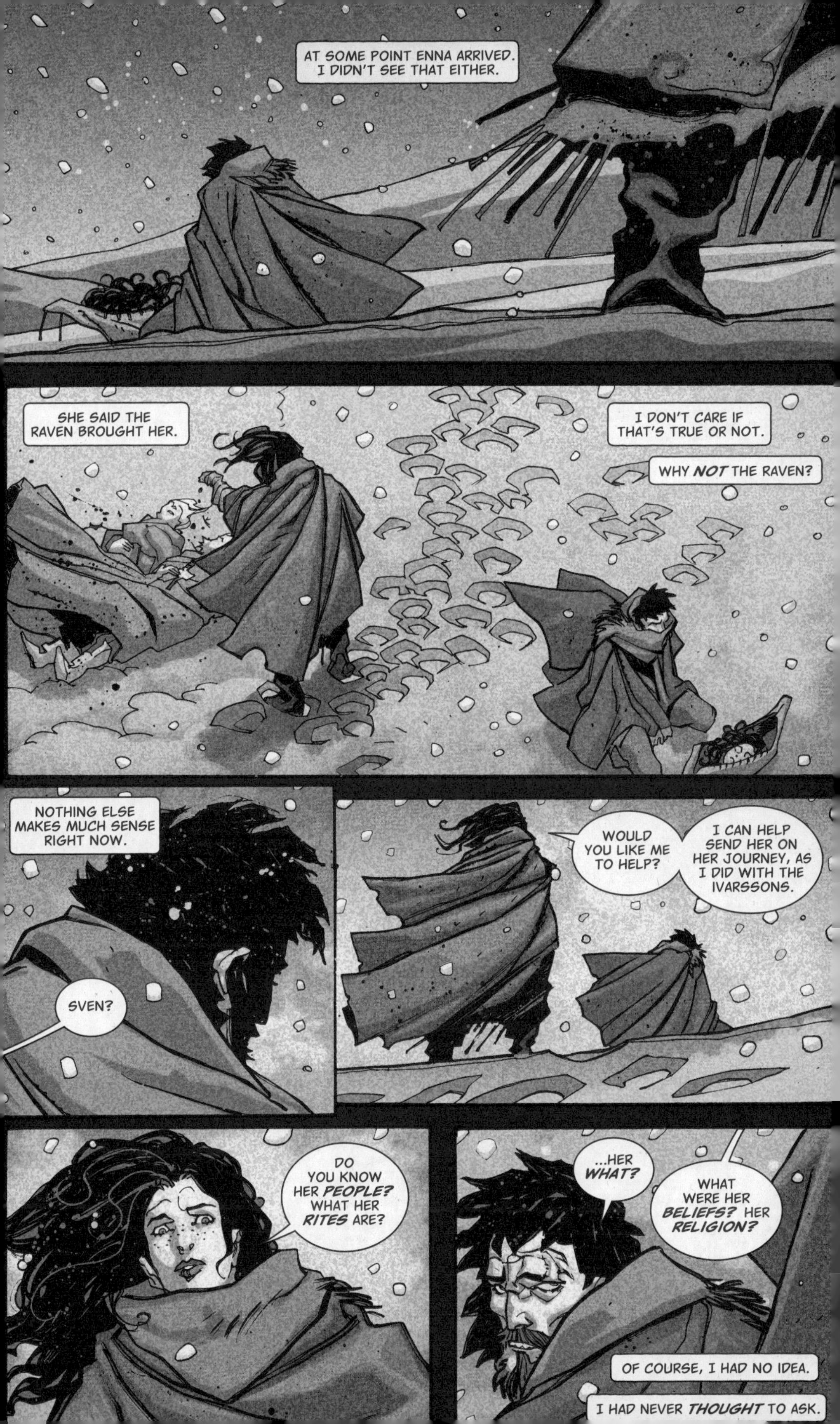
AT SOME POINT ENNA ARRIVED. I DIDN'T SEE THAT EITHER.
SHE SAID THE RAVEN BROUGHT HER.
I DON'T CARE IF THAT'S TRUE OR NOT.
WHY *NOT* THE RAVEN?
NOTHING ELSE MAKES MUCH SENSE RIGHT NOW.
SVEN?
WOULD YOU LIKE ME TO HELP?
I CAN HELP SEND HER ON HER JOURNEY, AS I DID WITH THE IVARSSONS.
DO YOU KNOW HER *PEOPLE?* WHAT HER *RITES* ARE?
...HER *WHAT?*
WHAT WERE HER *BELIEFS?* HER *RELIGION?*
OF COURSE, I HAD NO IDEA.
I HAD NEVER *THOUGHT* TO ASK.

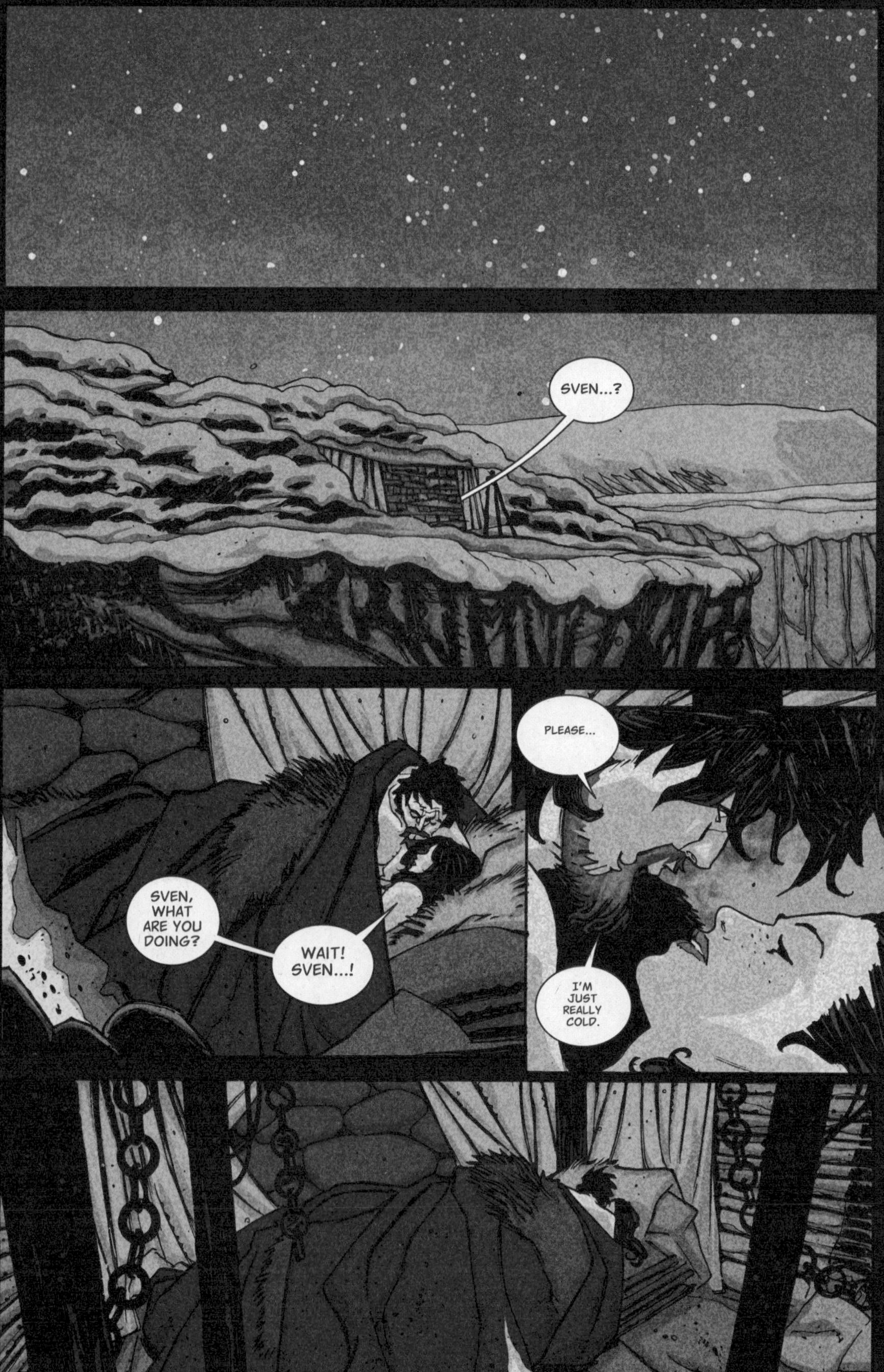
SVEN...?
SVEN, WHAT ARE YOU DOING?
WAIT! SVEN...!
PLEASE...
I'M JUST REALLY COLD.

5 The Land of the Leal

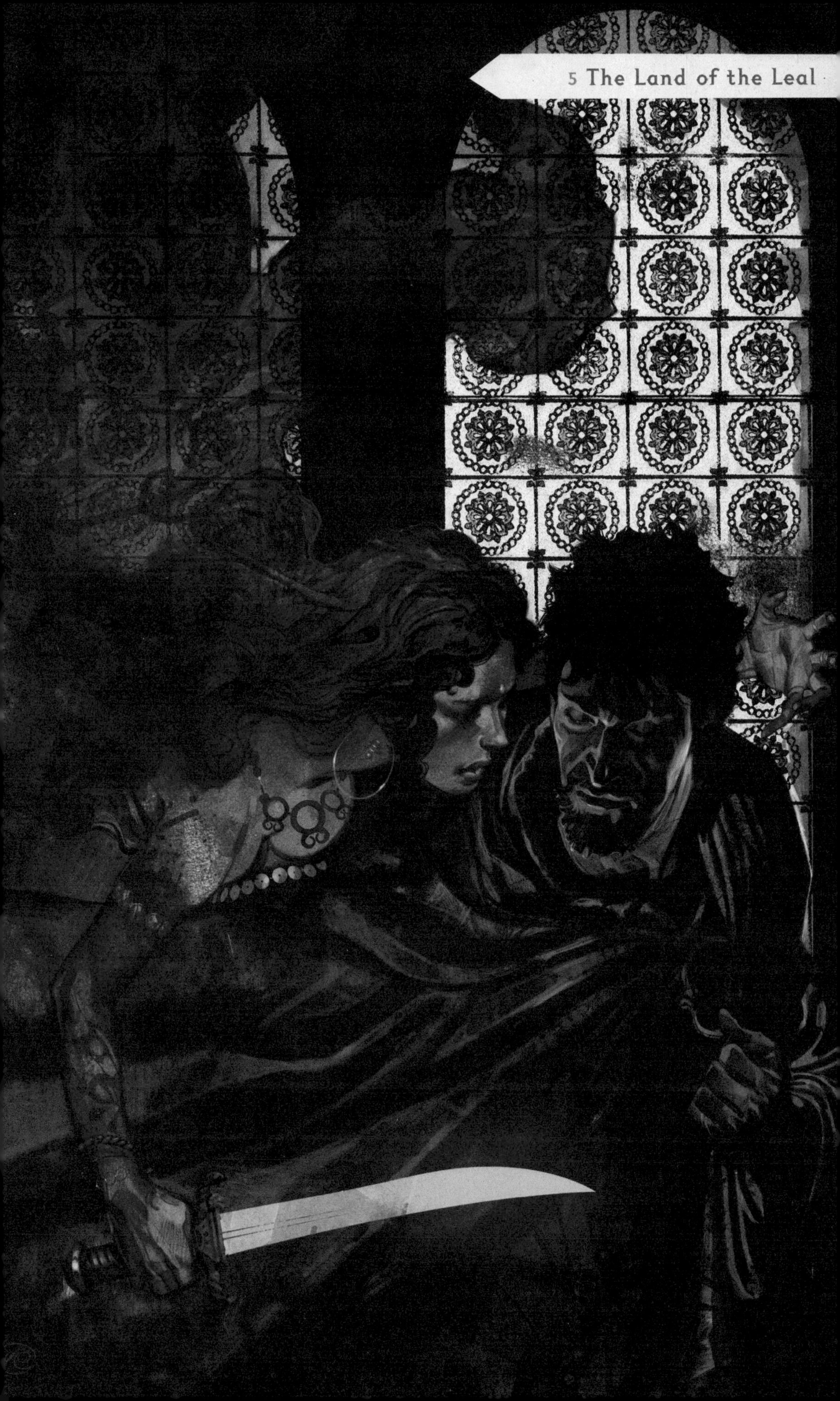

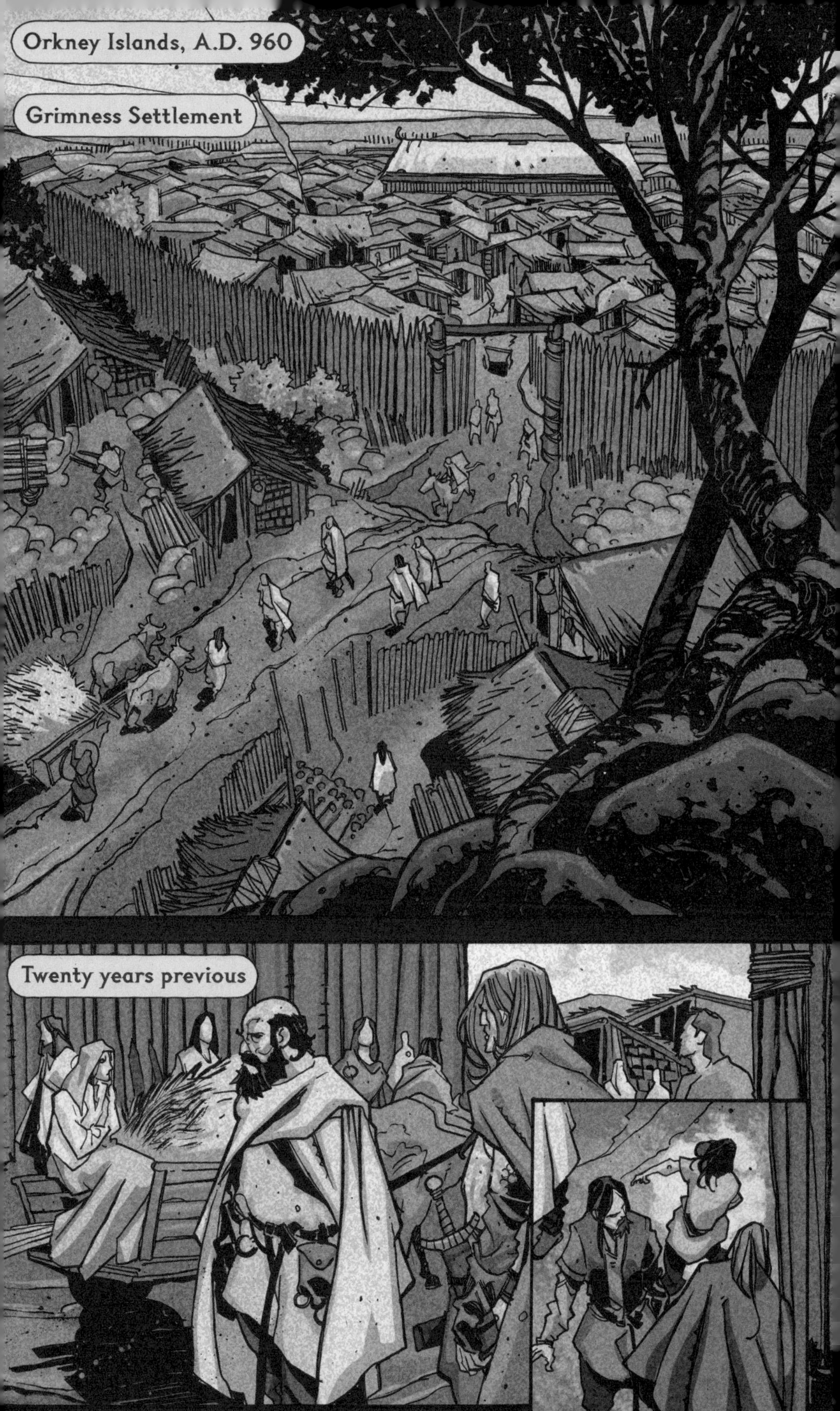
Orkney Islands, A.D. 960
Grimness Settlement
Twenty years previous

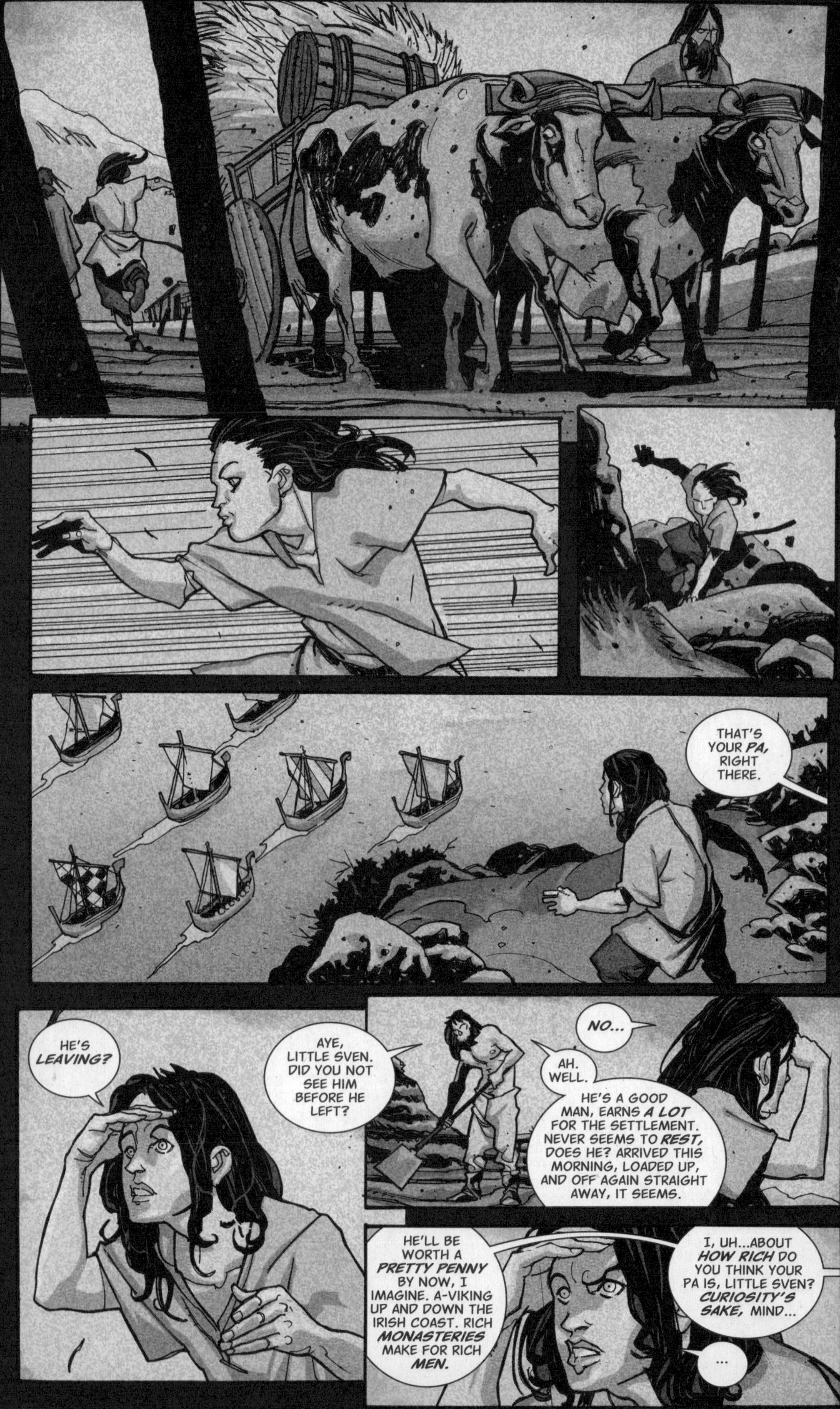

THAT'S YOUR *PA,* RIGHT THERE.
HE'S *LEAVING?*
AYE, LITTLE SVEN. DID YOU NOT SEE HIM BEFORE HE LEFT?
NO...
AH. WELL.
HE'S A GOOD MAN, EARNS *A LOT* FOR THE SETTLEMENT. NEVER SEEMS TO *REST,* DOES HE? ARRIVED THIS MORNING, LOADED UP, AND OFF AGAIN STRAIGHT AWAY, IT SEEMS.
HE'LL BE WORTH A *PRETTY PENNY* BY NOW, I IMAGINE. A-VIKING UP AND DOWN THE IRISH COAST. RICH *MONASTERIES* MAKE FOR RICH *MEN.*
I, UH...ABOUT *HOW RICH* DO YOU THINK YOUR PA IS, LITTLE SVEN? *CURIOSITY'S SAKE,* MIND...
...

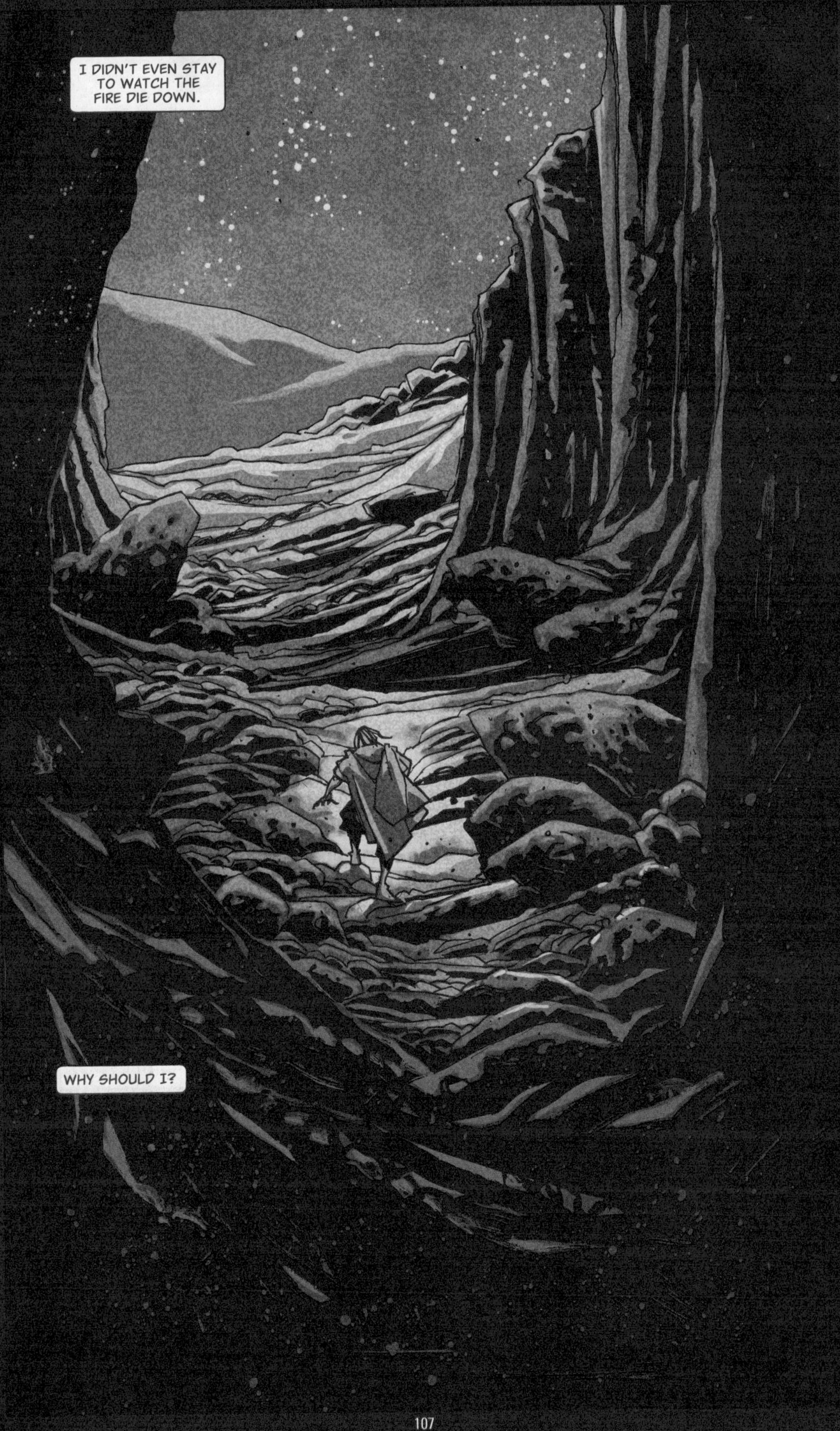
I DIDN'T EVEN STAY TO WATCH THE FIRE DIE DOWN.
WHY SHOULD I?

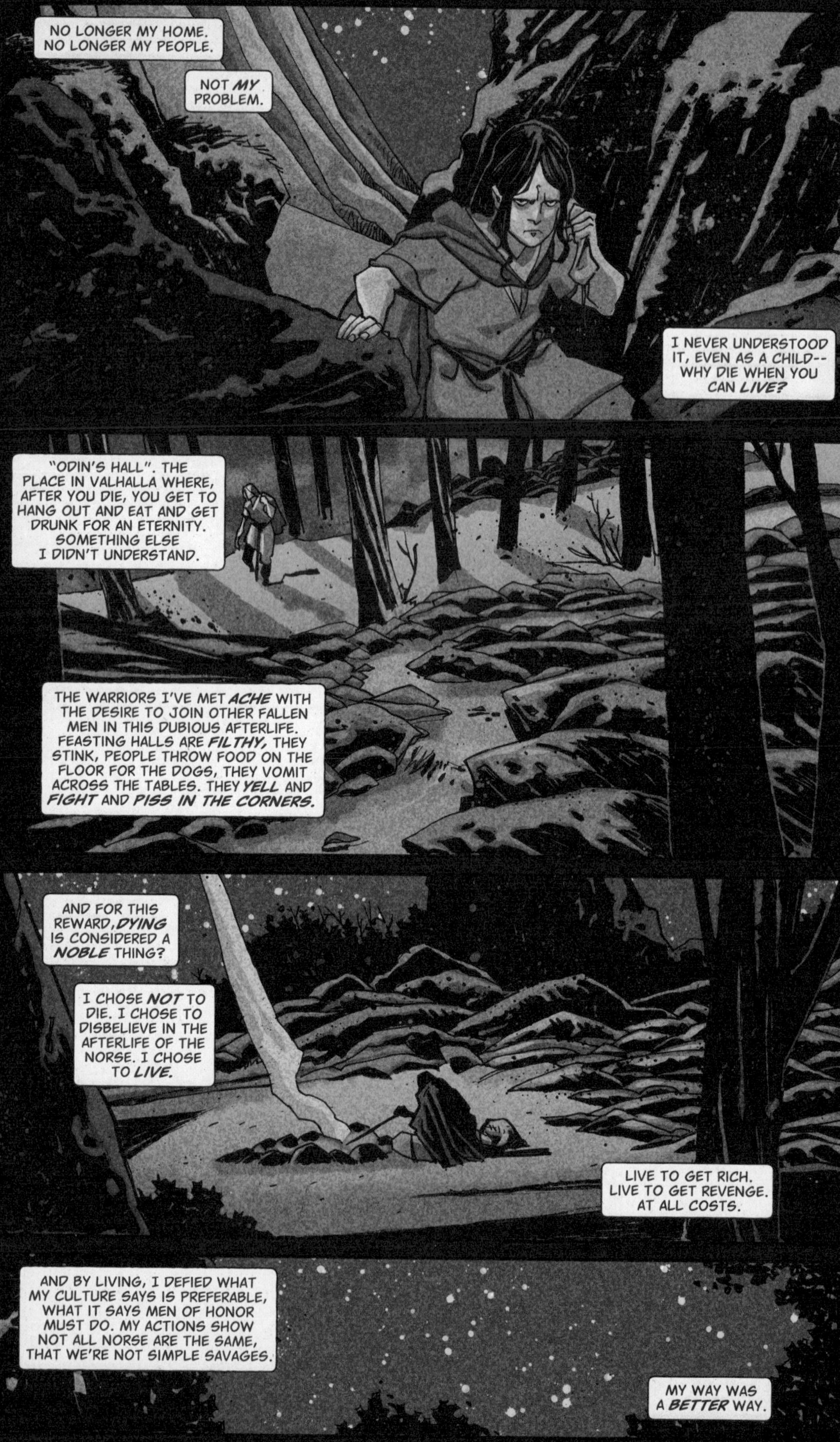
NO LONGER MY HOME.
NO LONGER MY PEOPLE.
NOT MY PROBLEM.
I NEVER UNDERSTOOD IT, EVEN AS A CHILD-- WHY DIE WHEN YOU CAN LIVE?
"ODIN'S HALL". THE PLACE IN VALHALLA WHERE, AFTER YOU DIE, YOU GET TO HANG OUT AND EAT AND GET DRUNK FOR AN ETERNITY. SOMETHING ELSE I DIDN'T UNDERSTAND.
THE WARRIORS I'VE MET ACHE WITH THE DESIRE TO JOIN OTHER FALLEN MEN IN THIS DUBIOUS AFTERLIFE. FEASTING HALLS ARE FILTHY, THEY STINK, PEOPLE THROW FOOD ON THE FLOOR FOR THE DOGS, THEY VOMIT ACROSS THE TABLES. THEY YELL AND FIGHT AND PISS IN THE CORNERS.
AND FOR THIS REWARD, DYING IS CONSIDERED A NOBLE THING?
I CHOSE NOT TO DIE. I CHOSE TO DISBELIEVE IN THE AFTERLIFE OF THE NORSE. I CHOSE TO LIVE.
LIVE TO GET RICH. LIVE TO GET REVENGE. AT ALL COSTS.
AND BY LIVING, I DEFIED WHAT MY CULTURE SAYS IS PREFERABLE, WHAT IT SAYS MEN OF HONOR MUST DO. MY ACTIONS SHOW NOT ALL NORSE ARE THE SAME, THAT WE'RE NOT SIMPLE SAVAGES.
MY WAY WAS A BETTER WAY.

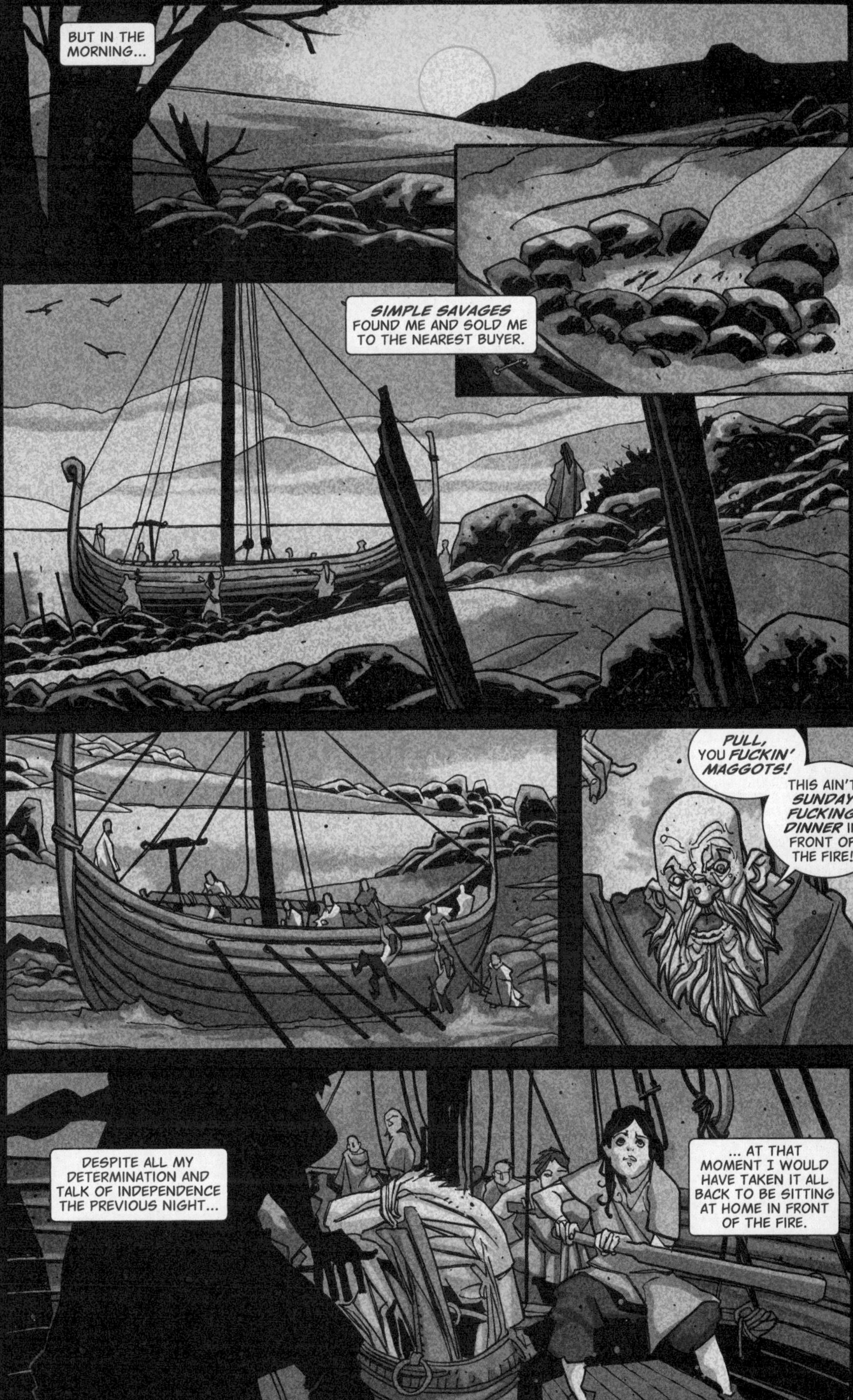
BUT IN THE MORNING...
SIMPLE SAVAGES FOUND ME AND SOLD ME TO THE NEAREST BUYER.
PULL, YOU FUCKIN' MAGGOTS!
THIS AIN'T SUNDAY FUCKING DINNER IN FRONT OF THE FIRE!
DESPITE ALL MY DETERMINATION AND TALK OF INDEPENDENCE THE PREVIOUS NIGHT...
... AT THAT MOMENT I WOULD HAVE TAKEN IT ALL BACK TO BE SITTING AT HOME IN FRONT OF THE FIRE.

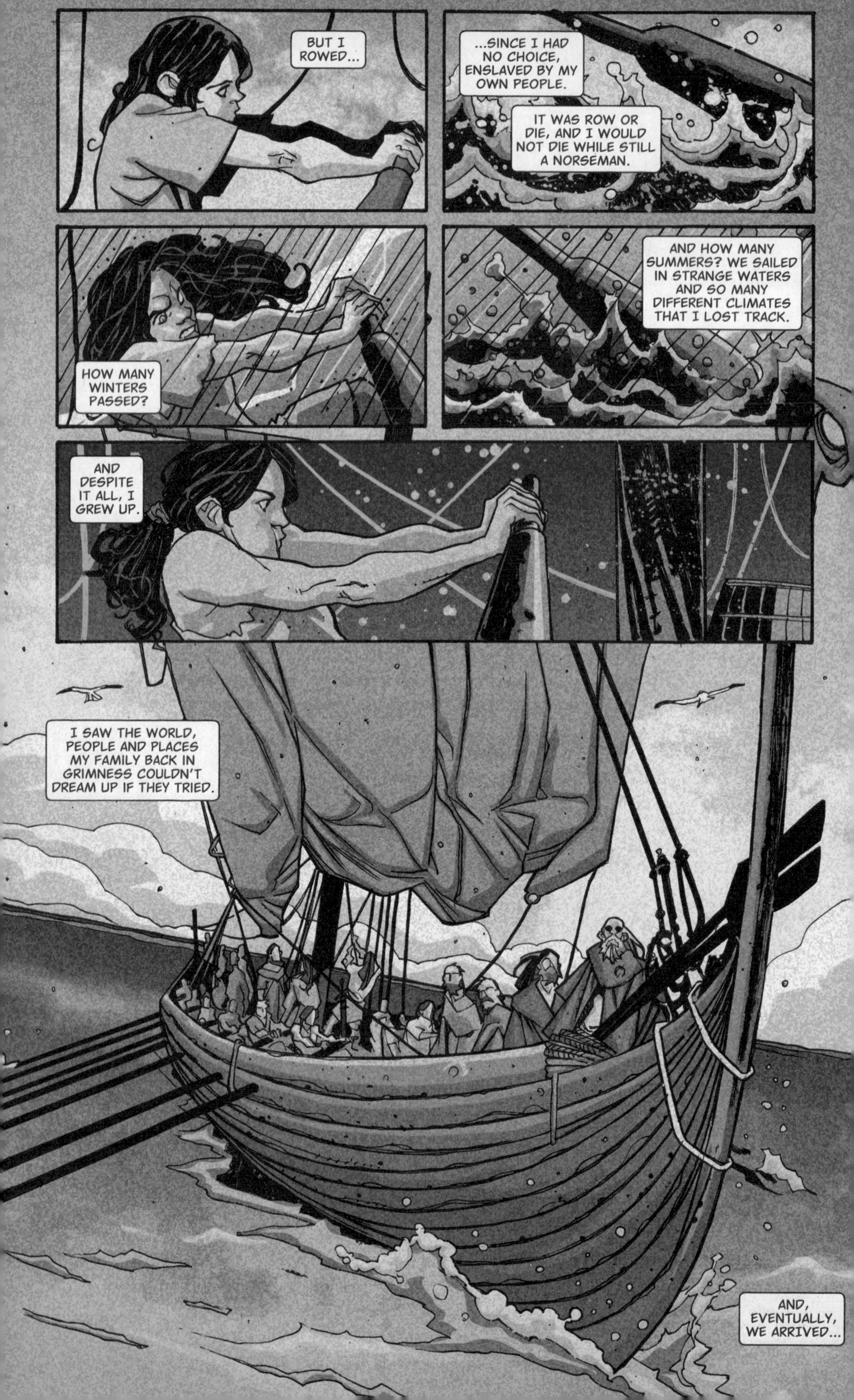
BUT I ROWED...
...SINCE I HAD NO CHOICE, ENSLAVED BY MY OWN PEOPLE.
IT WAS ROW OR DIE, AND I WOULD NOT DIE WHILE STILL A NORSEMAN.
HOW MANY WINTERS PASSED?
AND HOW MANY SUMMERS? WE SAILED IN STRANGE WATERS AND SO MANY DIFFERENT CLIMATES THAT I LOST TRACK.
AND DESPITE IT ALL, I GREW UP.
I SAW THE WORLD, PEOPLE AND PLACES MY FAMILY BACK IN GRIMNESS COULDN'T DREAM UP IF THEY TRIED.
AND, EVENTUALLY, WE ARRIVED...

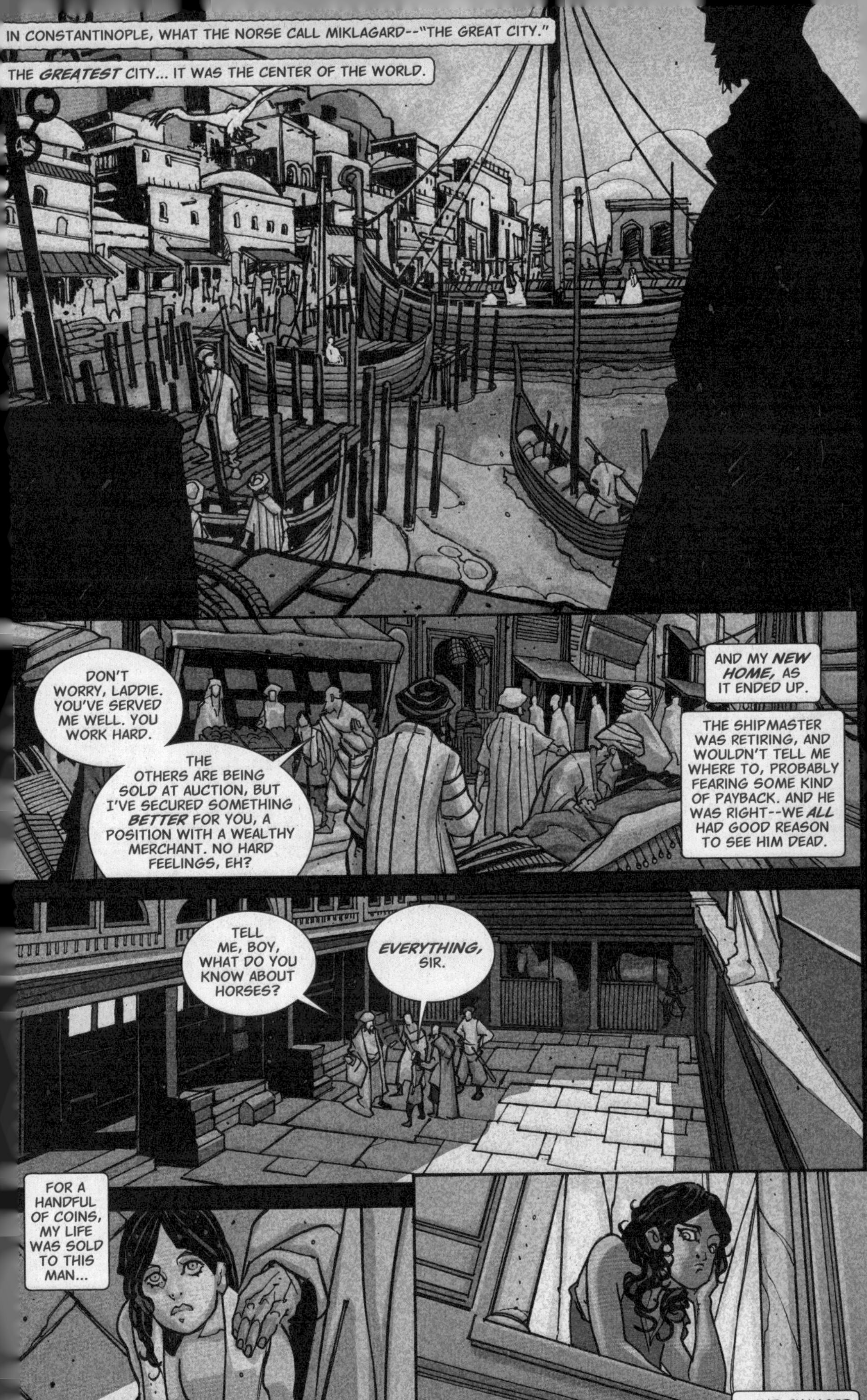
IN CONSTANTINOPLE, WHAT THE NORSE CALL MIKLAGARD--"THE GREAT CITY."
THE *GREATEST* CITY... IT WAS THE CENTER OF THE WORLD.
AND MY *NEW HOME,* AS IT ENDED UP.
DON'T WORRY, LADDIE. YOU'VE SERVED ME WELL. YOU WORK HARD.
THE OTHERS ARE BEING SOLD AT AUCTION, BUT I'VE SECURED SOMETHING *BETTER* FOR YOU, A POSITION WITH A WEALTHY MERCHANT. NO HARD FEELINGS, EH?
THE SHIPMASTER WAS RETIRING, AND WOULDN'T TELL ME WHERE TO, PROBABLY FEARING SOME KIND OF PAYBACK. AND HE WAS RIGHT--WE *ALL* HAD GOOD REASON TO SEE HIM DEAD.
TELL ME, BOY, WHAT DO YOU KNOW ABOUT HORSES?
EVERYTHING, SIR.
FOR A HANDFUL OF COINS, MY LIFE WAS SOLD TO THIS MAN...
...AND CHANGED *FOREVER.*

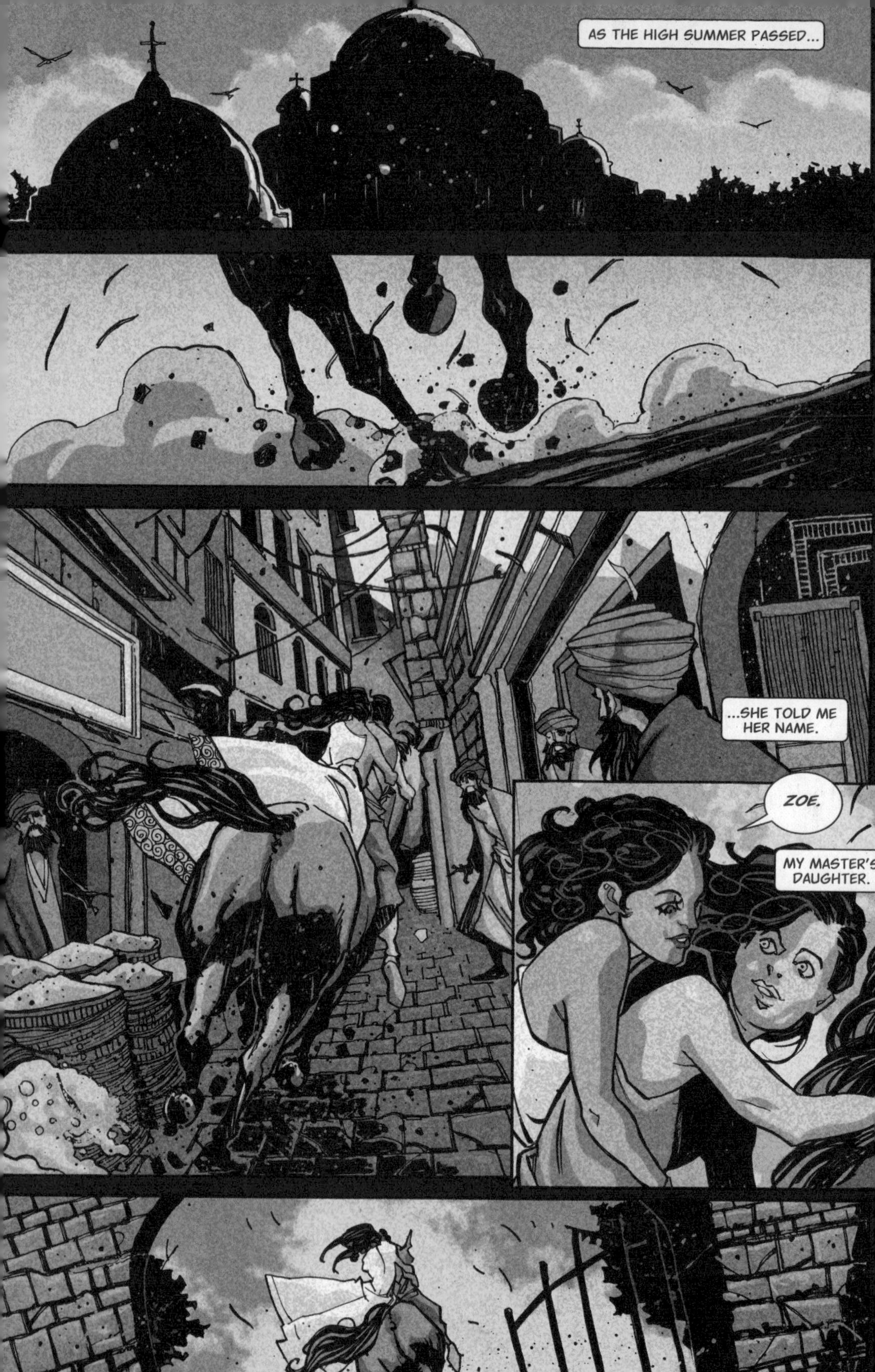
AS THE HIGH SUMMER PASSED...
...SHE TOLD ME HER NAME.
ZOE.
MY MASTER'S DAUGHTER.
AND SHE HAD MY HEART.

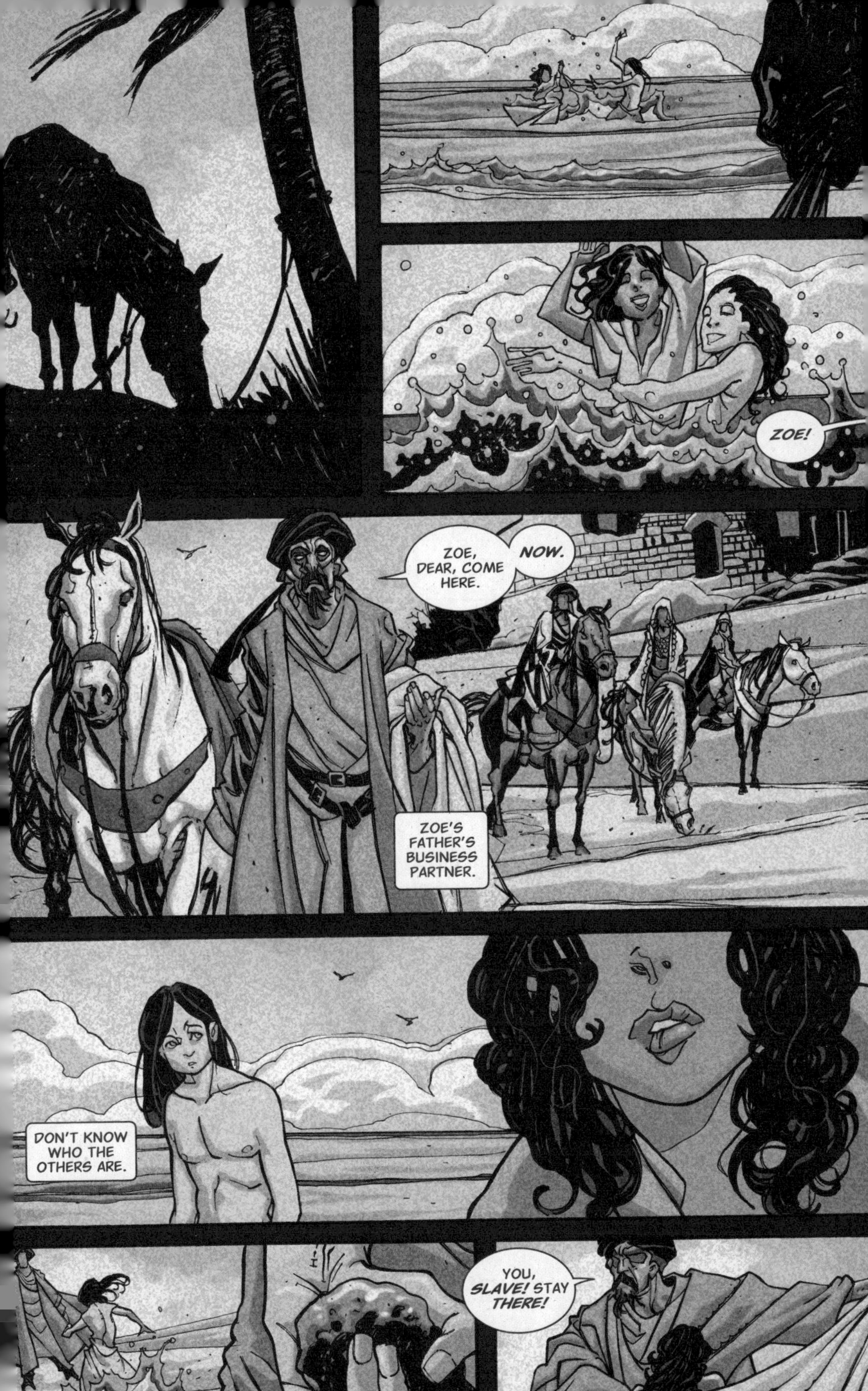
ZOE!
ZOE, DEAR, COME HERE.
NOW.
ZOE'S FATHER'S BUSINESS PARTNER.
DON'T KNOW WHO THE OTHERS ARE.
YOU, SLAVE! STAY THERE!

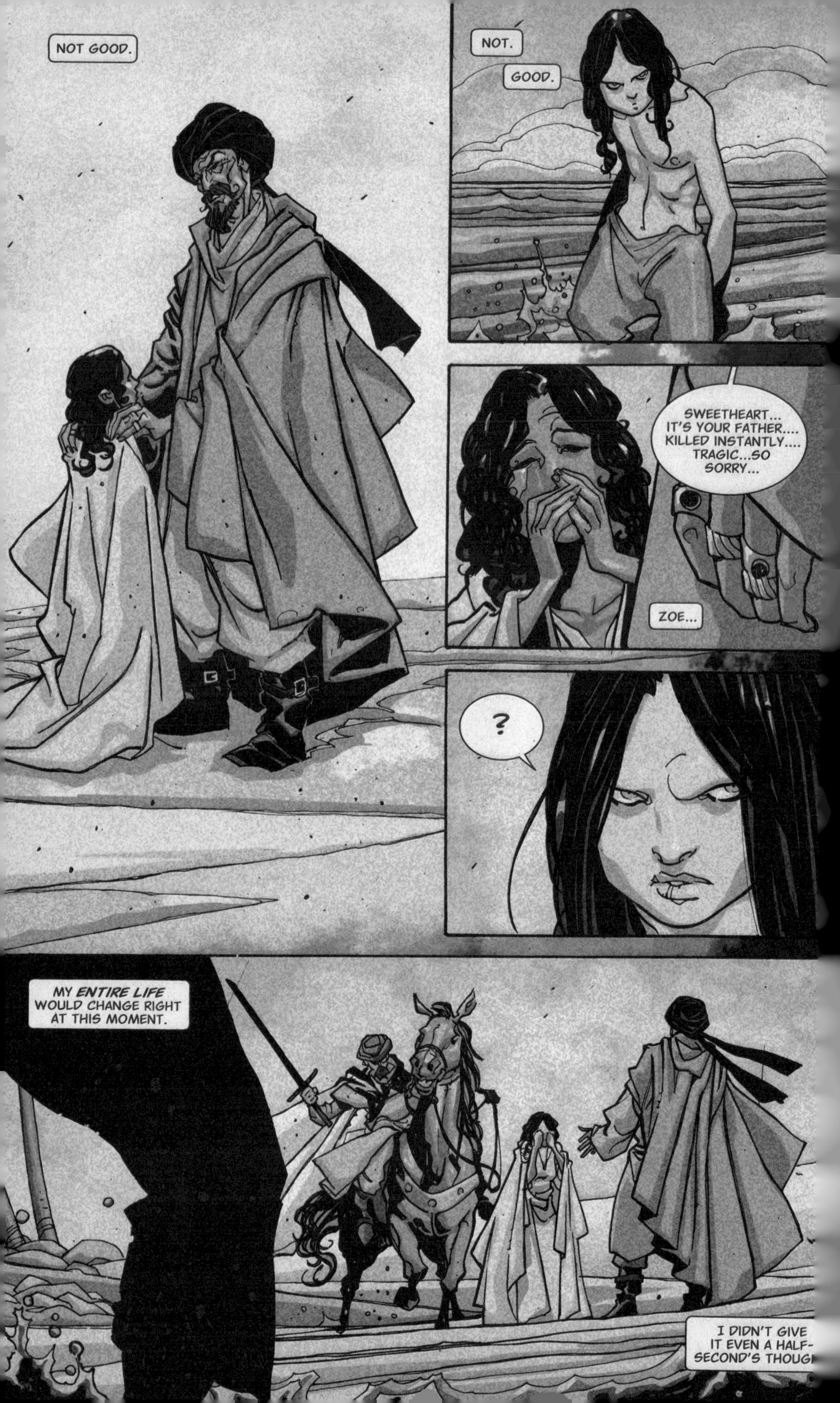
NOT GOOD.
NOT.
GOOD.
SWEETHEART... IT'S YOUR FATHER.... KILLED INSTANTLY.... TRAGIC...SO SORRY...
ZOE...
?
MY ENTIRE LIFE WOULD CHANGE RIGHT AT THIS MOMENT.
I DIDN'T GIVE IT EVEN A HALF-SECOND'S THOUG

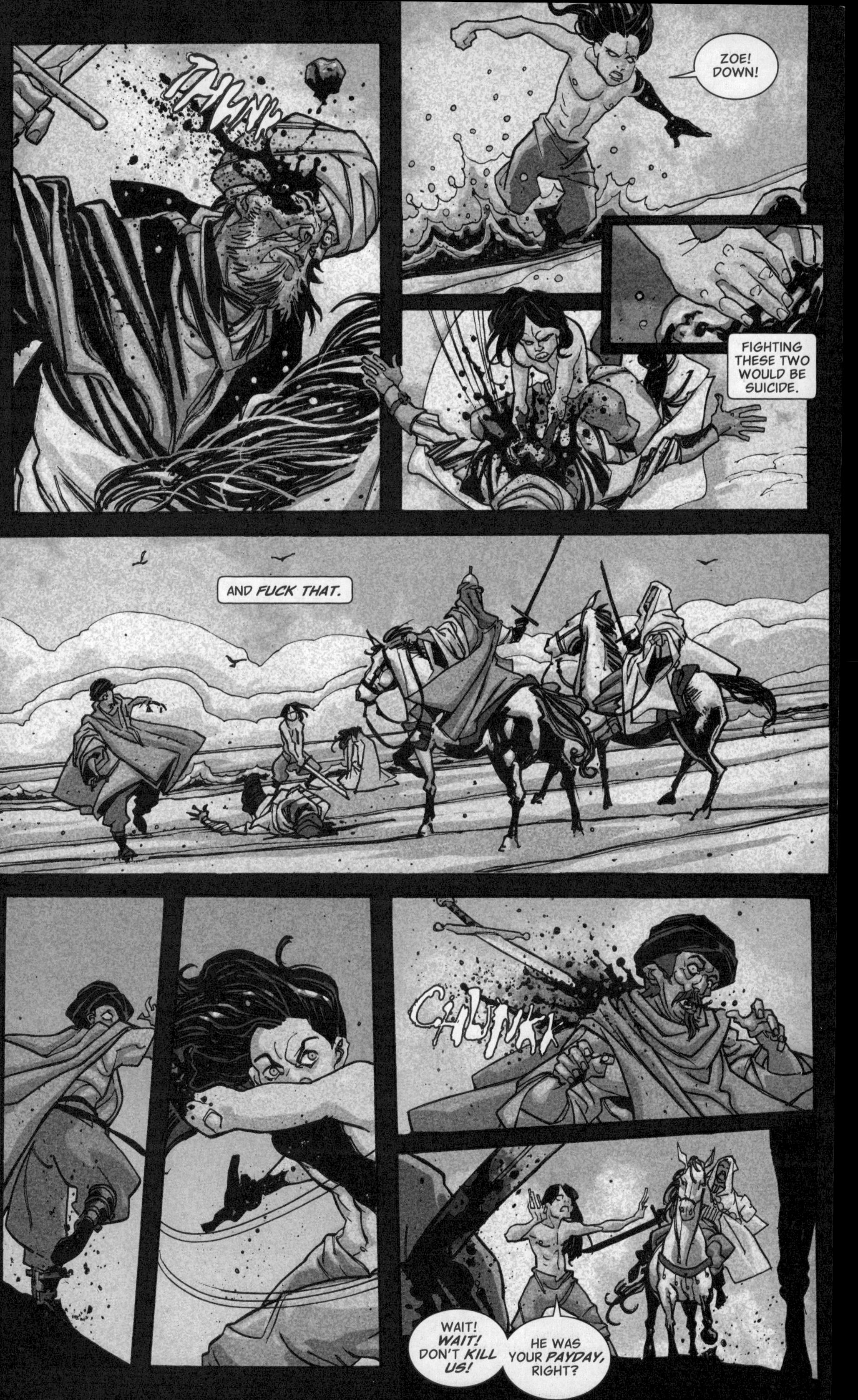
THHUNK
ZOE! DOWN!
FIGHTING THESE TWO WOULD BE SUICIDE.
AND *FUCK THAT.*
CHUNK
WAIT! *WAIT!* DON'T *KILL US!*
HE WAS YOUR *PAYDAY,* RIGHT?

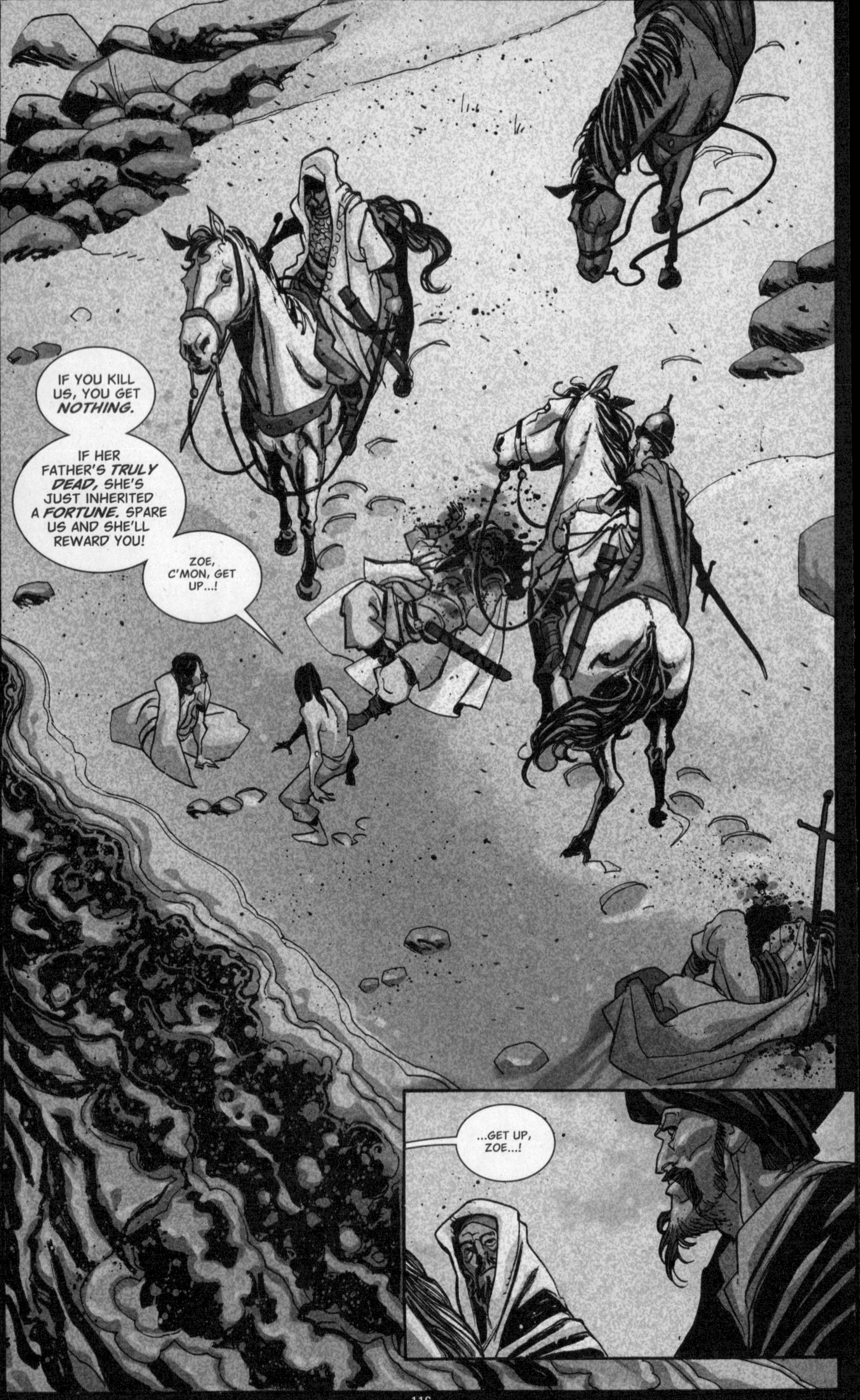
IF YOU KILL US, YOU GET NOTHING.
IF HER FATHER'S TRULY DEAD, SHE'S JUST INHERITED A FORTUNE. SPARE US AND SHE'LL REWARD YOU!
ZOE, C'MON, GET UP...!
...GET UP, ZOE...!

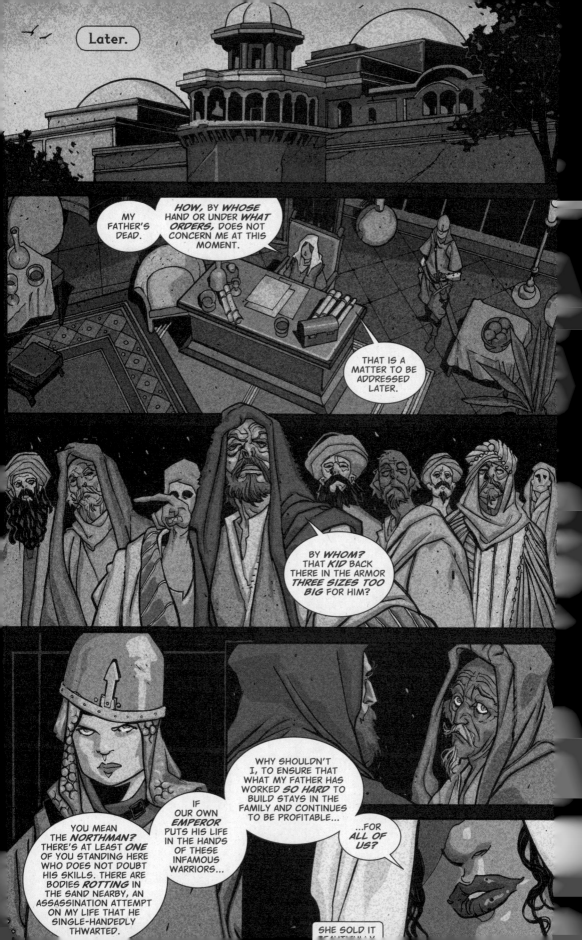

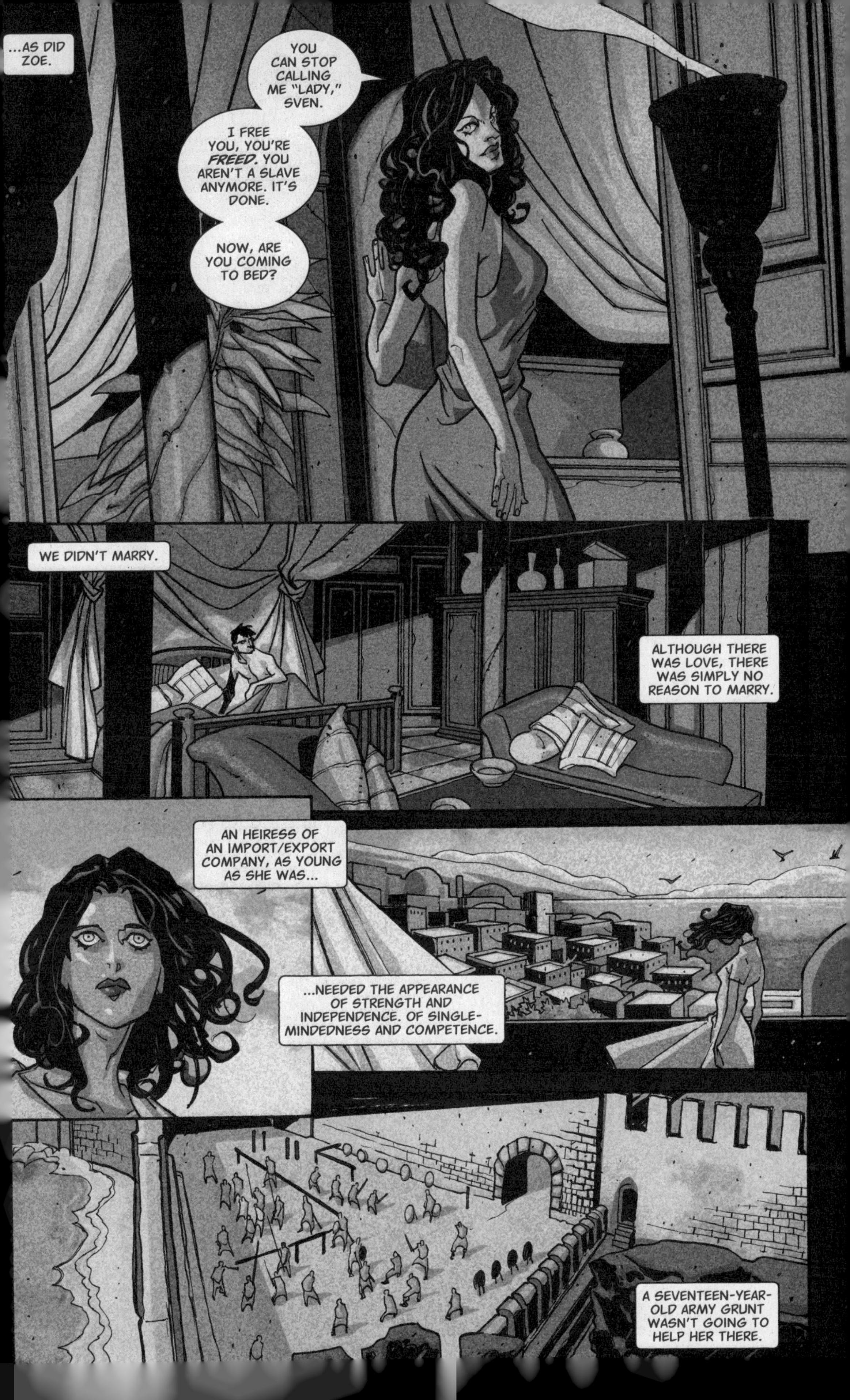

...AS DID ZOE.
YOU CAN STOP CALLING ME "LADY," SVEN.
I FREE YOU, YOU'RE FREED. YOU AREN'T A SLAVE ANYMORE. IT'S DONE.
NOW, ARE YOU COMING TO BED?
WE DIDN'T MARRY.
ALTHOUGH THERE WAS LOVE, THERE WAS SIMPLY NO REASON TO MARRY.
AN HEIRESS OF AN IMPORT/EXPORT COMPANY, AS YOUNG AS SHE WAS...
...NEEDED THE APPEARANCE OF STRENGTH AND INDEPENDENCE. OF SINGLE-MINDEDNESS AND COMPETENCE.
A SEVENTEEN-YEAR-OLD ARMY GRUNT WASN'T GOING TO HELP HER THERE.

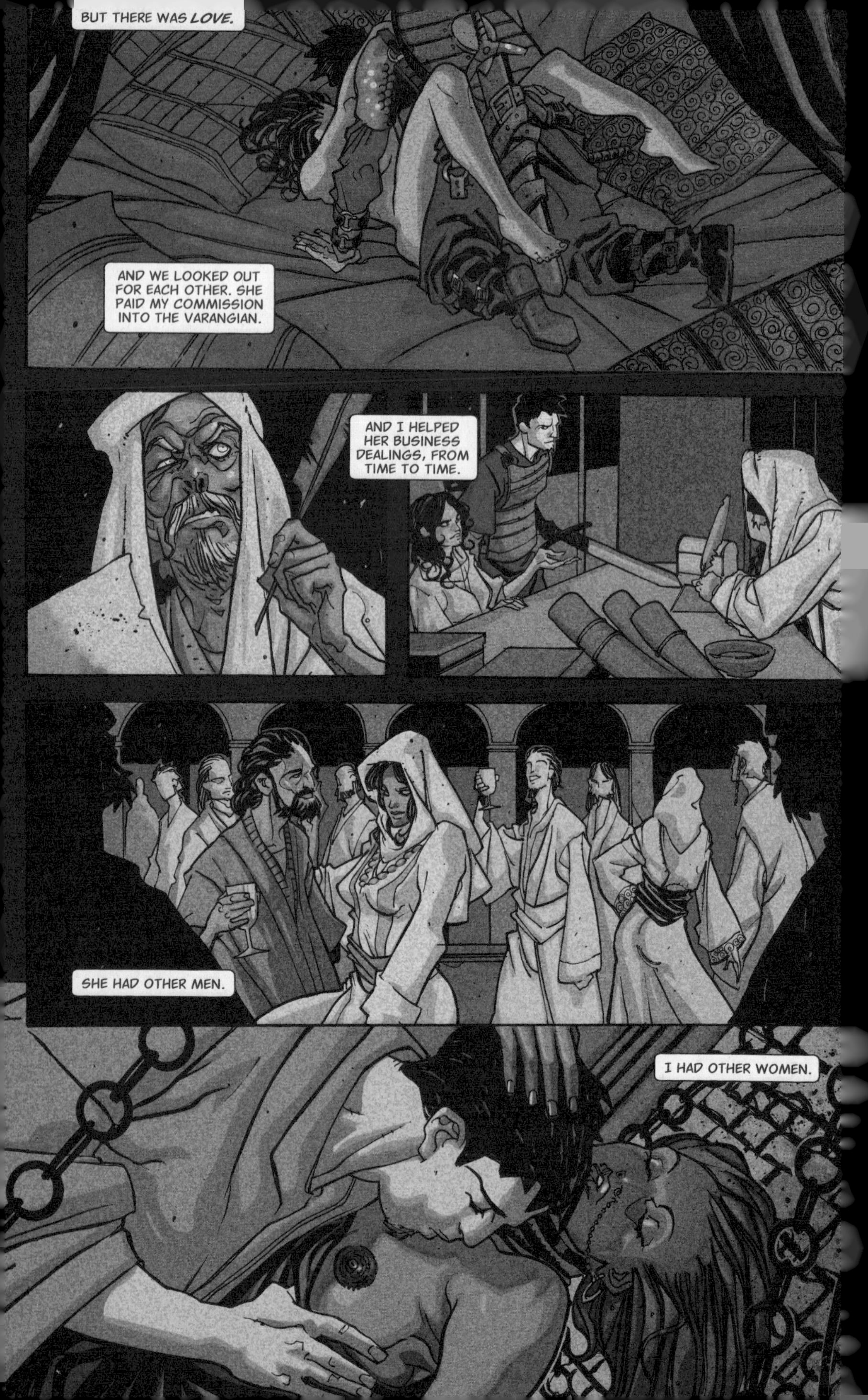
BUT THERE WAS *LOVE.*
AND WE LOOKED OUT FOR EACH OTHER. SHE PAID MY COMMISSION INTO THE VARANGIAN.
AND I HELPED HER BUSINESS DEALINGS, FROM TIME TO TIME.
SHE HAD OTHER MEN.
I HAD OTHER WOMEN.

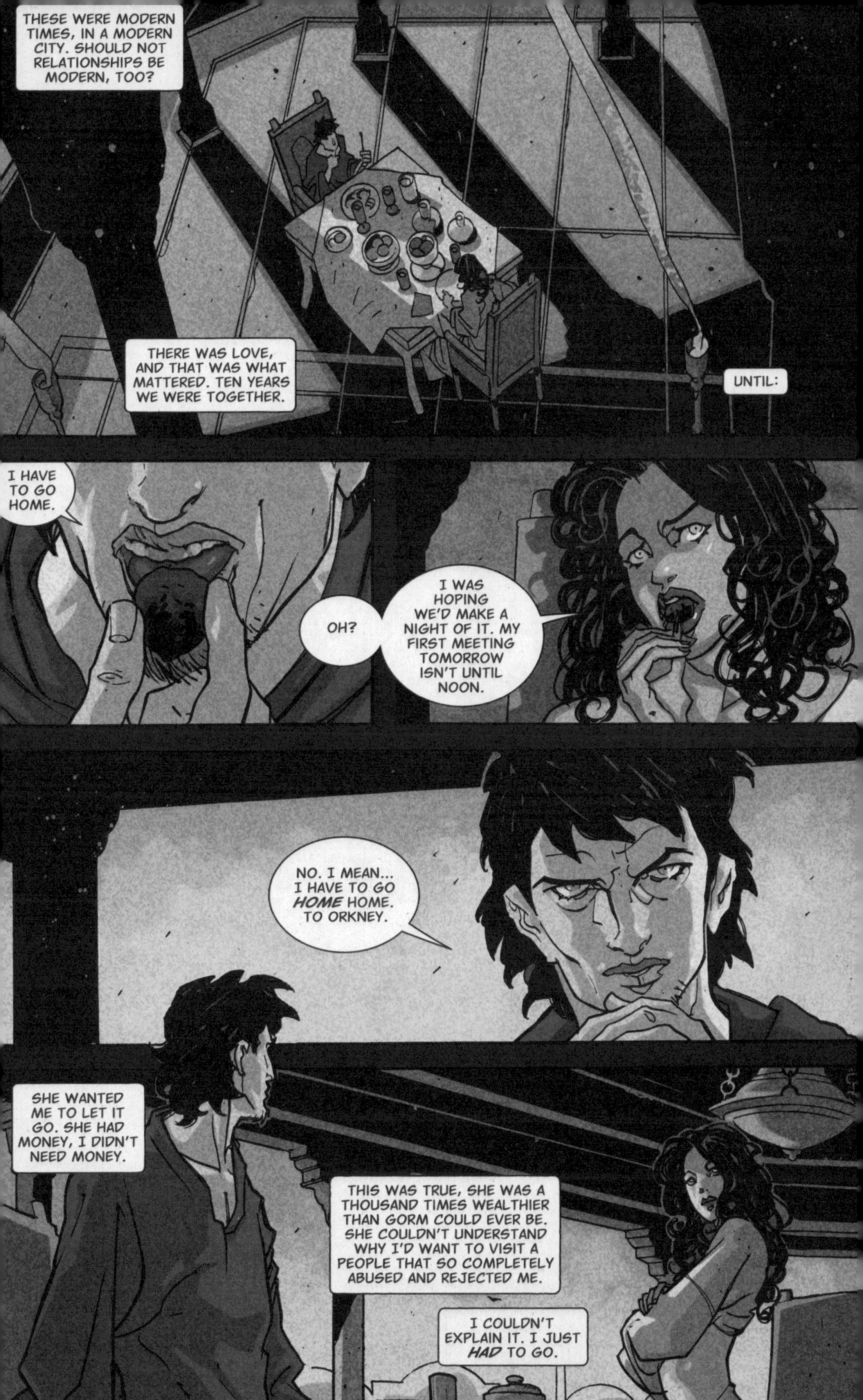

THESE WERE MODERN TIMES, IN A MODERN CITY. SHOULD NOT RELATIONSHIPS BE MODERN, TOO?
THERE WAS LOVE, AND THAT WAS WHAT MATTERED. TEN YEARS WE WERE TOGETHER.
UNTIL:
I HAVE TO GO HOME.
OH?
I WAS HOPING WE'D MAKE A NIGHT OF IT. MY FIRST MEETING TOMORROW ISN'T UNTIL NOON.
NO. I MEAN... I HAVE TO GO *HOME* HOME. TO ORKNEY.
SHE WANTED ME TO LET IT GO. SHE HAD MONEY, I DIDN'T NEED MONEY.
THIS WAS TRUE, SHE WAS A THOUSAND TIMES WEALTHIER THAN GORM COULD EVER BE. SHE COULDN'T UNDERSTAND WHY I'D WANT TO VISIT A PEOPLE THAT SO COMPLETELY ABUSED AND REJECTED ME.
I COULDN'T EXPLAIN IT. I JUST *HAD* TO GO.

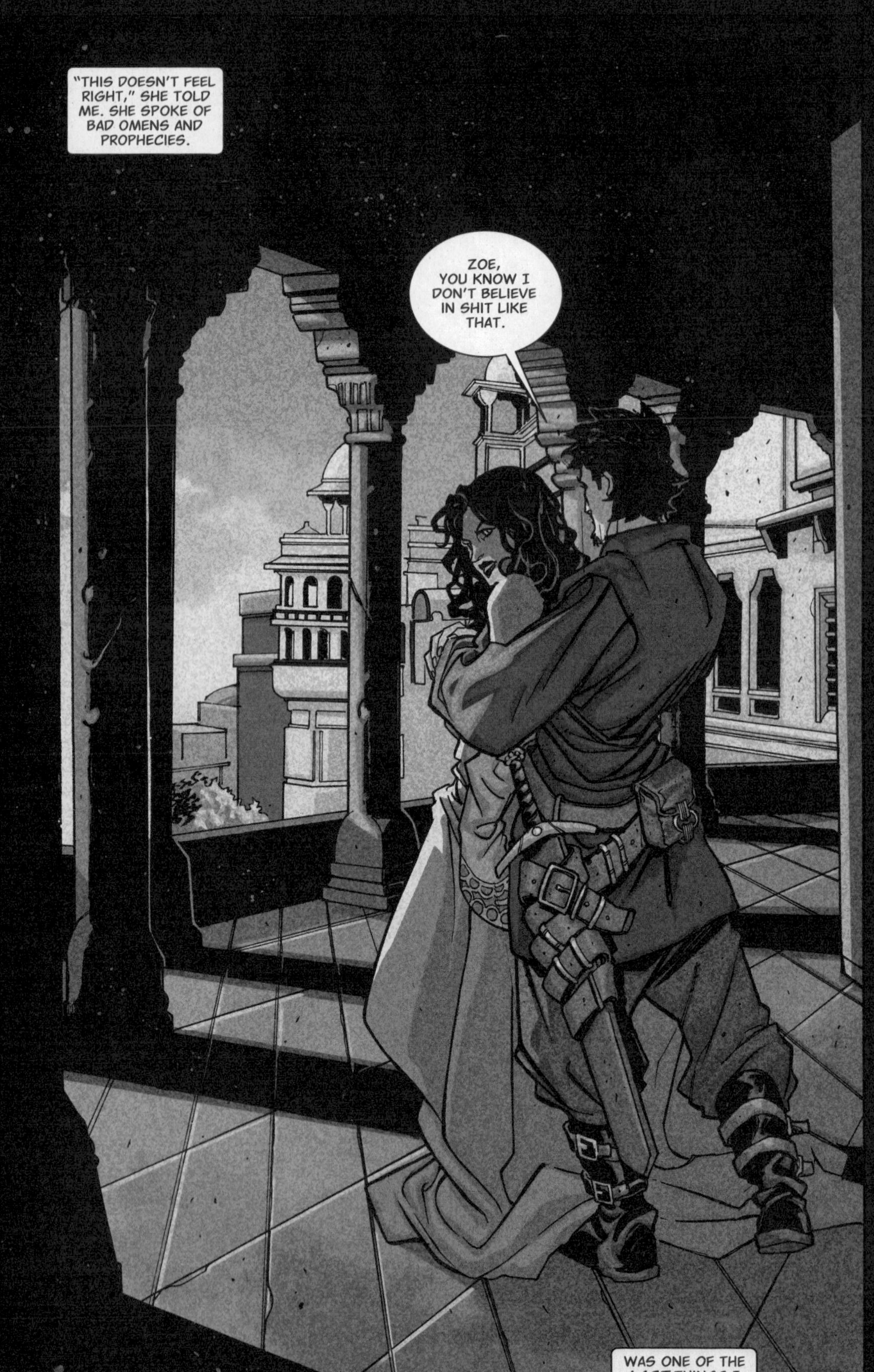
"THIS DOESN'T FEEL RIGHT," SHE TOLD ME. SHE SPOKE OF BAD OMENS AND PROPHECIES.
ZOE, YOU KNOW I DON'T BELIEVE IN SHIT LIKE THAT.
WAS ONE OF THE *LAST* THINGS I EVER SAID TO HER.

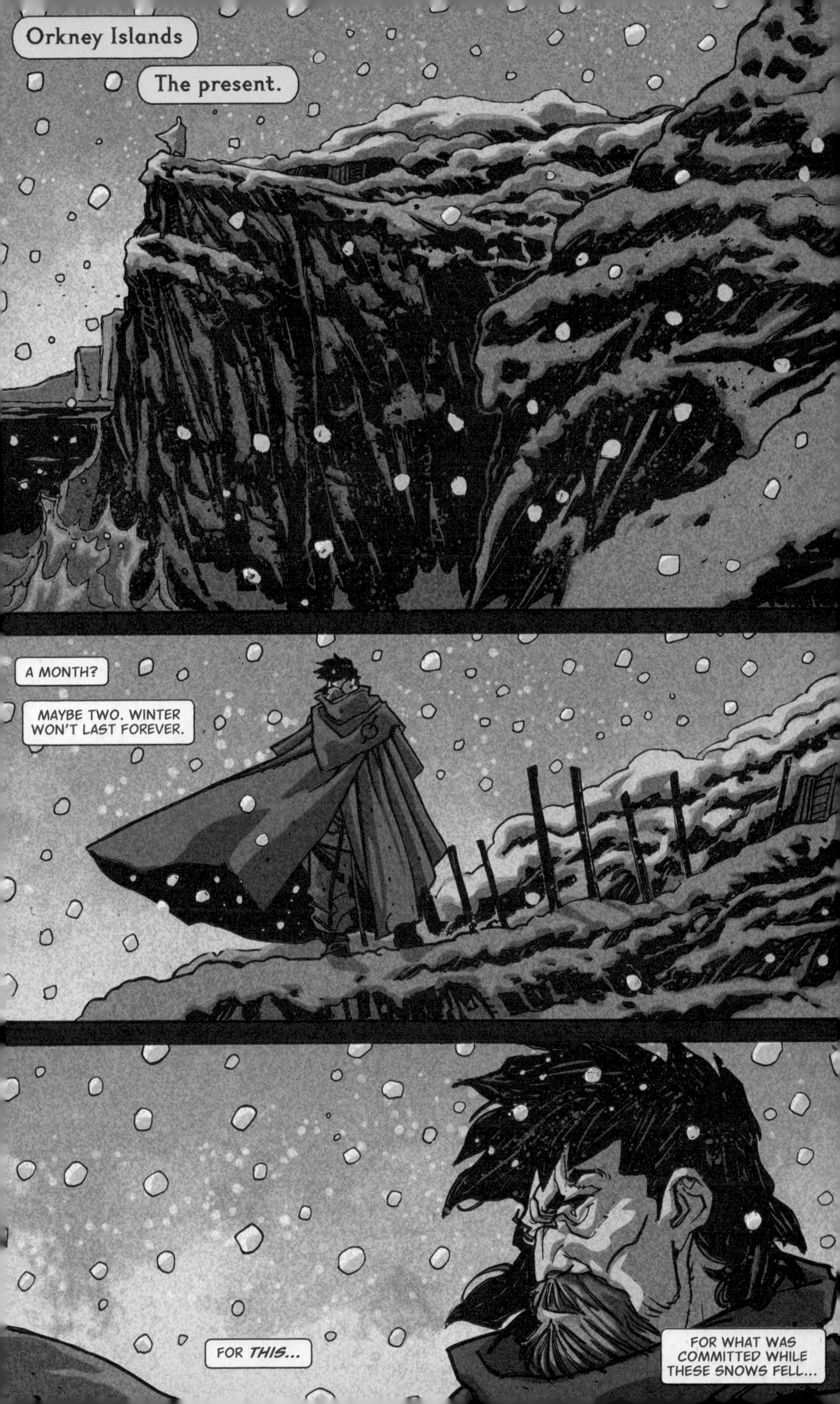
Orkney Islands
The present.
A MONTH?
MAYBE TWO. WINTER WON'T LAST FOREVER.
FOR *THIS*...
FOR WHAT WAS COMMITTED WHILE THESE SNOWS FELL...

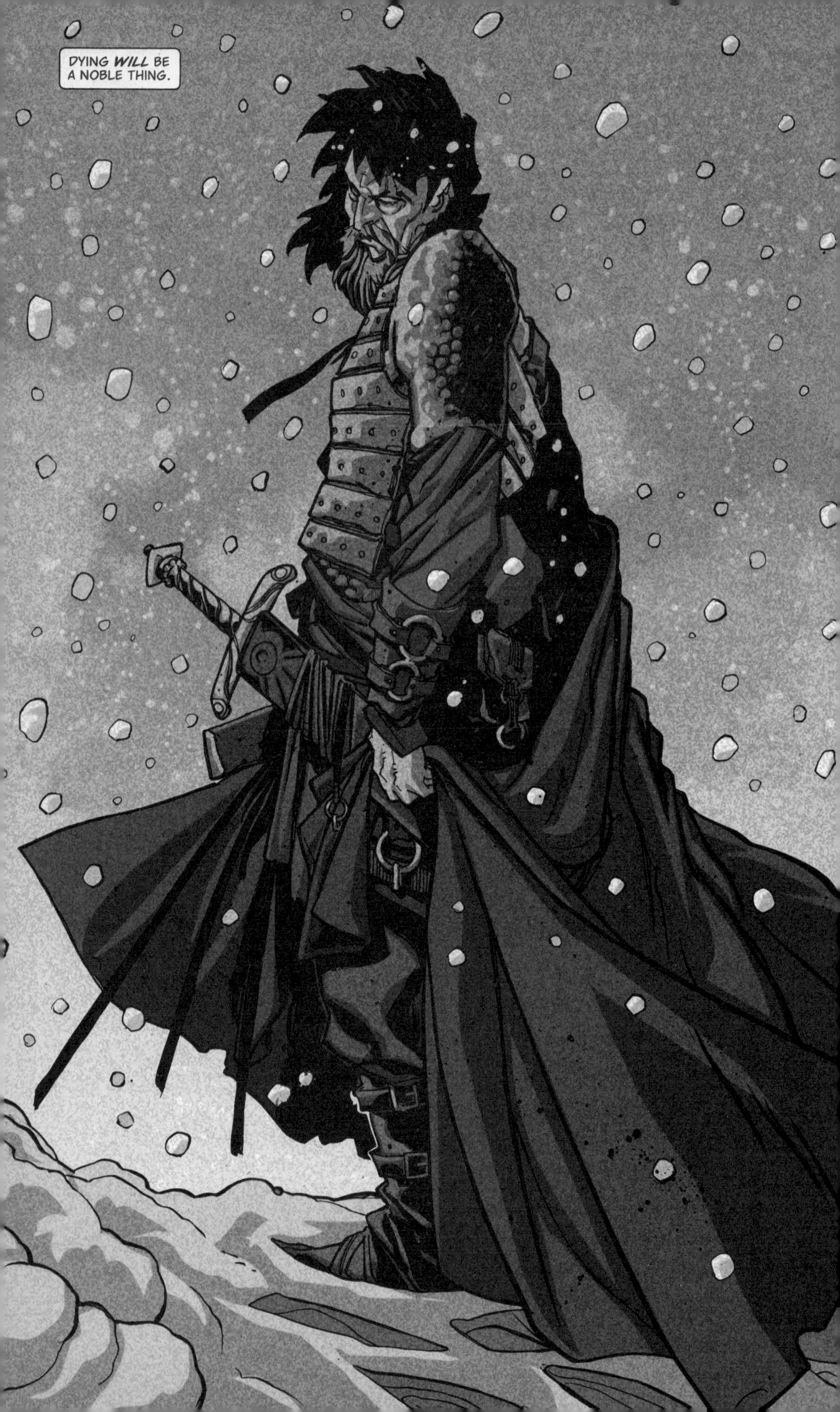
DYING WILL BE A NOBLE THING.

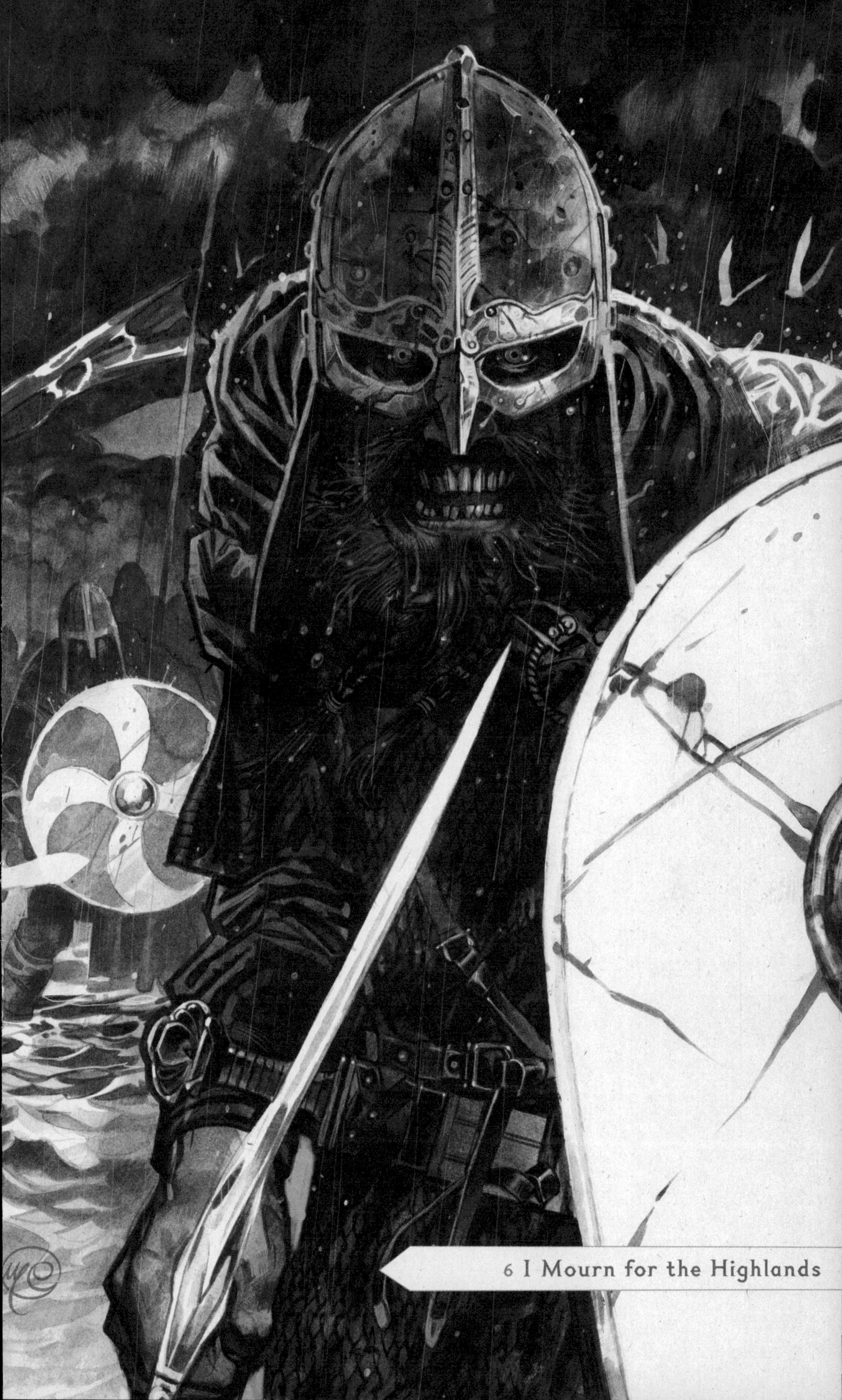

6 I Mourn for the Highlands

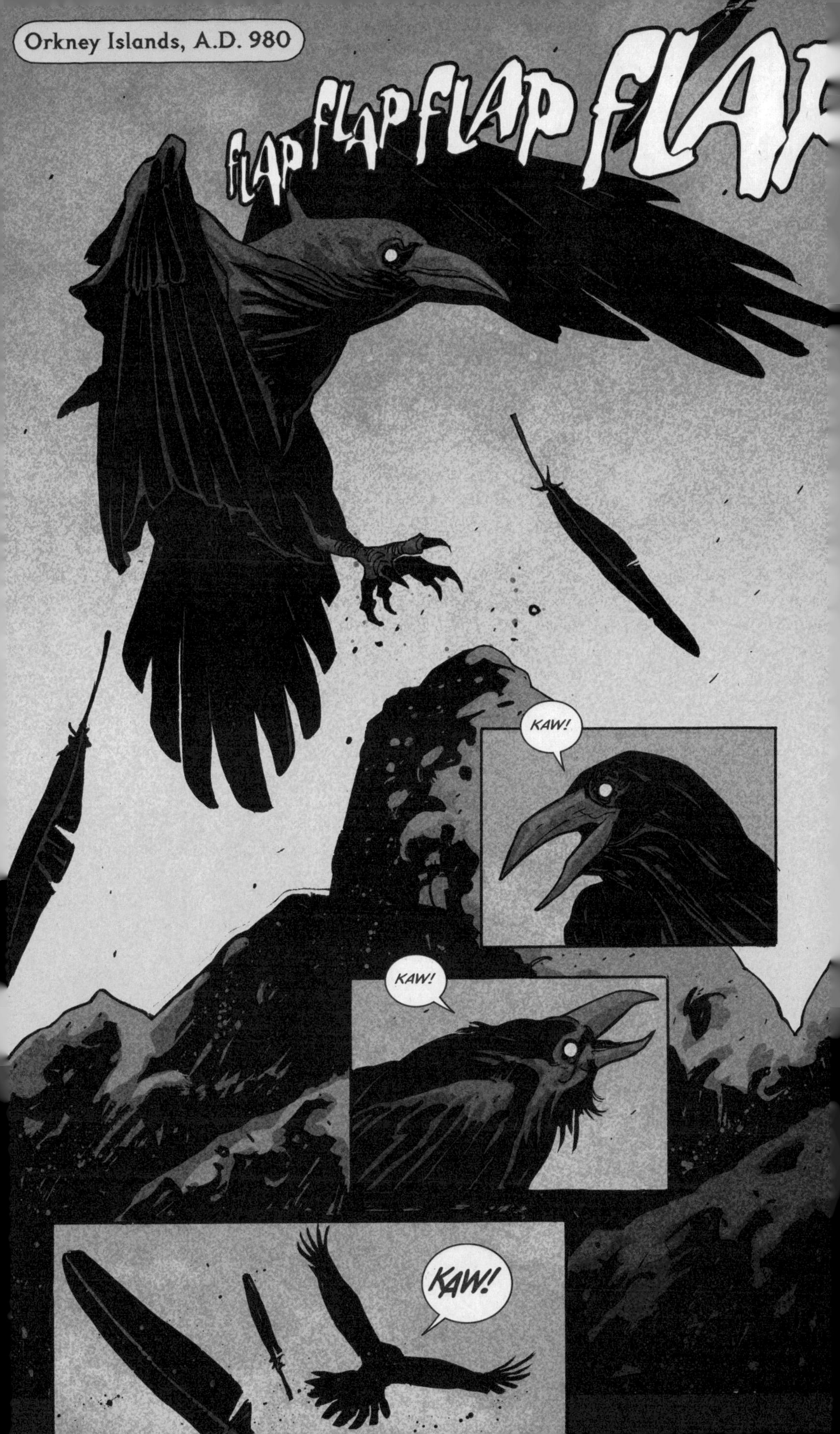
Orkney Islands, A.D. 980
FLAP FLAP FLAP FLAP
KAW!
KAW!
KAW!

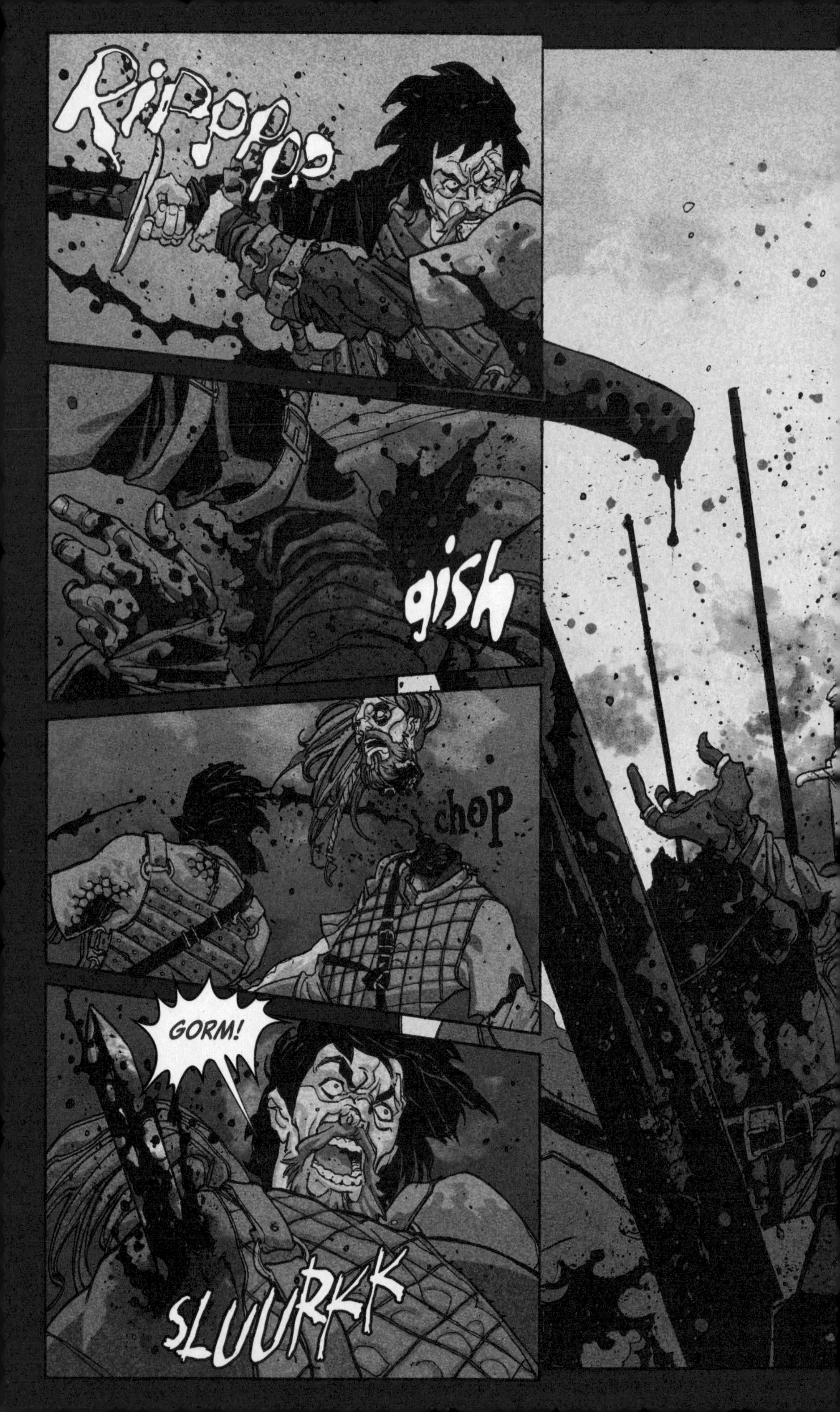
RIPPPPP
gish
chop
GORM!
SLUURKK

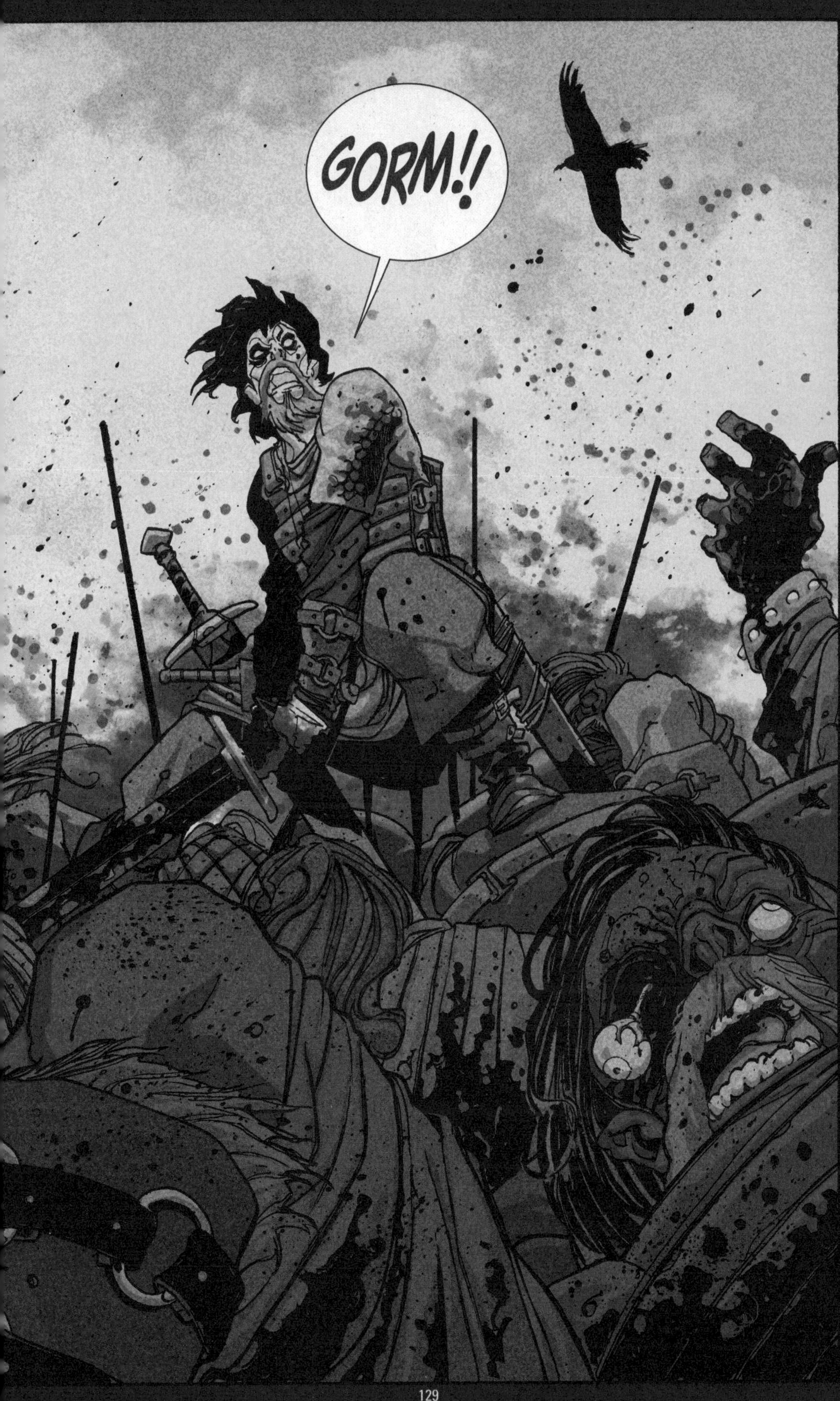
GORM!!

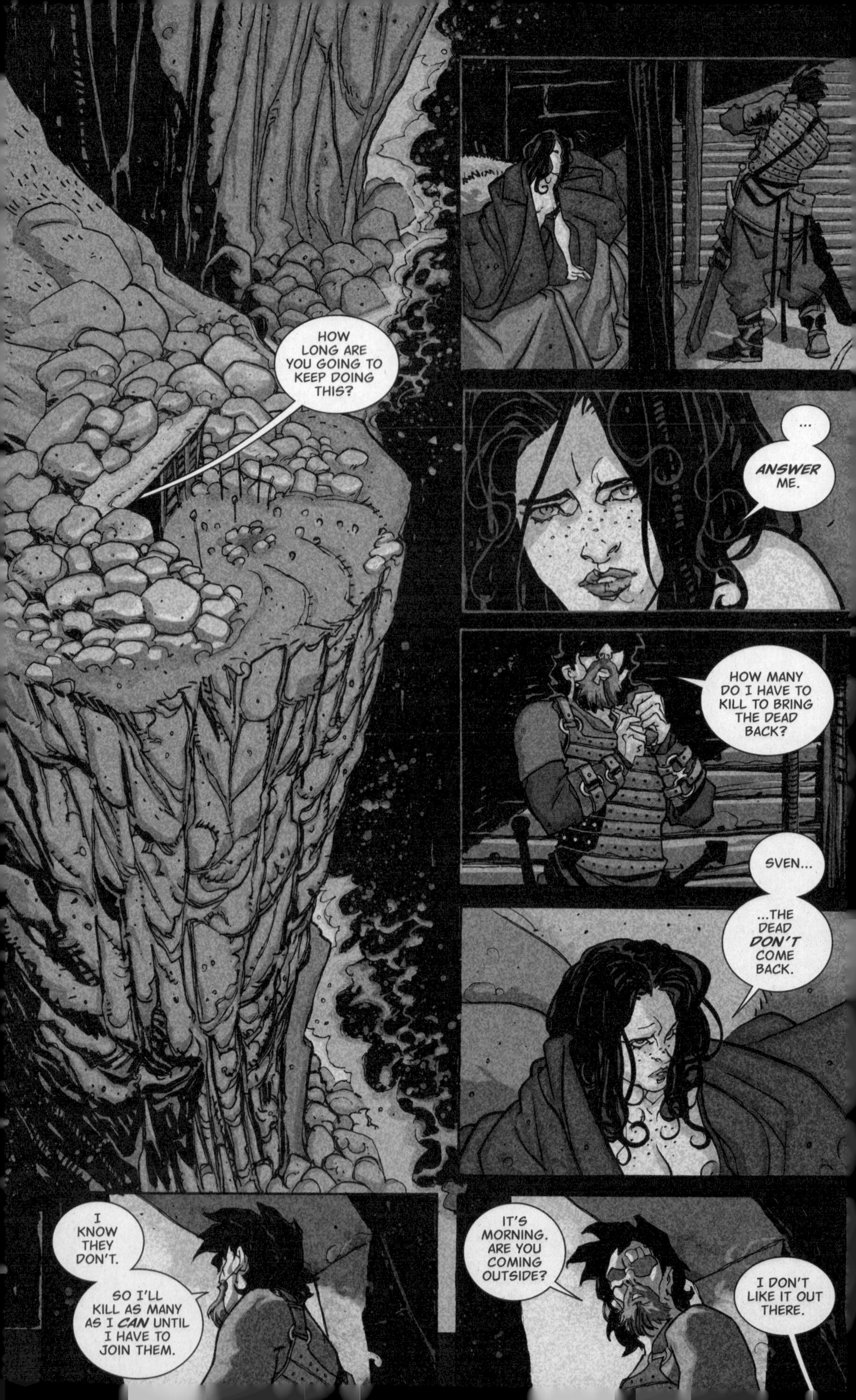
HOW LONG ARE YOU GOING TO KEEP DOING THIS?
... ANSWER ME.
HOW MANY DO I HAVE TO KILL TO BRING THE DEAD BACK?
SVEN...
...THE DEAD DON'T COME BACK.
I KNOW THEY DON'T.
SO I'LL KILL AS MANY AS I CAN UNTIL I HAVE TO JOIN THEM.
IT'S MORNING. ARE YOU COMING OUTSIDE?
I DON'T LIKE IT OUT THERE.

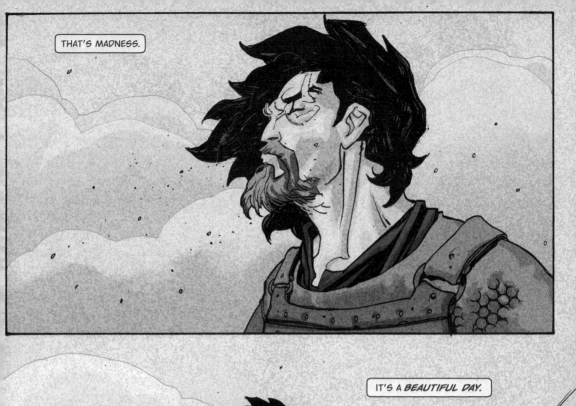

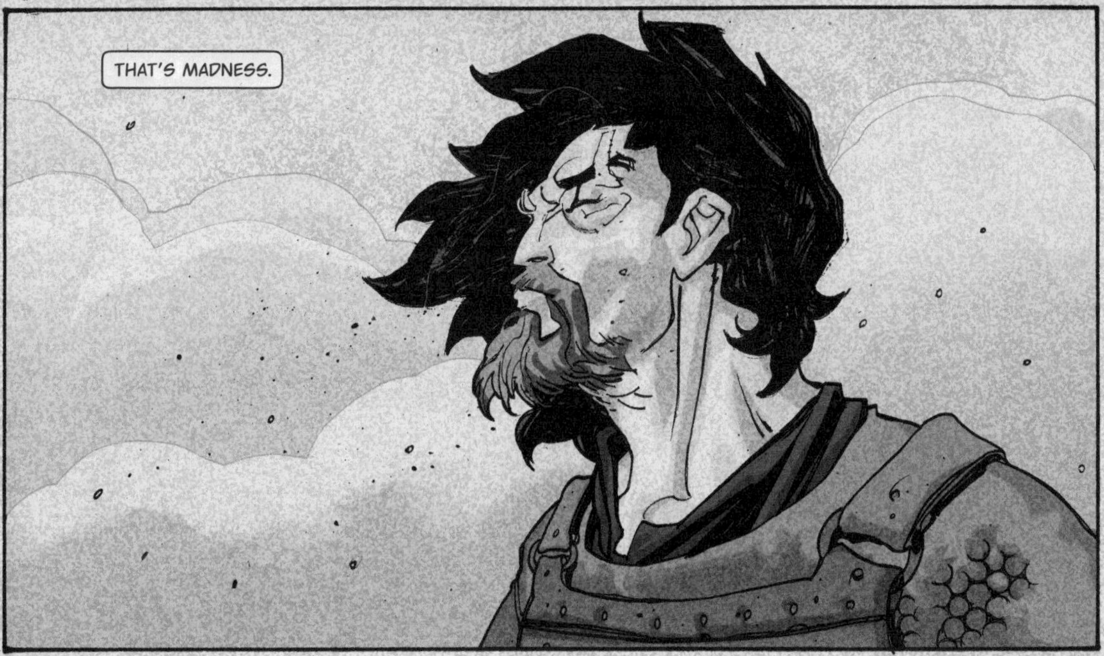
THAT'S MADNESS.

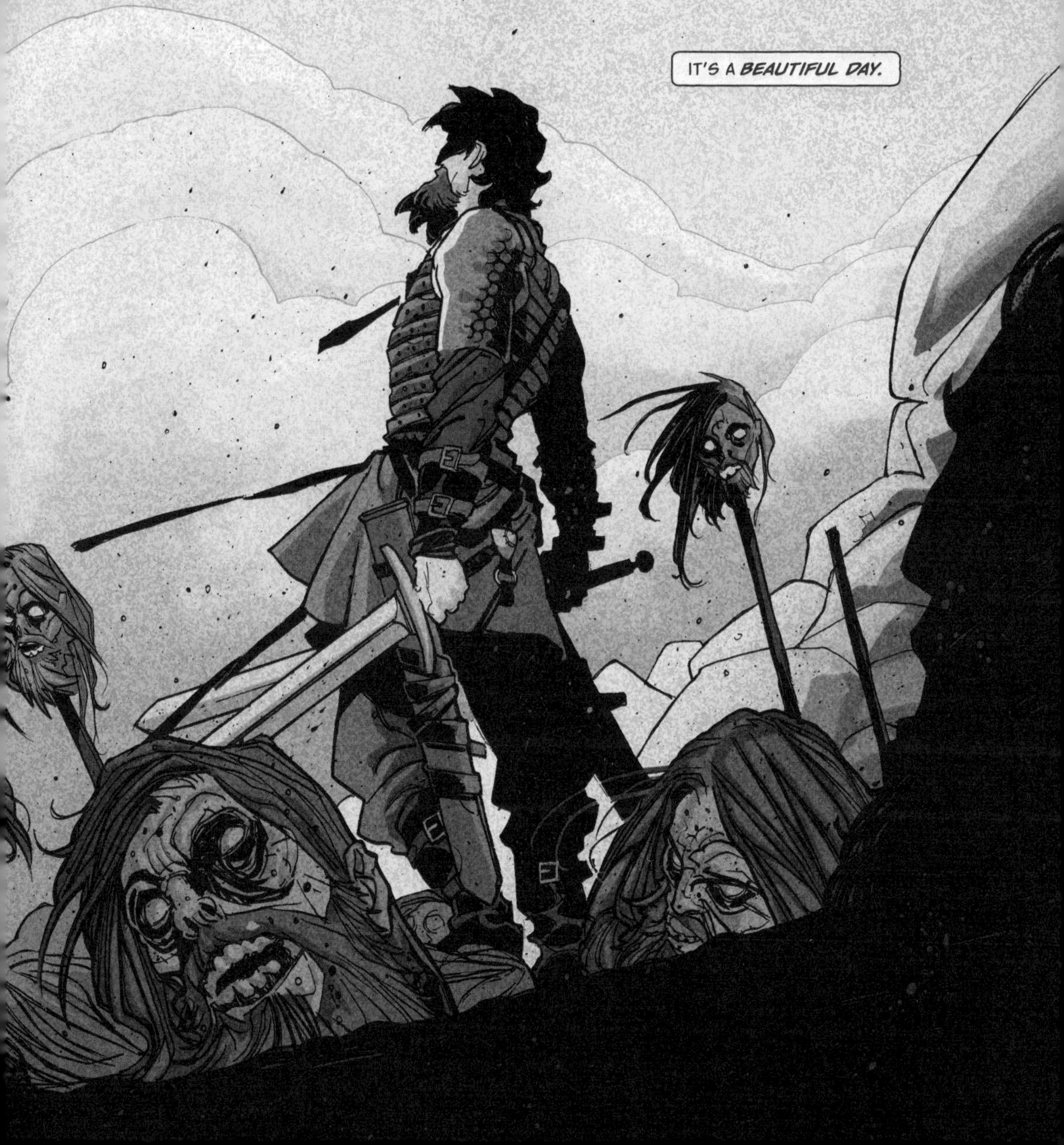
IT'S A *BEAUTIFUL DAY.*

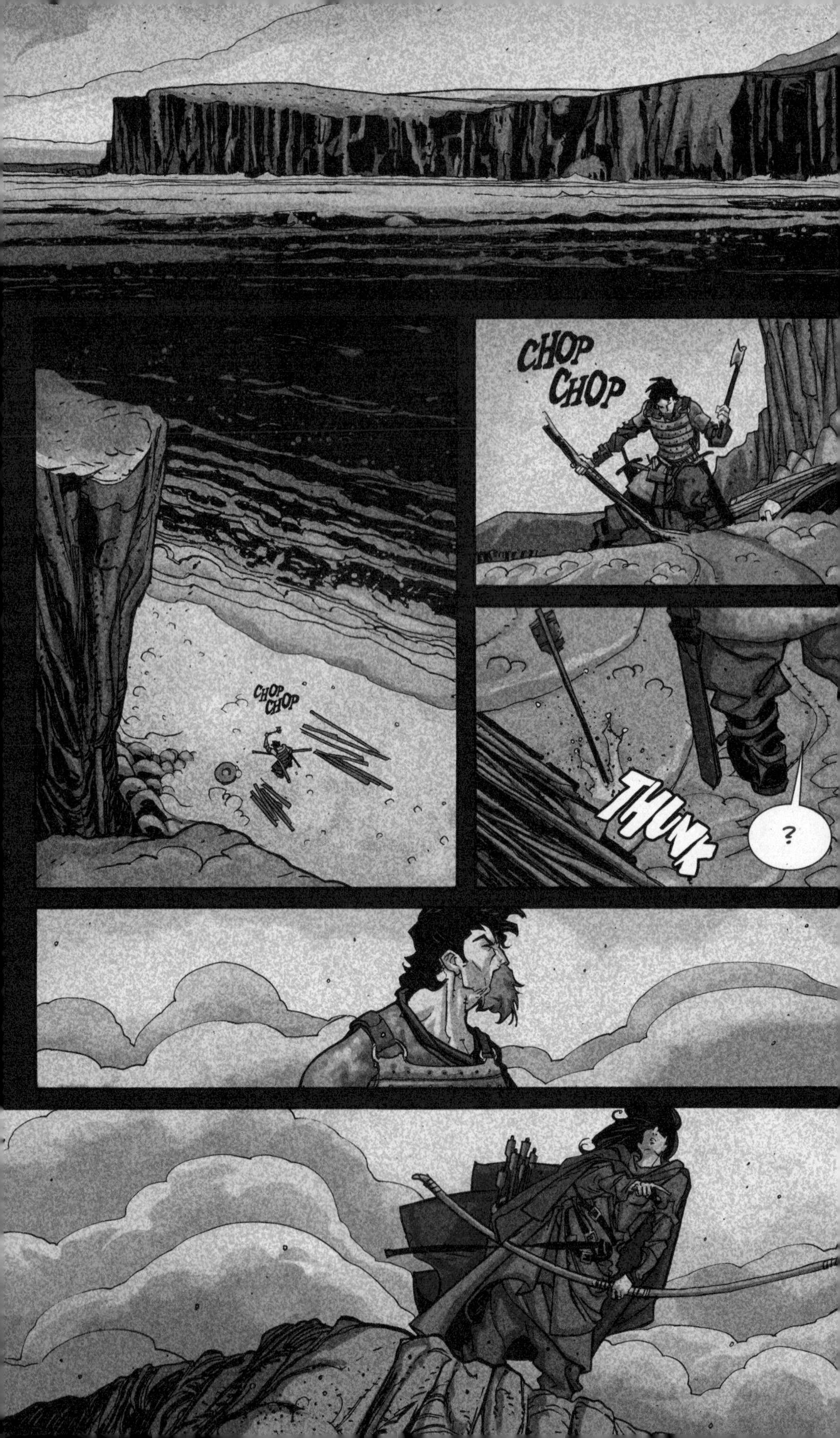

CHOP CHOP
CHOP CHOP
THUNK
?

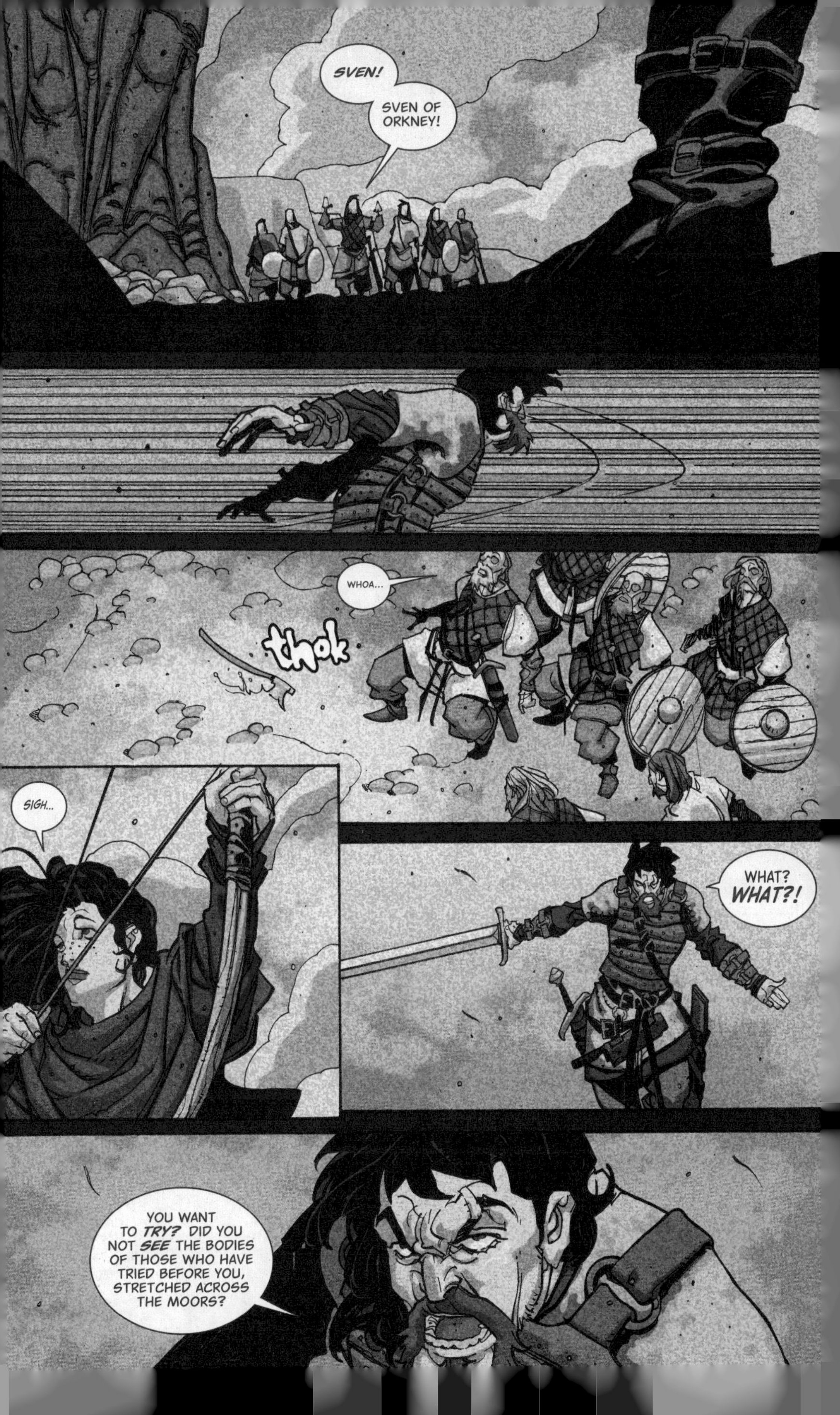
SVEN!
SVEN OF ORKNEY!
WHOA...
thok
SIGH...
WHAT? WHAT?!
YOU WANT TO TRY? DID YOU NOT SEE THE BODIES OF THOSE WHO HAVE TRIED BEFORE YOU, STRETCHED ACROSS THE MOORS?

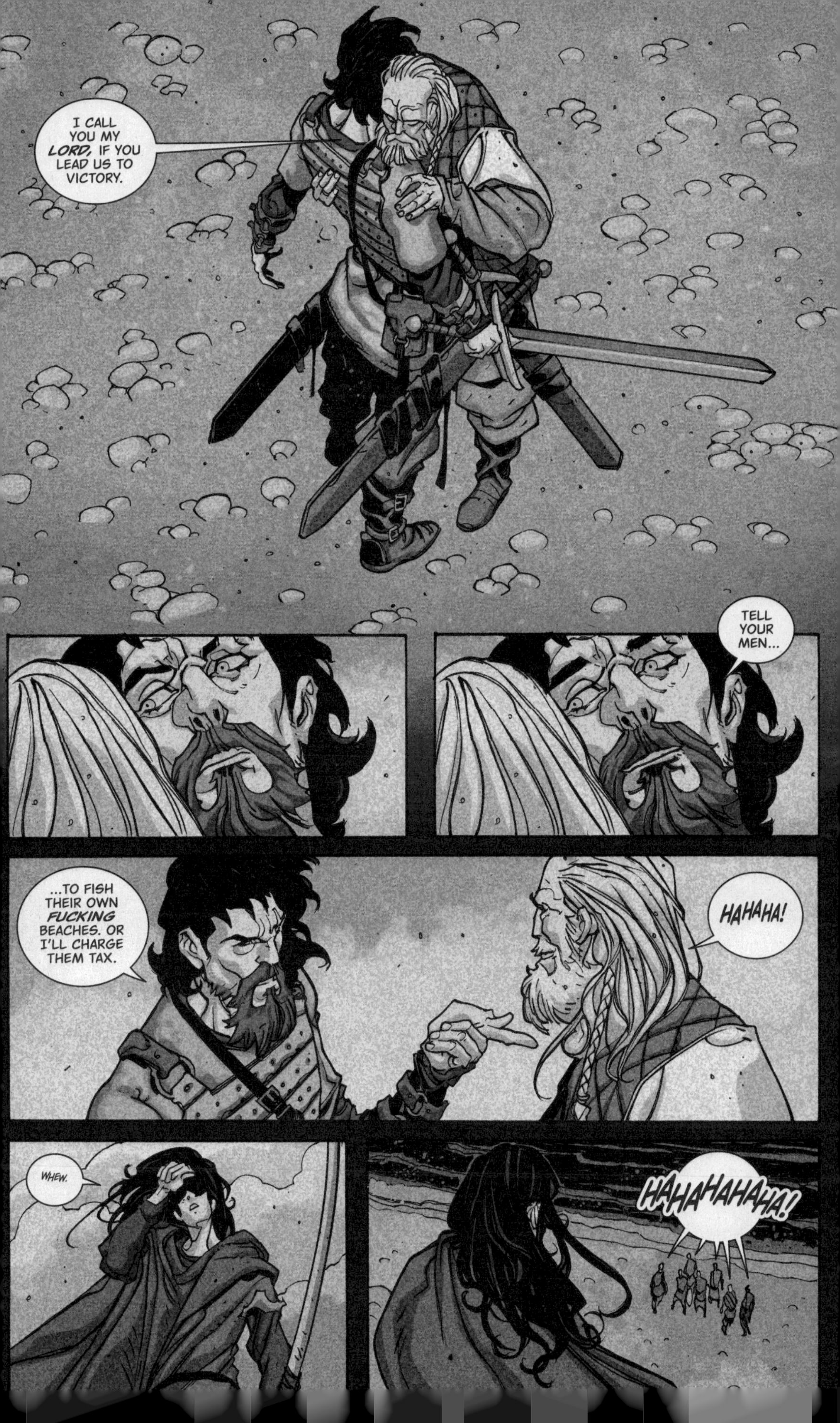
I CALL YOU MY LORD, IF YOU LEAD US TO VICTORY.
TELL YOUR MEN...
...TO FISH THEIR OWN FUCKING BEACHES. OR I'LL CHARGE THEM TAX.
HAHAHA!
WHEW.
HAHAHAHAHAHA!

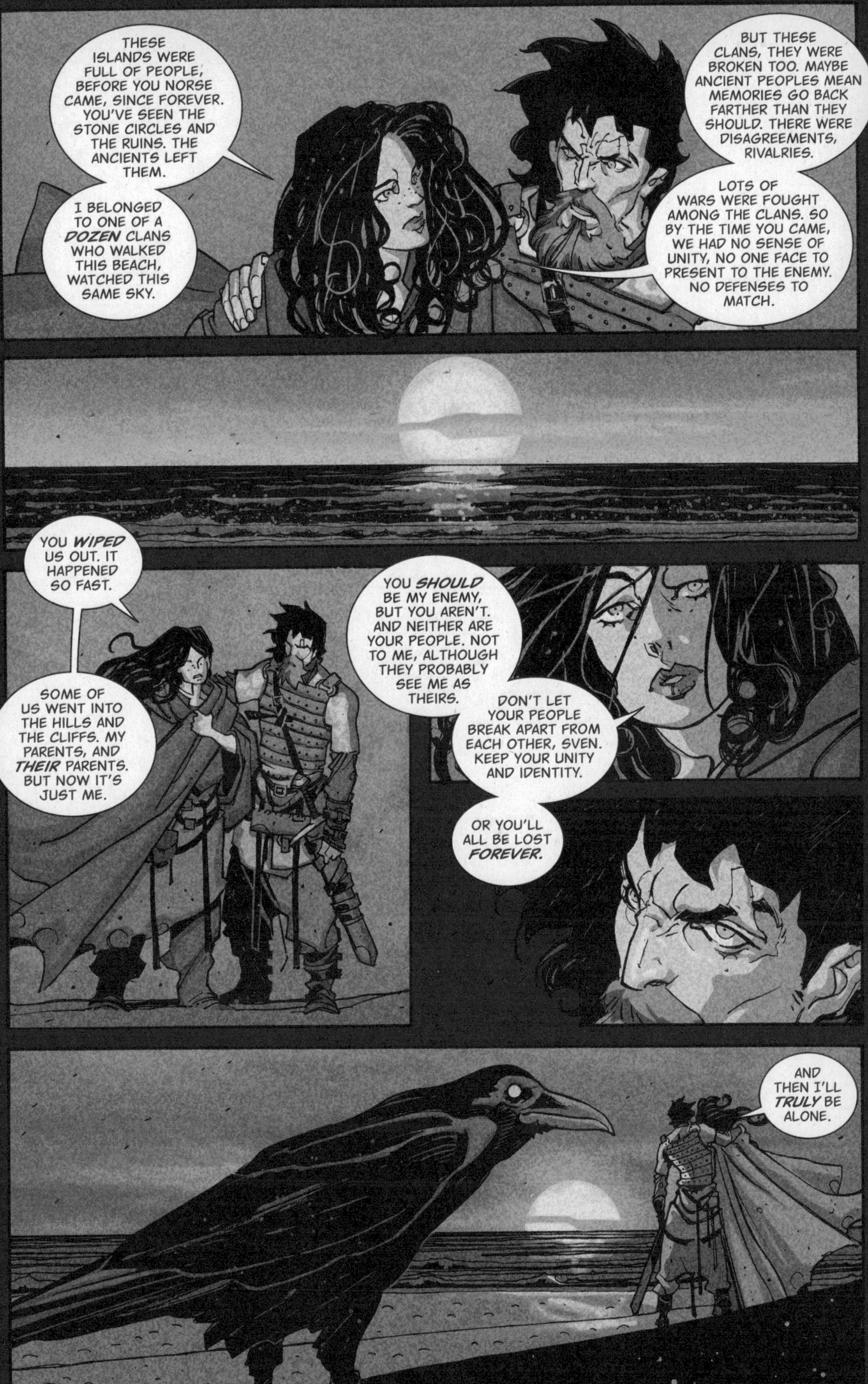

THESE ISLANDS WERE FULL OF PEOPLE, BEFORE YOU NORSE CAME, SINCE FOREVER. YOU'VE SEEN THE STONE CIRCLES AND THE RUINS. THE ANCIENTS LEFT THEM.
I BELONGED TO ONE OF A *DOZEN* CLANS WHO WALKED THIS BEACH, WATCHED THIS SAME SKY.
BUT THESE CLANS, THEY WERE BROKEN TOO. MAYBE ANCIENT PEOPLES MEAN MEMORIES GO BACK FARTHER THAN THEY SHOULD. THERE WERE DISAGREEMENTS, RIVALRIES.
LOTS OF WARS WERE FOUGHT AMONG THE CLANS. SO BY THE TIME YOU CAME, WE HAD NO SENSE OF UNITY, NO ONE FACE TO PRESENT TO THE ENEMY. NO DEFENSES TO MATCH.
YOU *WIPED* US OUT. IT HAPPENED SO FAST.
SOME OF US WENT INTO THE HILLS AND THE CLIFFS. MY PARENTS, AND *THEIR* PARENTS. BUT NOW IT'S JUST ME.
YOU *SHOULD* BE MY ENEMY, BUT YOU AREN'T. AND NEITHER ARE YOUR PEOPLE. NOT TO ME, ALTHOUGH THEY PROBABLY SEE ME AS THEIRS.
DON'T LET YOUR PEOPLE BREAK APART FROM EACH OTHER, SVEN. KEEP YOUR UNITY AND IDENTITY.
OR YOU'LL ALL BE LOST *FOREVER.*
AND THEN I'LL *TRULY* BE ALONE.

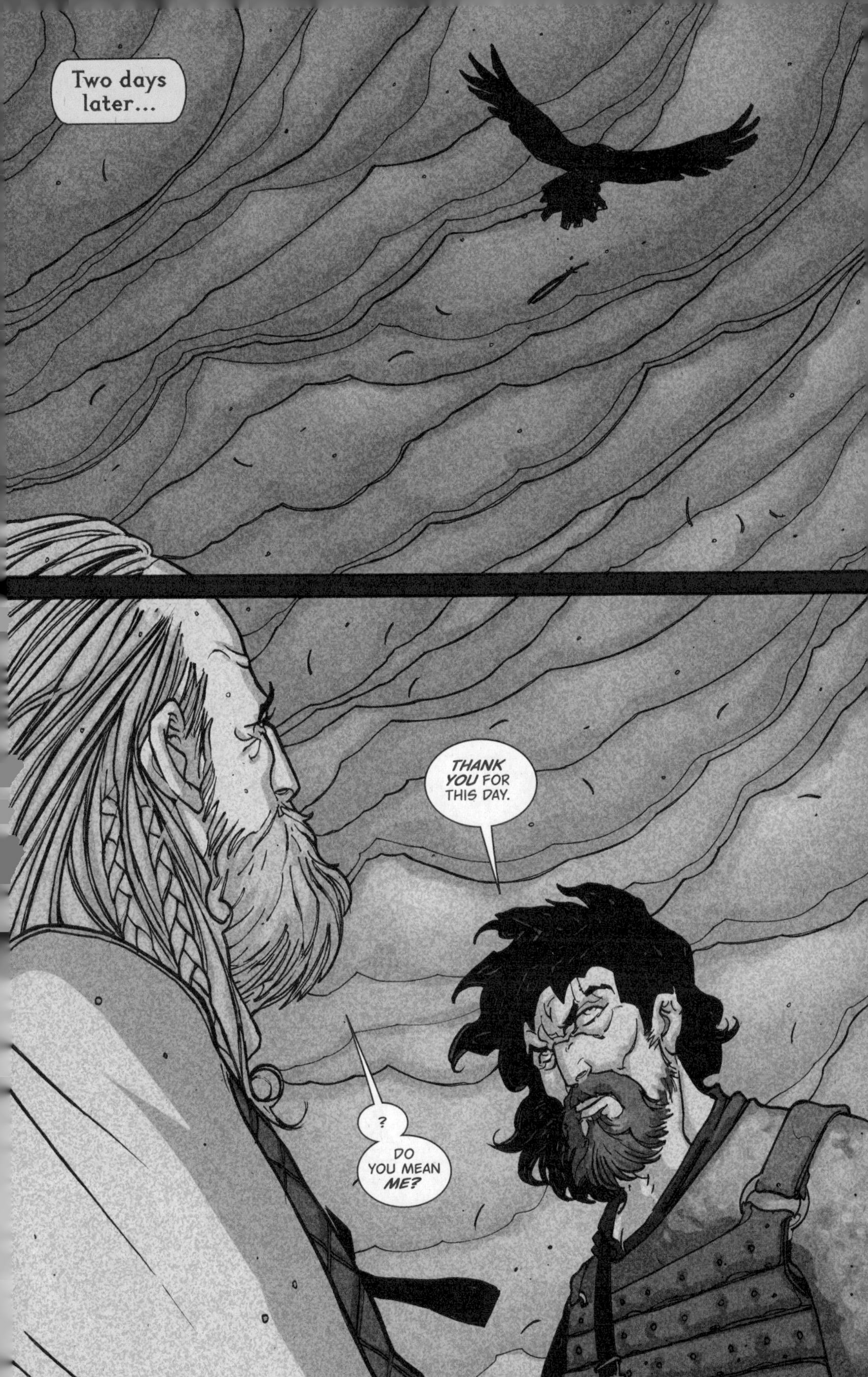
Two days later...
THANK YOU FOR THIS DAY.
?
DO YOU MEAN ME?

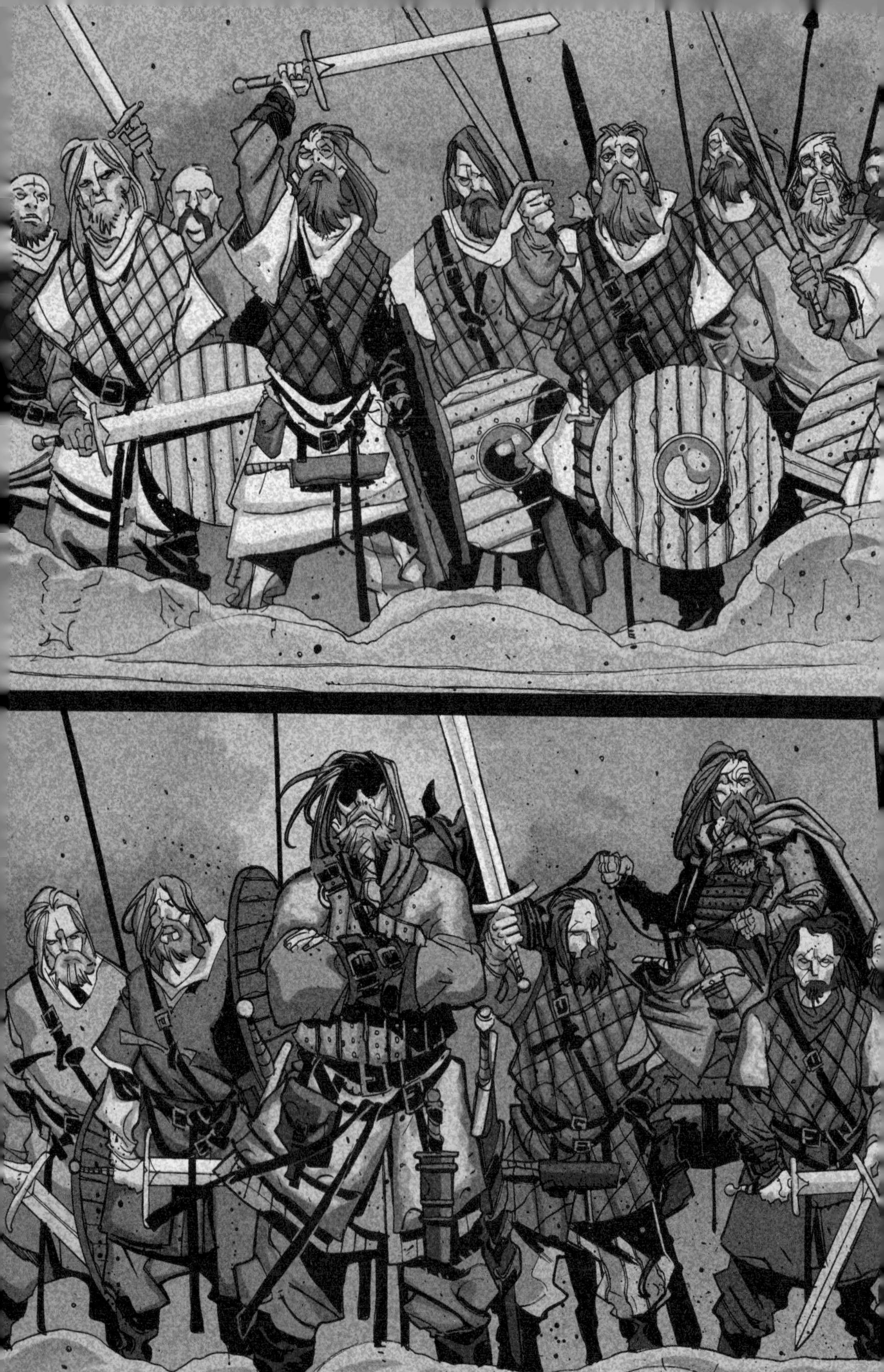

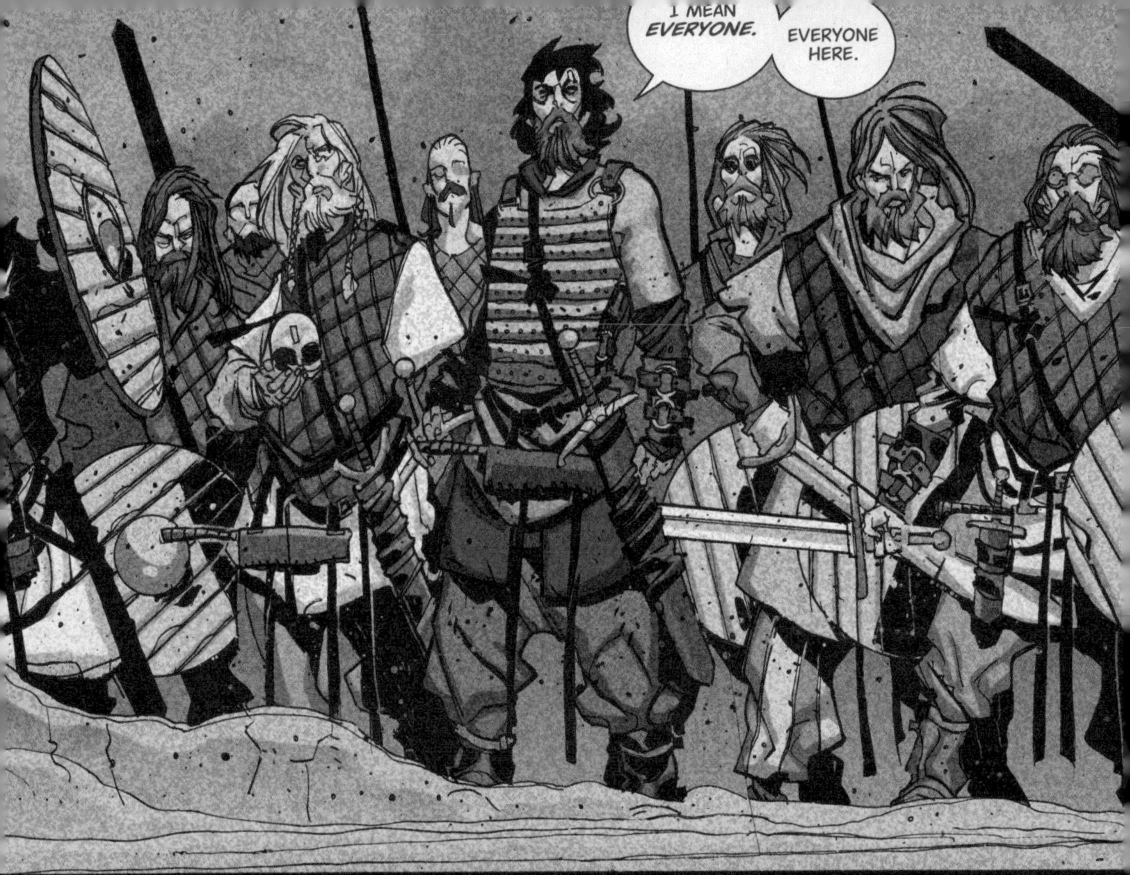
I MEAN EVERYONE.
EVERYONE HERE.

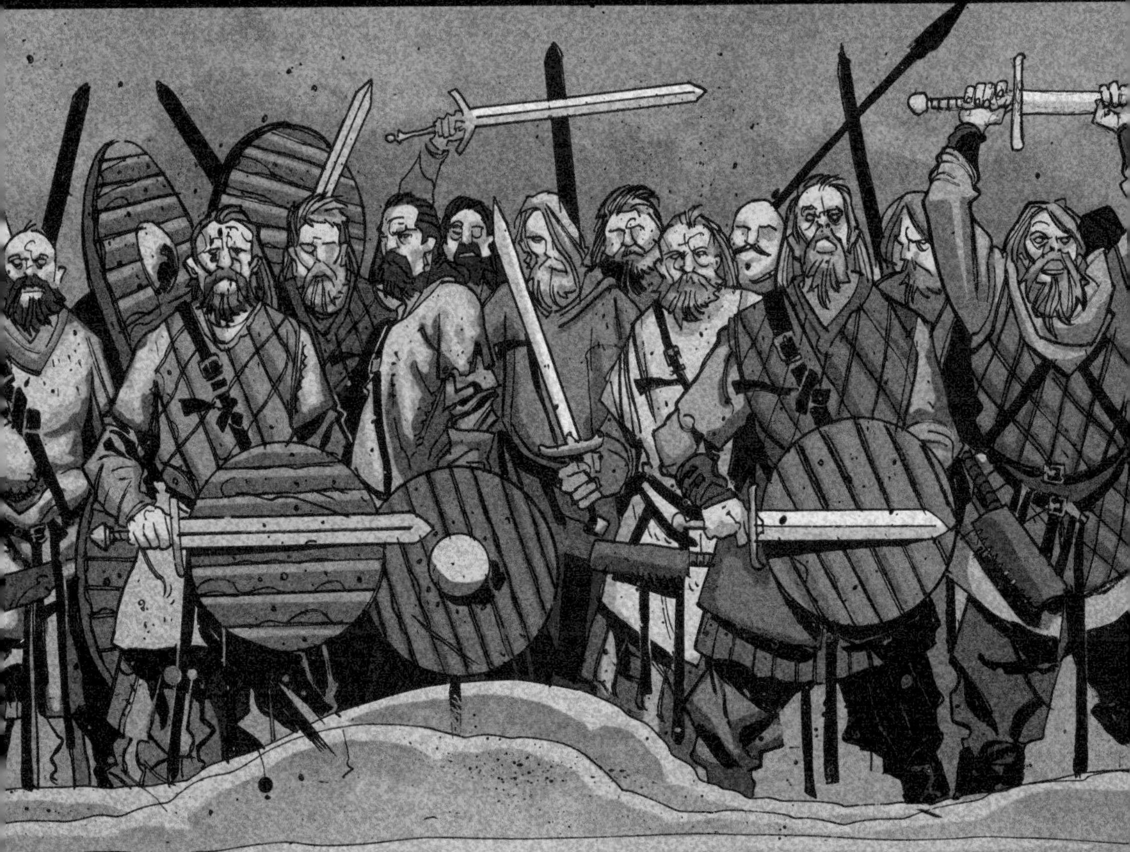
EVEN THEM.

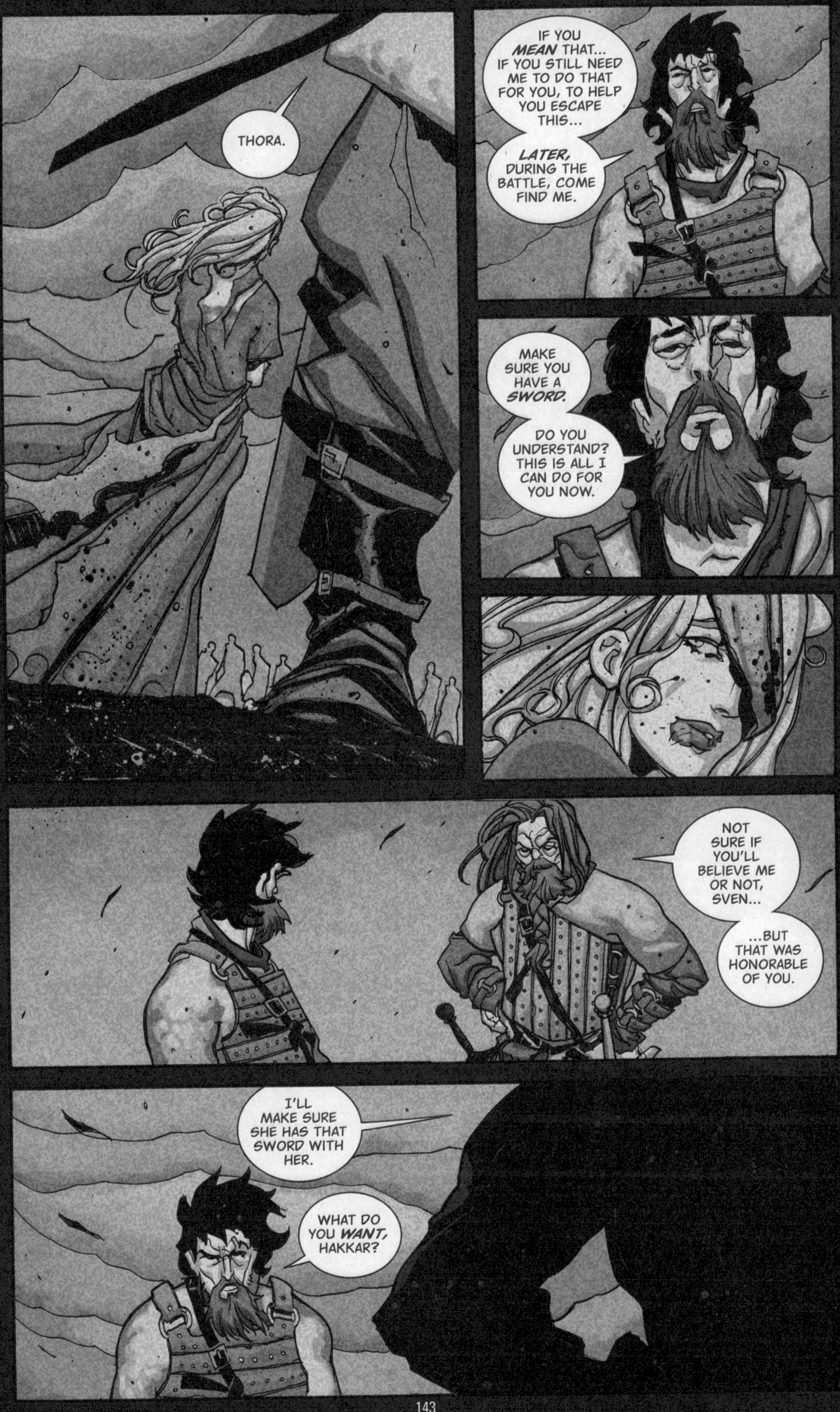
THORA.
IF YOU MEAN THAT... IF YOU STILL NEED ME TO DO THAT FOR YOU, TO HELP YOU ESCAPE THIS...
LATER, DURING THE BATTLE, COME FIND ME.
MAKE SURE YOU HAVE A SWORD.
DO YOU UNDERSTAND? THIS IS ALL I CAN DO FOR YOU NOW.
NOT SURE IF YOU'LL BELIEVE ME OR NOT, SVEN...
...BUT THAT WAS HONORABLE OF YOU.
I'LL MAKE SURE SHE HAS THAT SWORD WITH HER.
WHAT DO YOU WANT, HAKKAR?

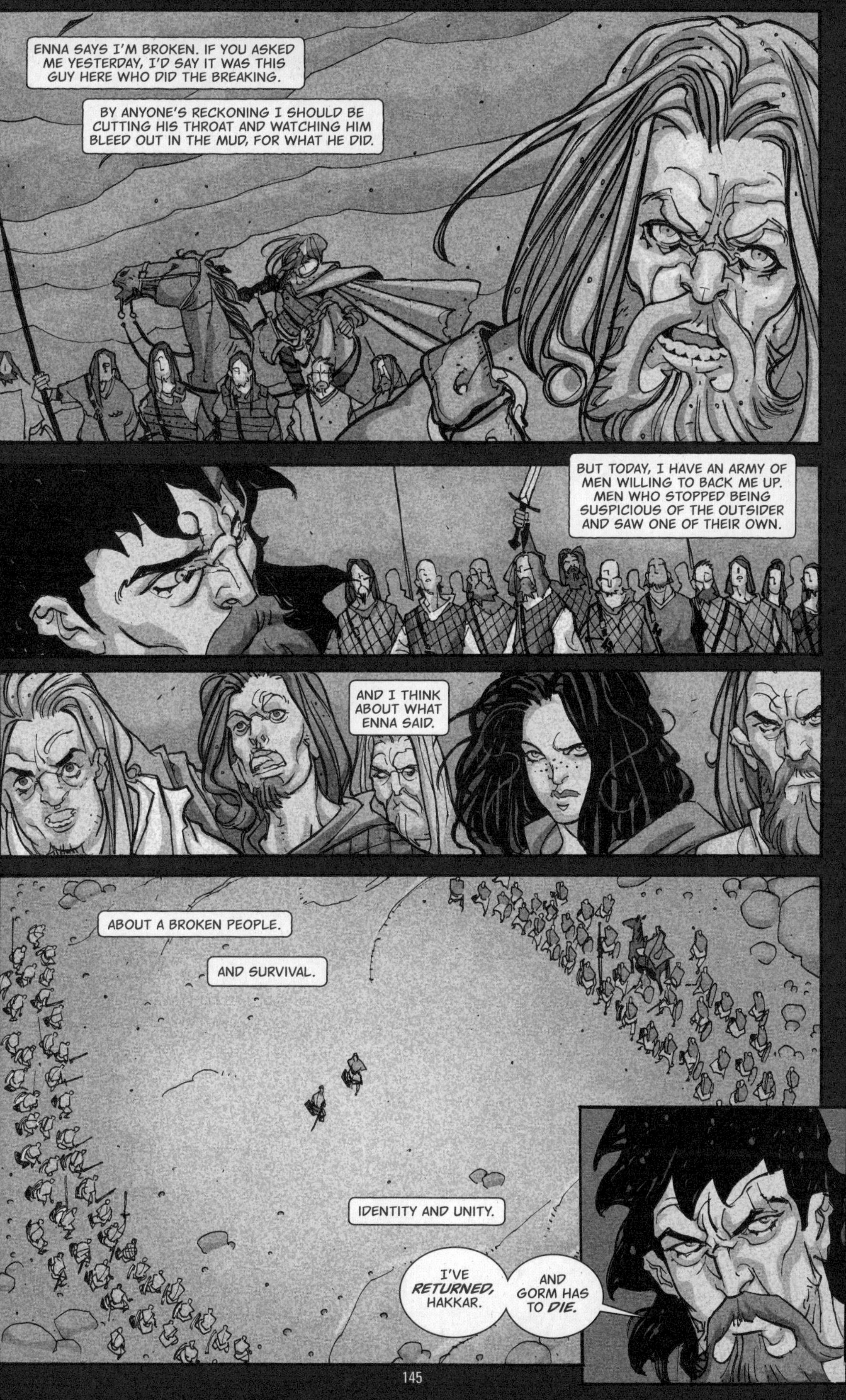
ENNA SAYS I'M BROKEN. IF YOU ASKED ME YESTERDAY, I'D SAY IT WAS THIS GUY HERE WHO DID THE BREAKING.
BY ANYONE'S RECKONING I SHOULD BE CUTTING HIS THROAT AND WATCHING HIM BLEED OUT IN THE MUD, FOR WHAT HE DID.
BUT TODAY, I HAVE AN ARMY OF MEN WILLING TO BACK ME UP. MEN WHO STOPPED BEING SUSPICIOUS OF THE OUTSIDER AND SAW ONE OF THEIR OWN.
AND I THINK ABOUT WHAT ENNA SAID.
ABOUT A BROKEN PEOPLE.
AND SURVIVAL.
IDENTITY AND UNITY.
I'VE *RETURNED,* HAKKAR.
AND GORM HAS TO *DIE.*

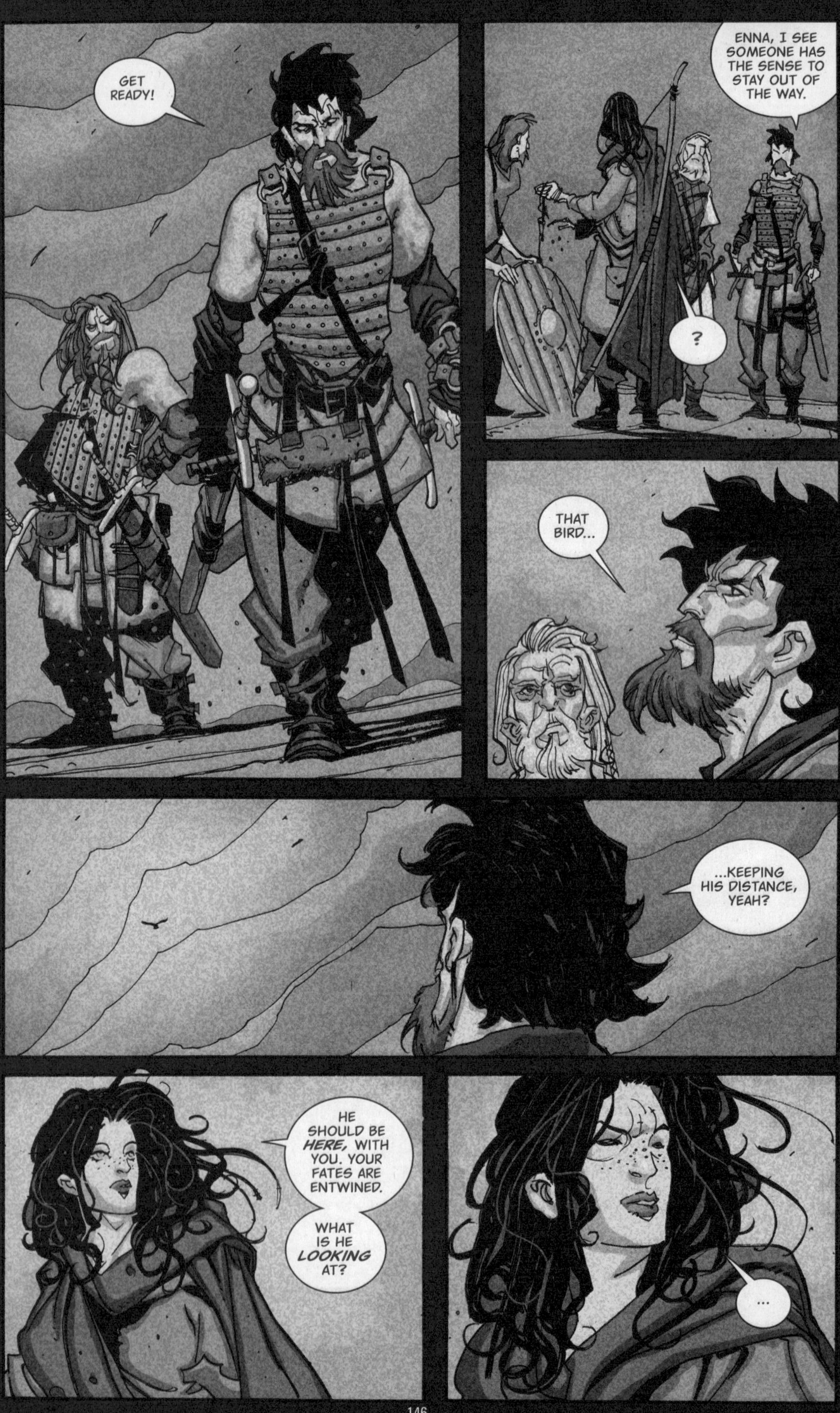

GET READY!
ENNA, I SEE SOMEONE HAS THE SENSE TO STAY OUT OF THE WAY.
?
THAT BIRD...
...KEEPING HIS DISTANCE, YEAH?
HE SHOULD BE *HERE,* WITH YOU. YOUR FATES ARE ENTWINED.
WHAT IS HE *LOOKING* AT?
...

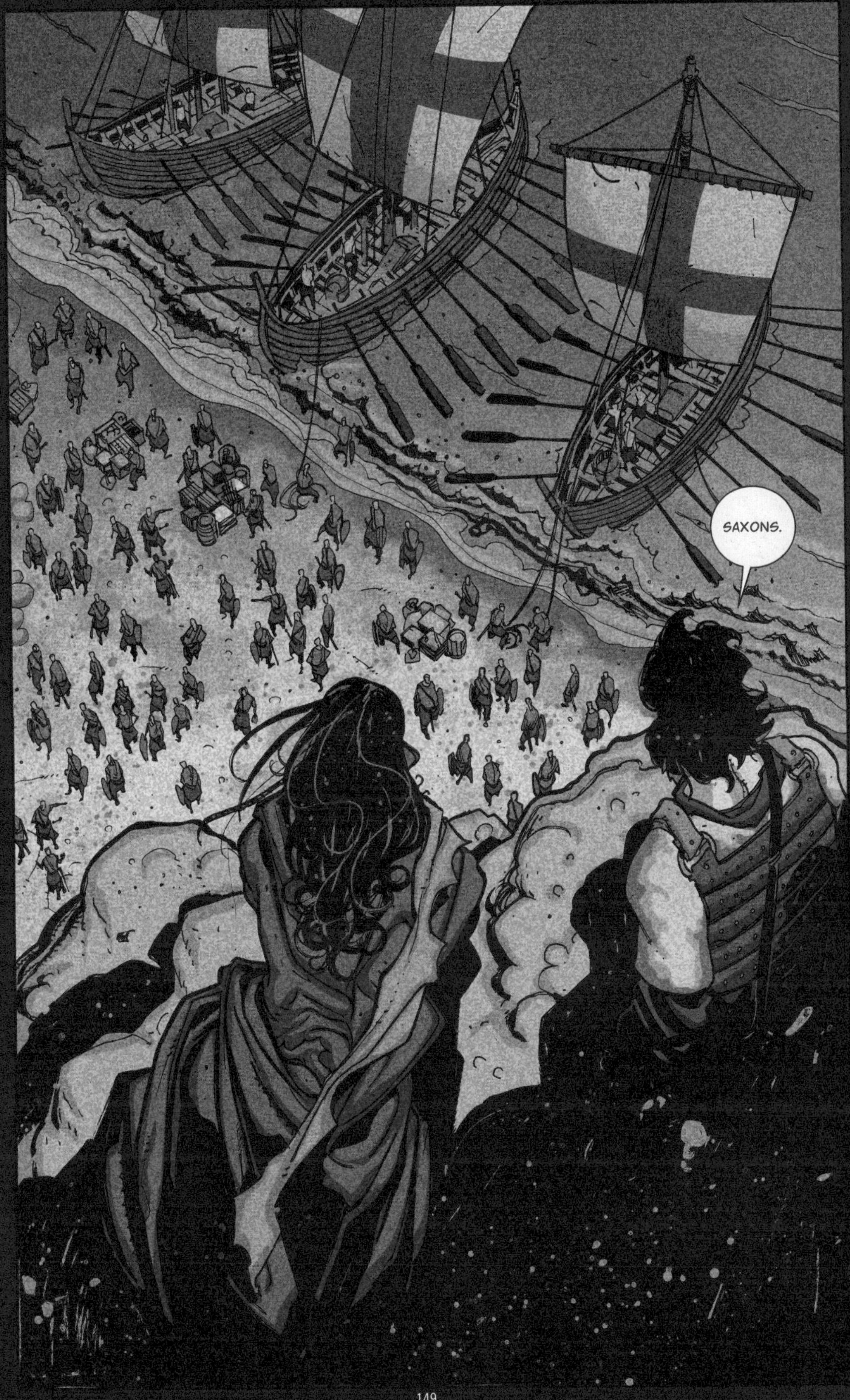
SAXONS.

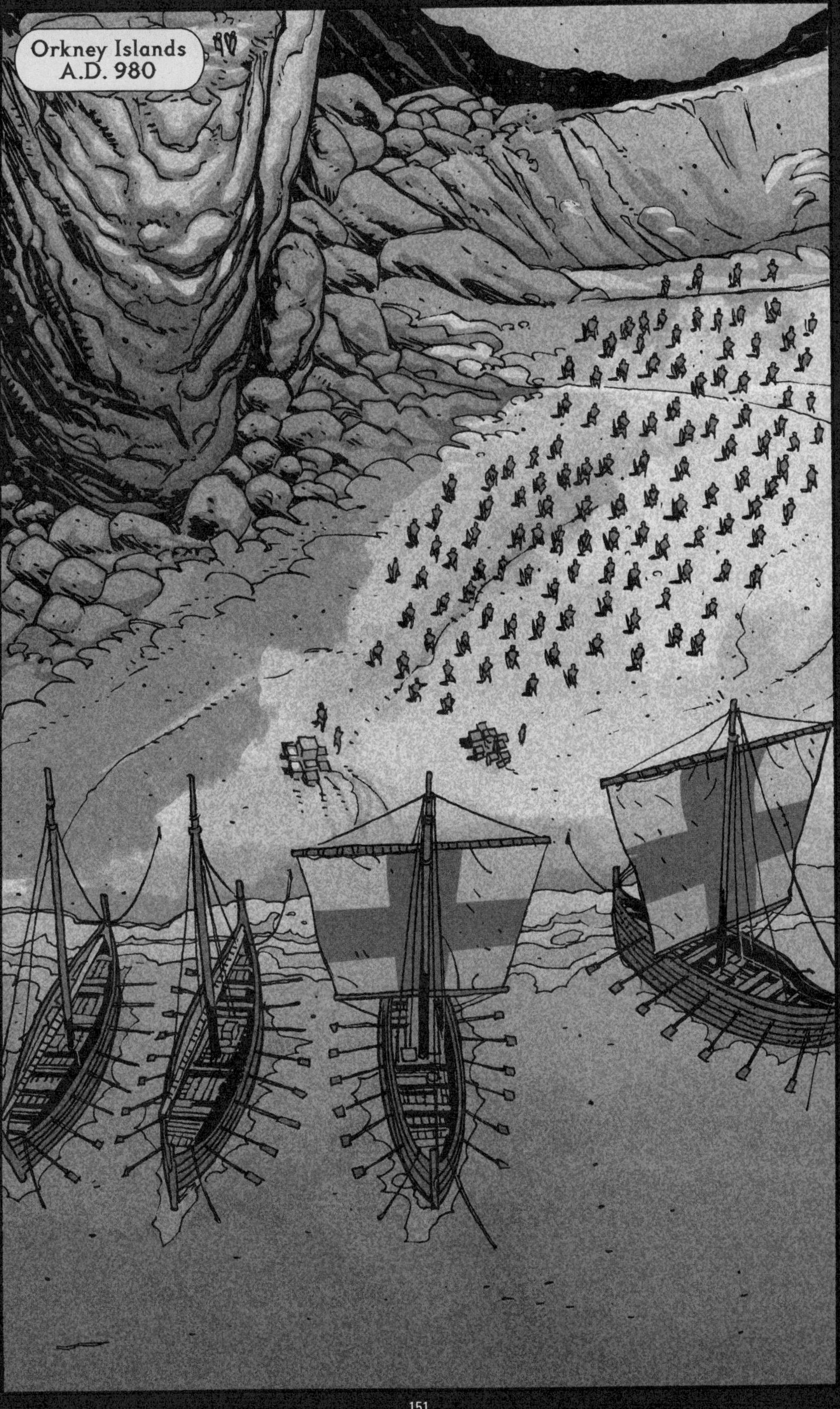
Orkney Islands
A.D. 980

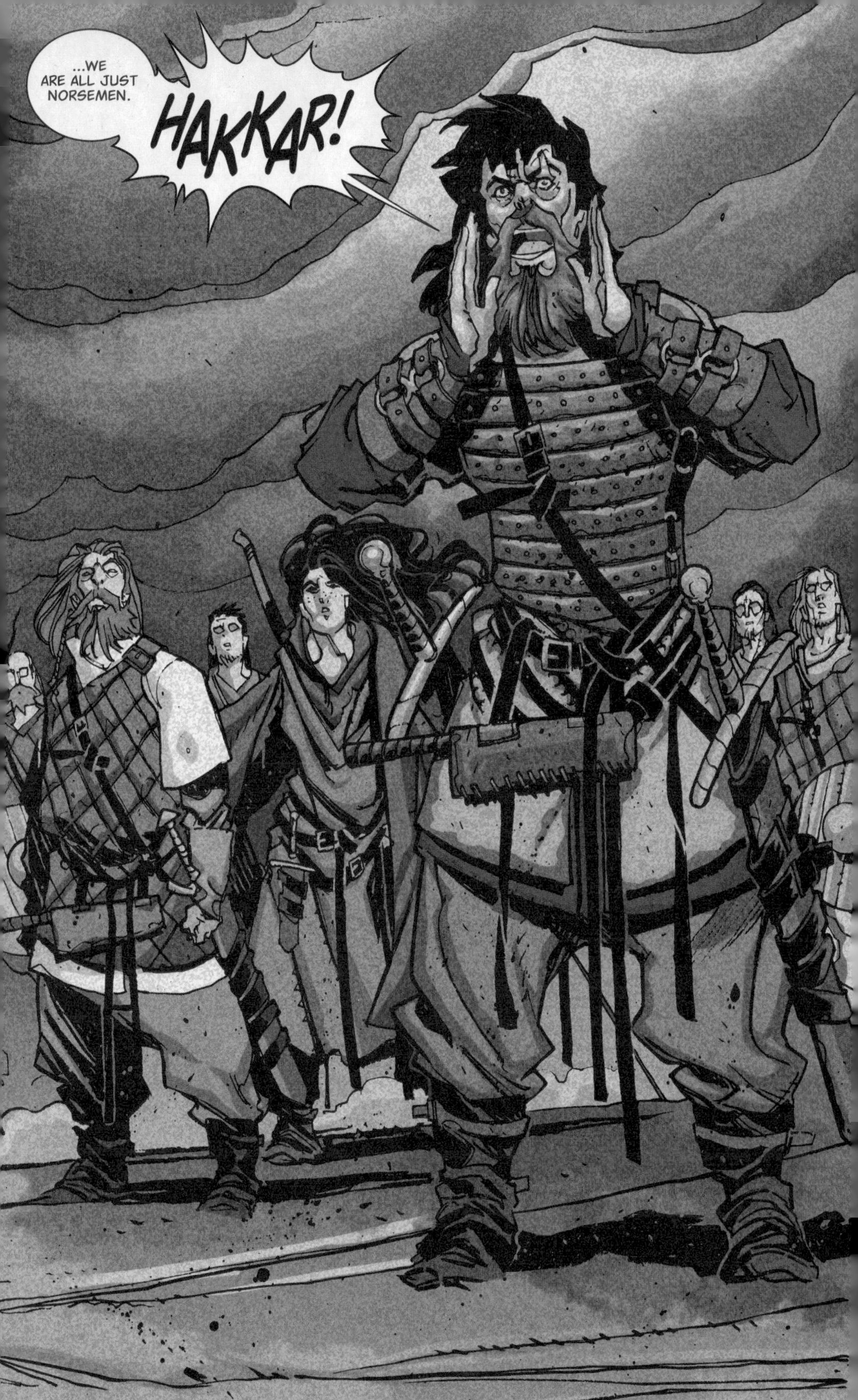
...WE ARE ALL JUST NORSEMEN.
HAKKAR!

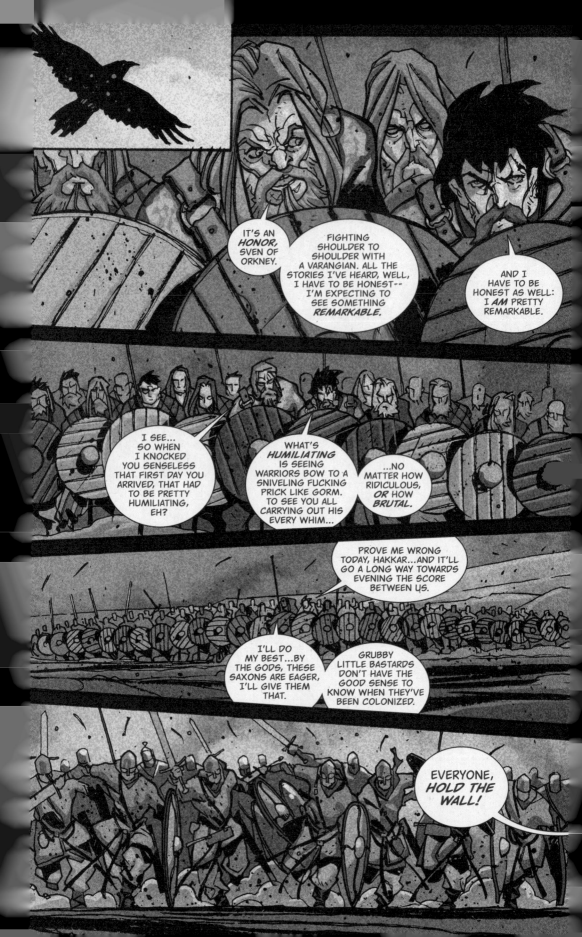

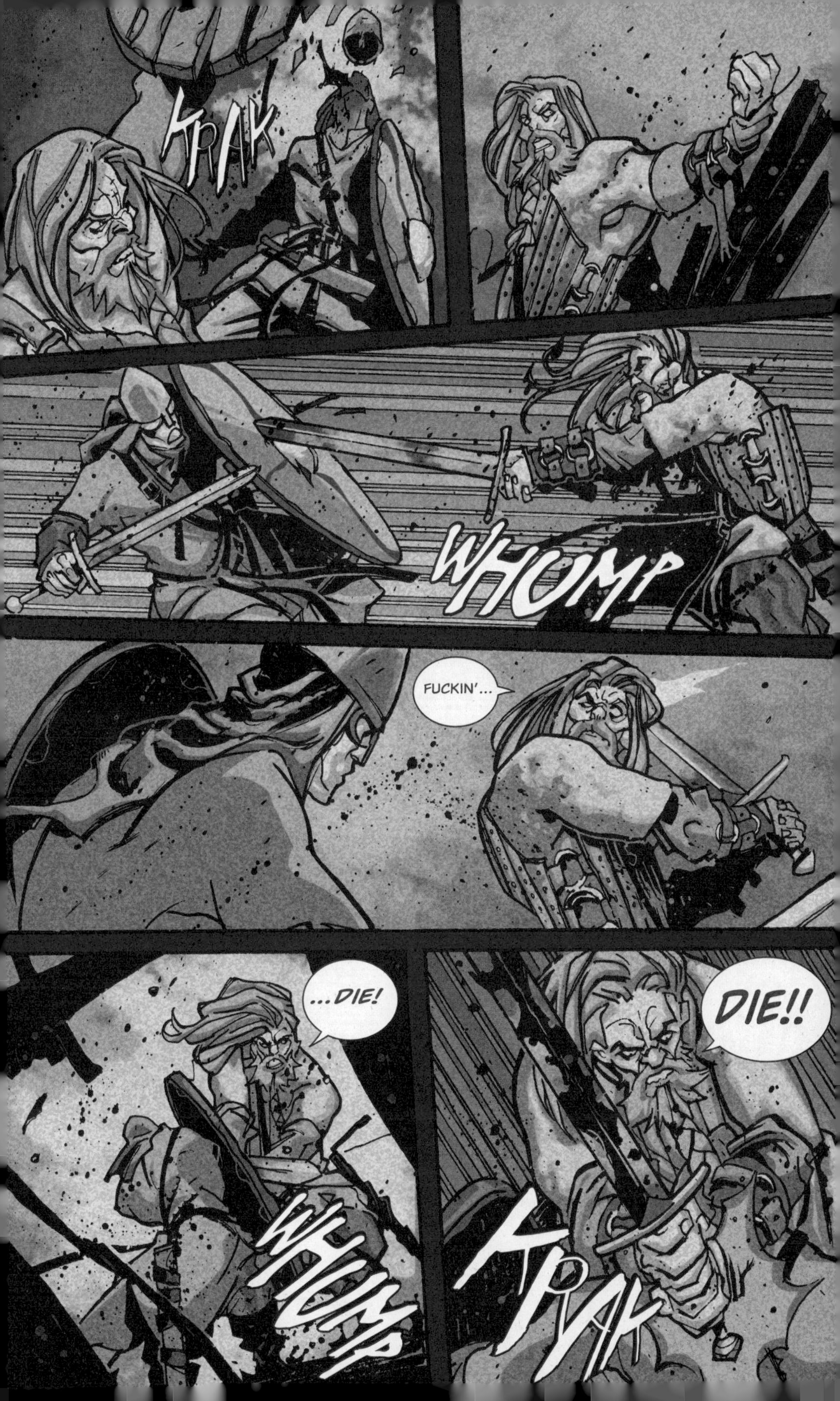
KRAK
WHUMP
FUCKIN'...
...DIE!
DIE!!
WHUMP
KRAK

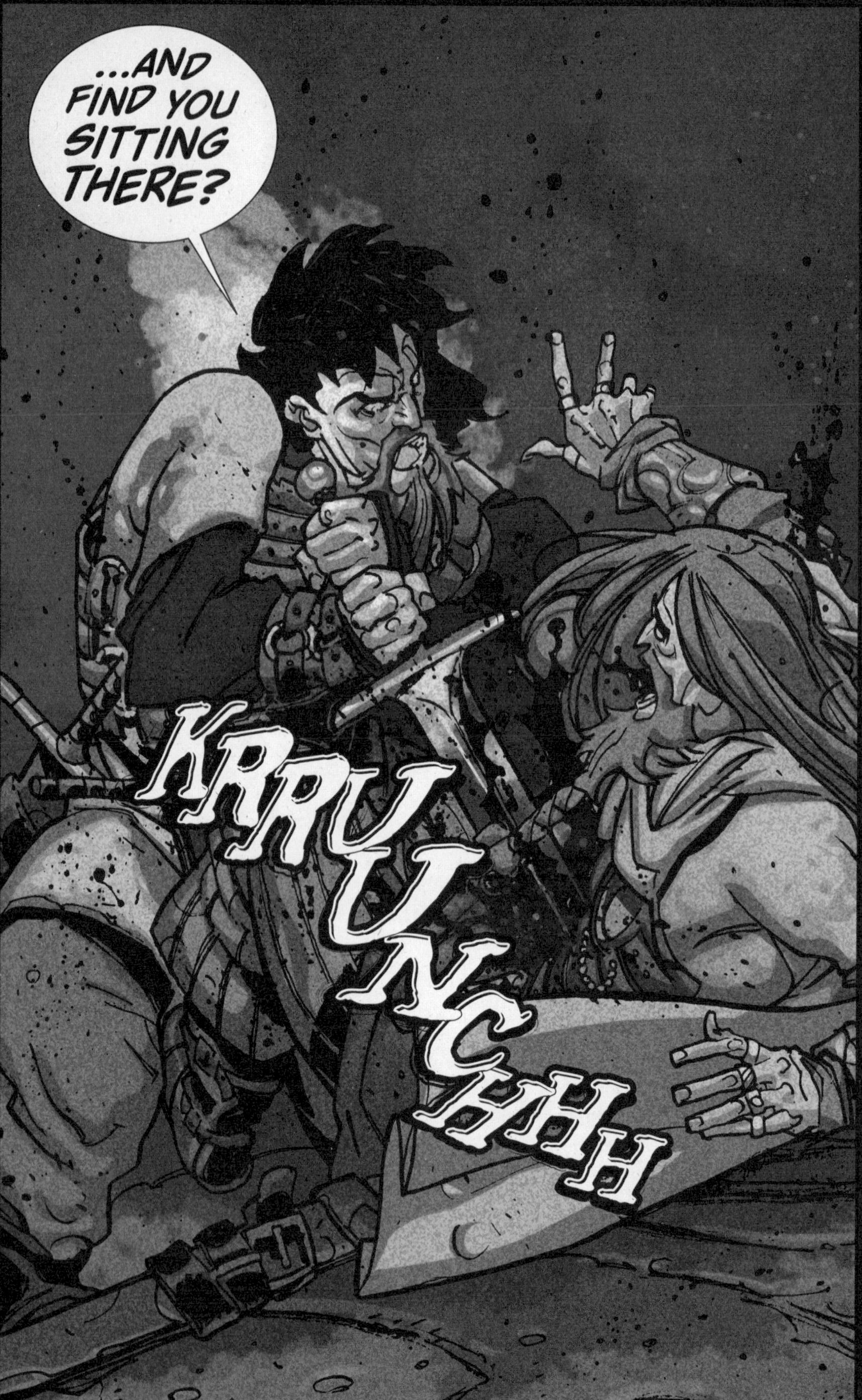
...AND FIND YOU SITTING THERE?
KRRUNCHHH

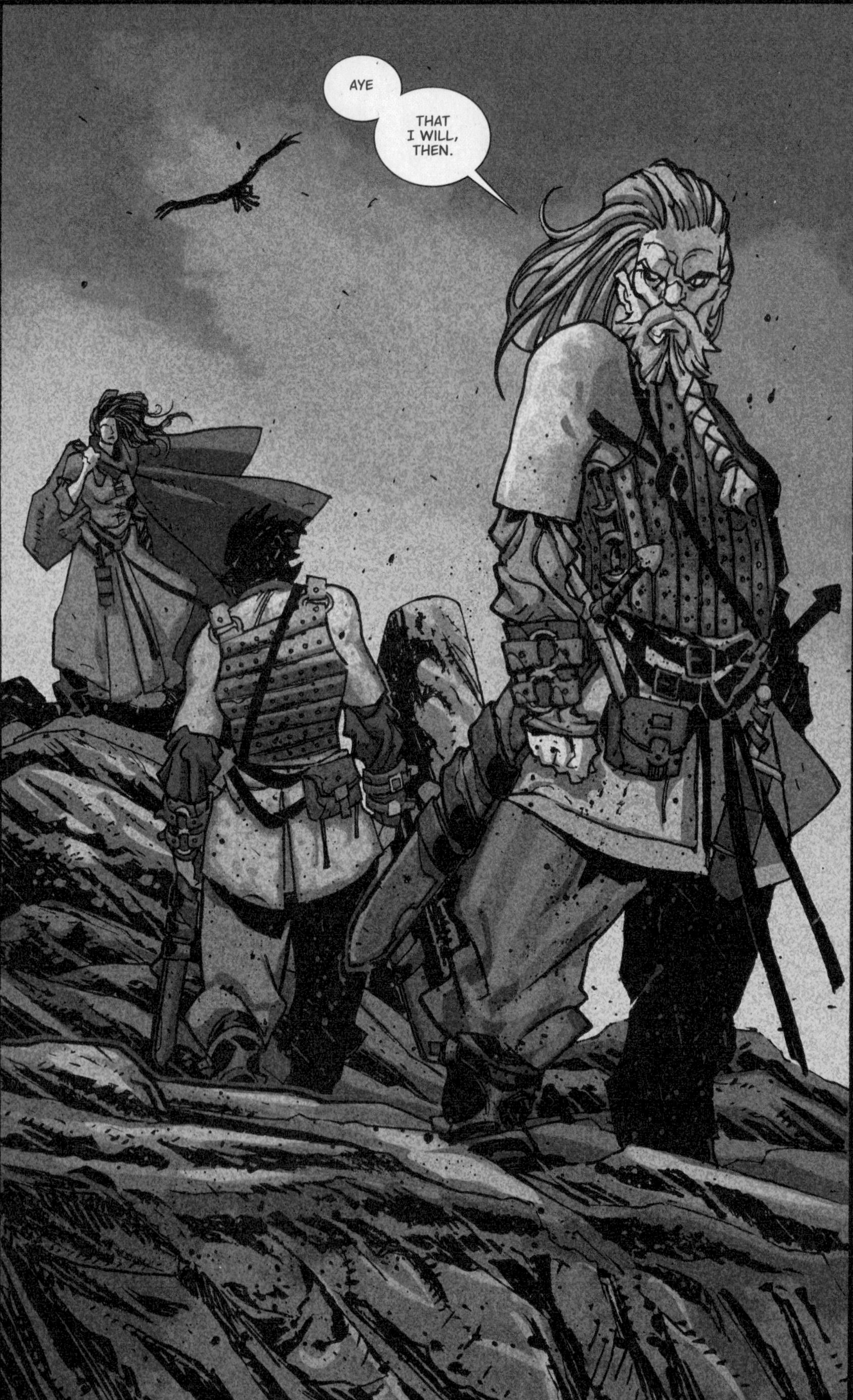
AYE
THAT I WILL, THEN.

8 The Return of the Exiled

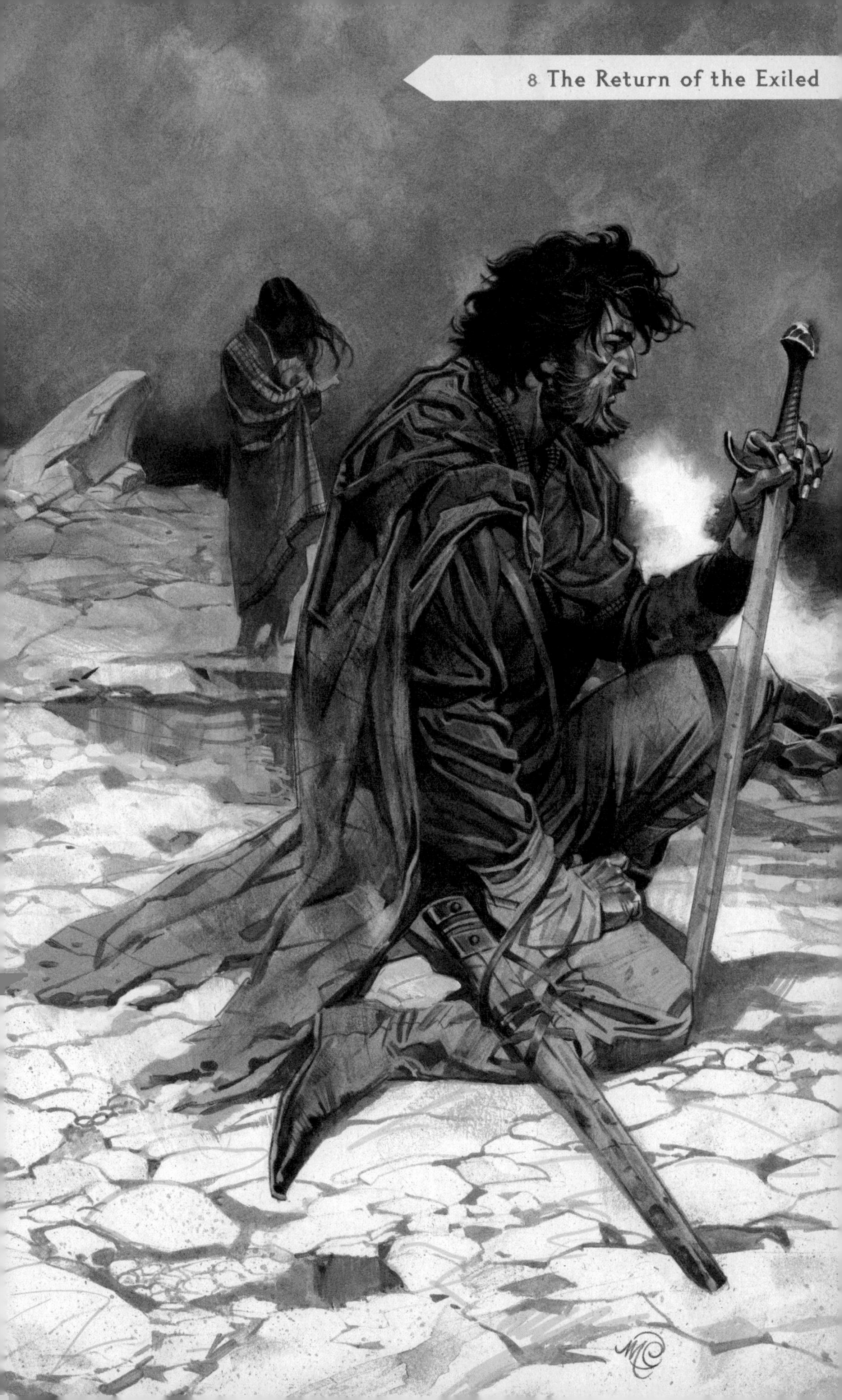

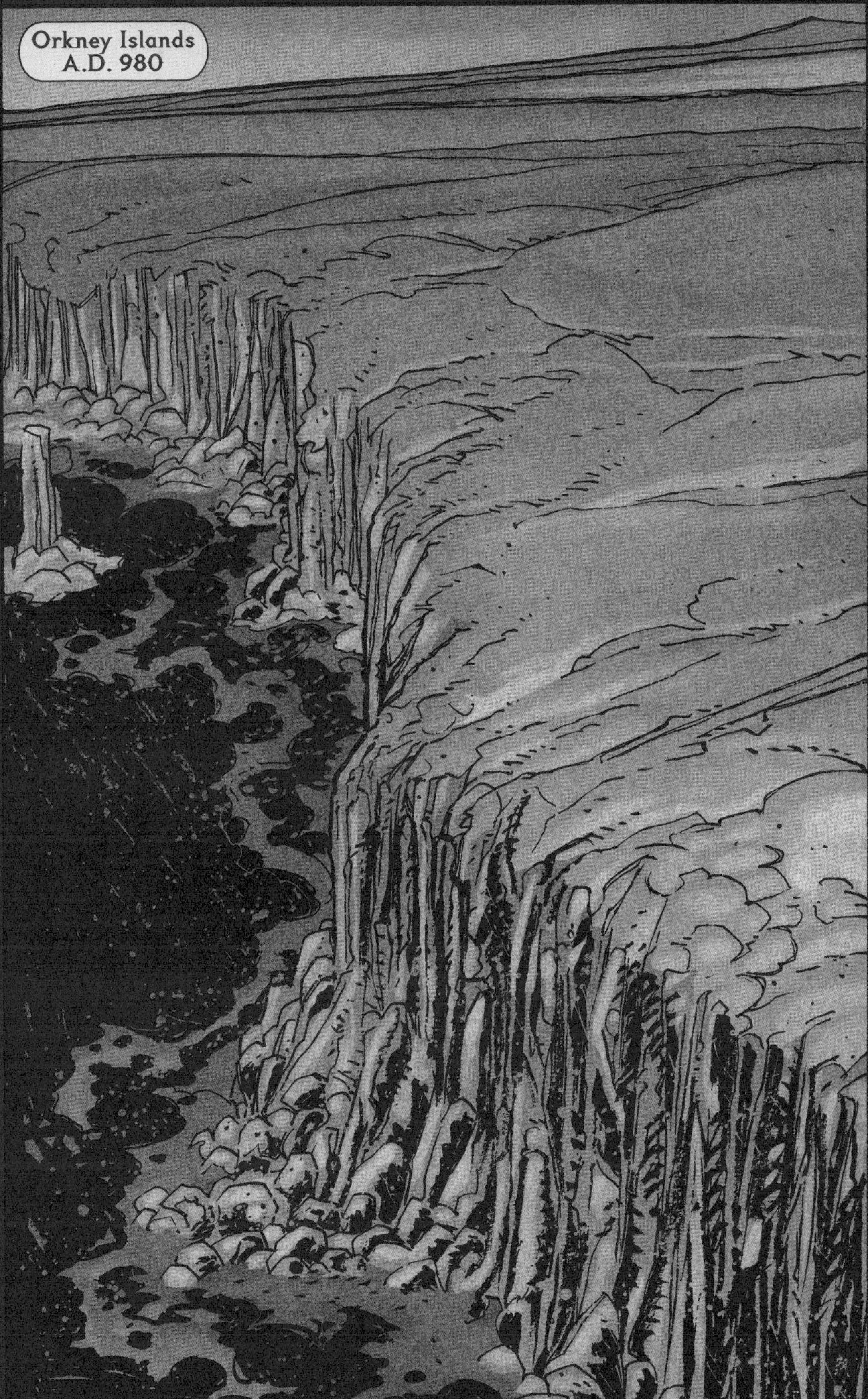
Orkney Islands
A.D. 980

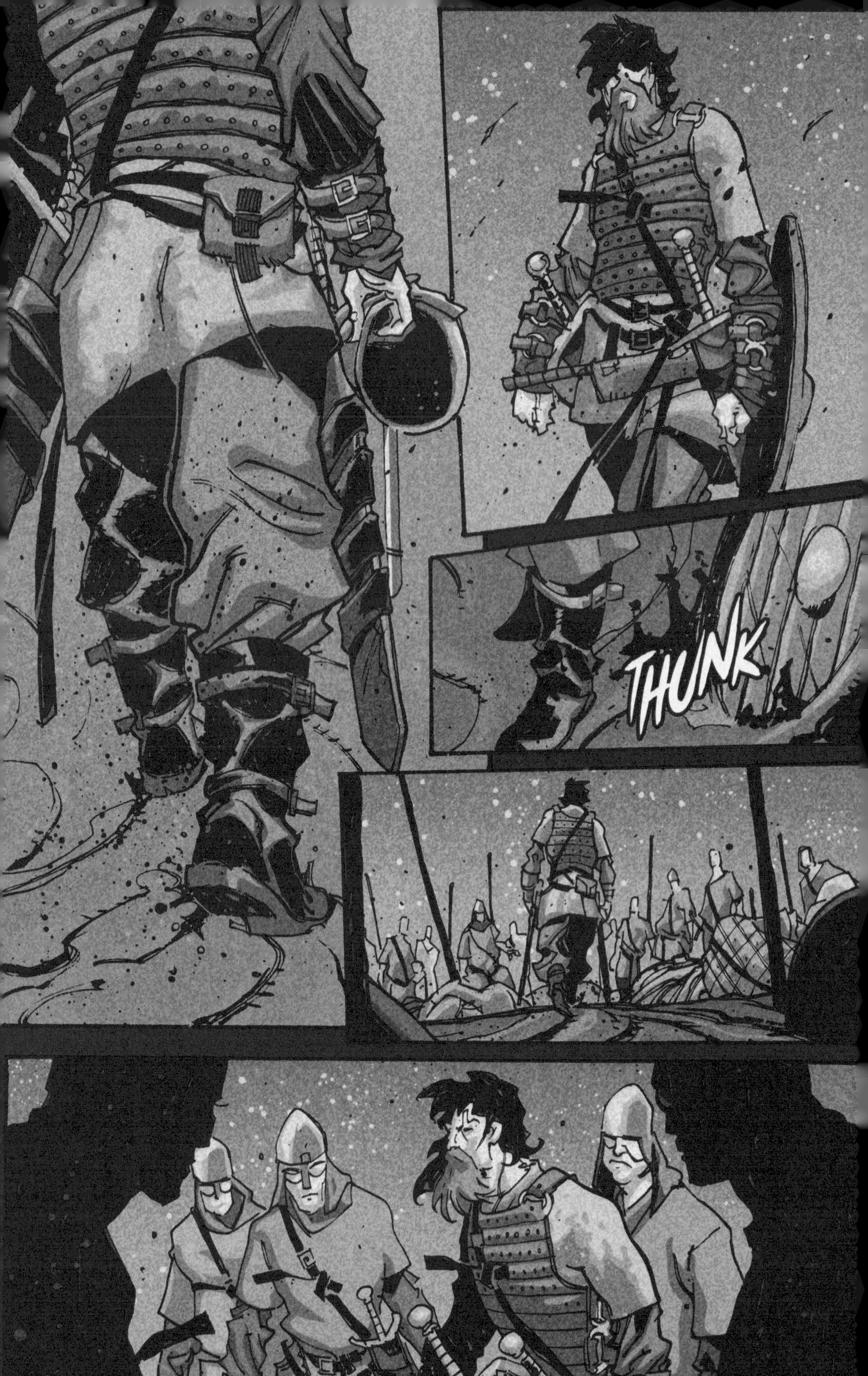
THUNK

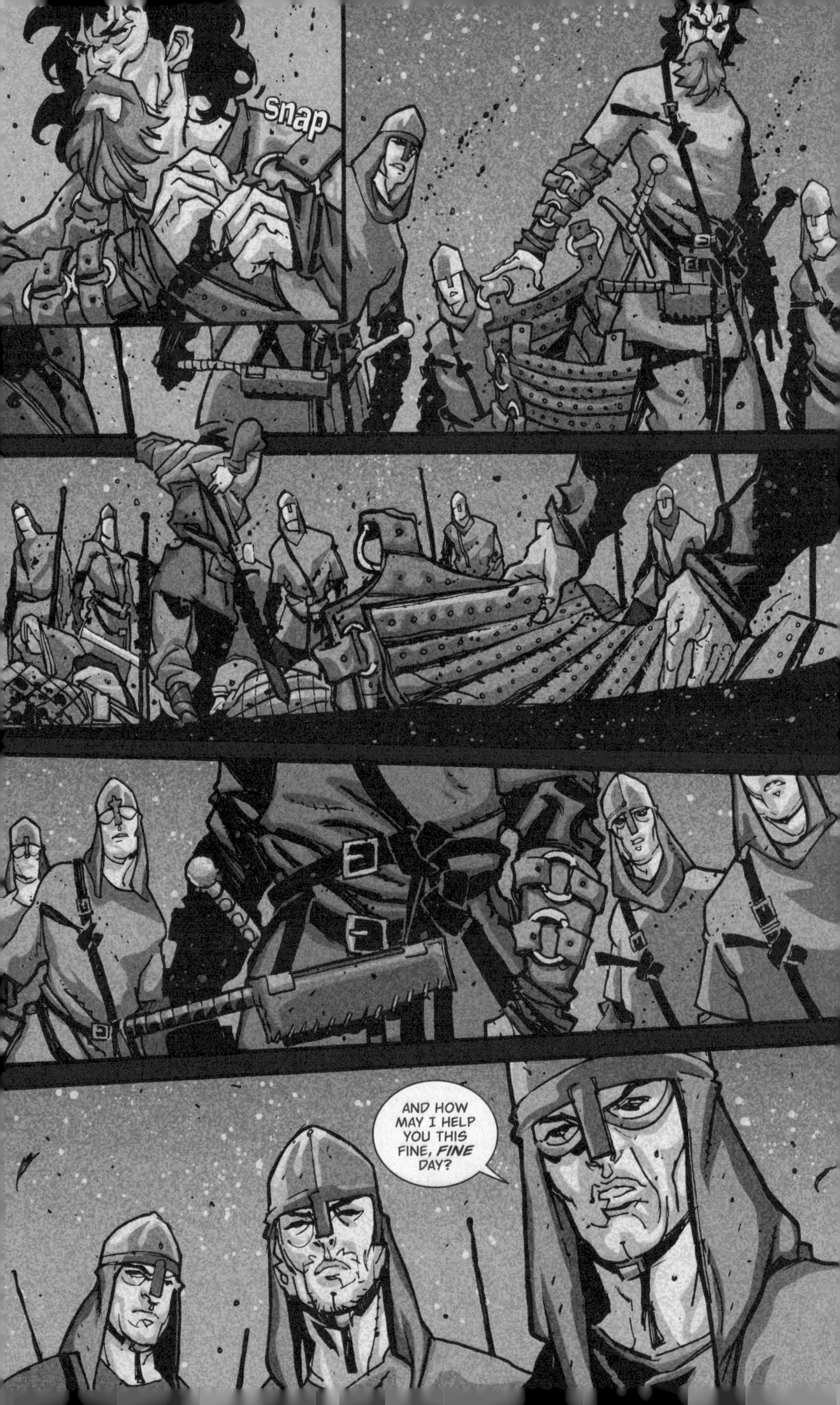
snap
AND HOW MAY I HELP YOU THIS FINE, *FINE* DAY?

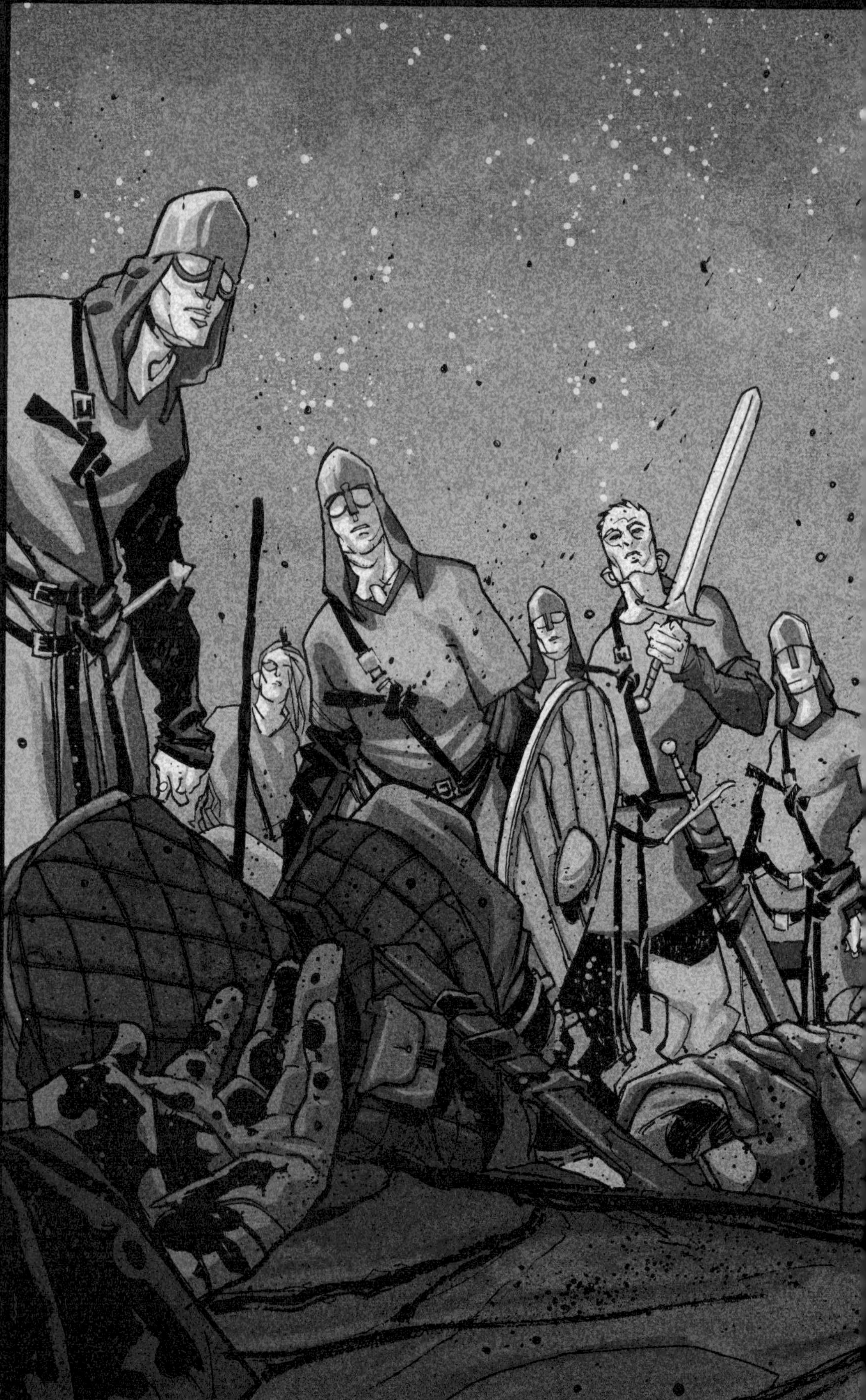

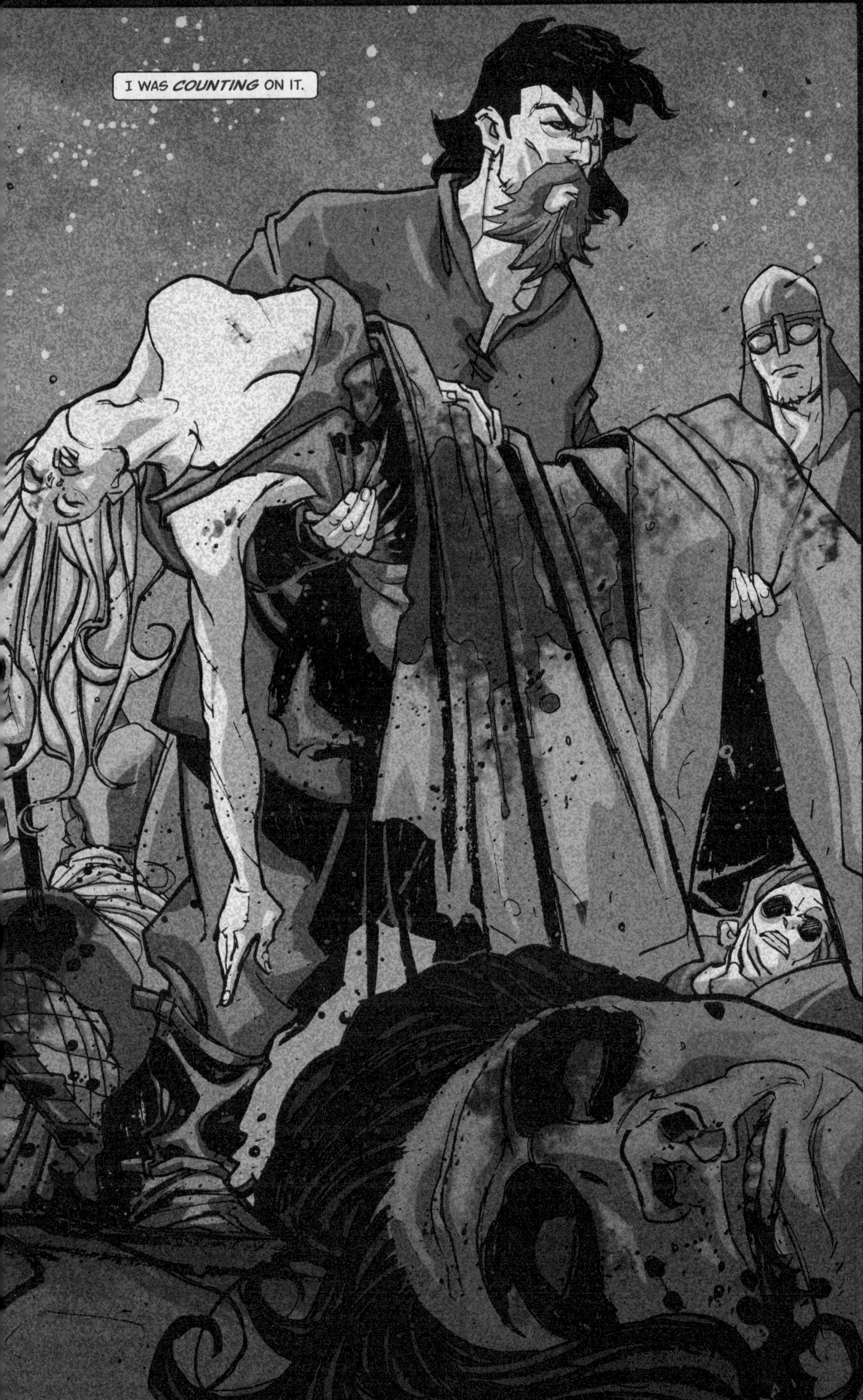
I WAS *COUNTING* ON IT.

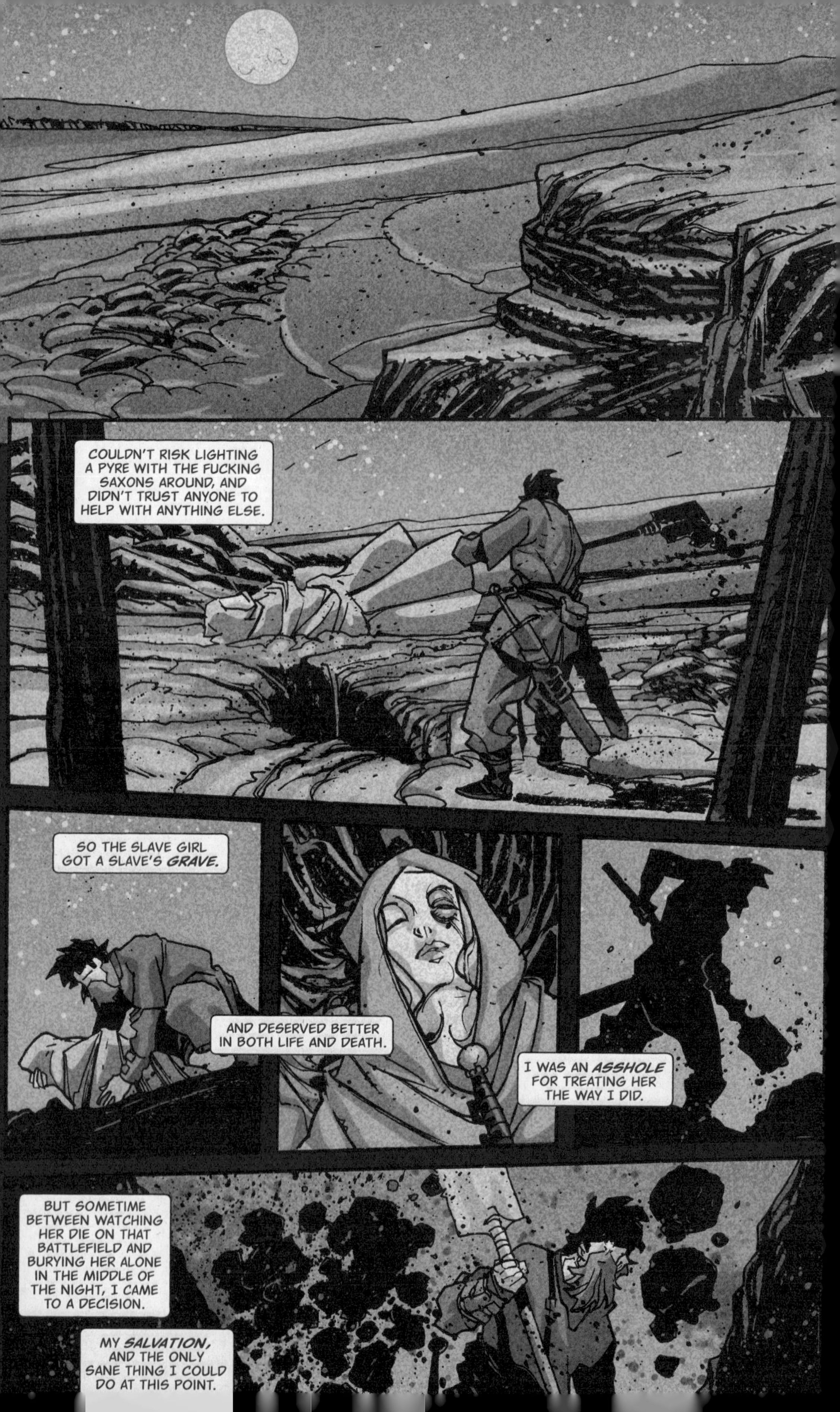
COULDN'T RISK LIGHTING A PYRE WITH THE FUCKING SAXONS AROUND, AND DIDN'T TRUST ANYONE TO HELP WITH ANYTHING ELSE.
SO THE SLAVE GIRL GOT A SLAVE'S GRAVE.
AND DESERVED BETTER IN BOTH LIFE AND DEATH.
I WAS AN ASSHOLE FOR TREATING HER THE WAY I DID.
BUT SOMETIME BETWEEN WATCHING HER DIE ON THAT BATTLEFIELD AND BURYING HER ALONE IN THE MIDDLE OF THE NIGHT, I CAME TO A DECISION.
MY SALVATION, AND THE ONLY SANE THING I COULD DO AT THIS POINT.

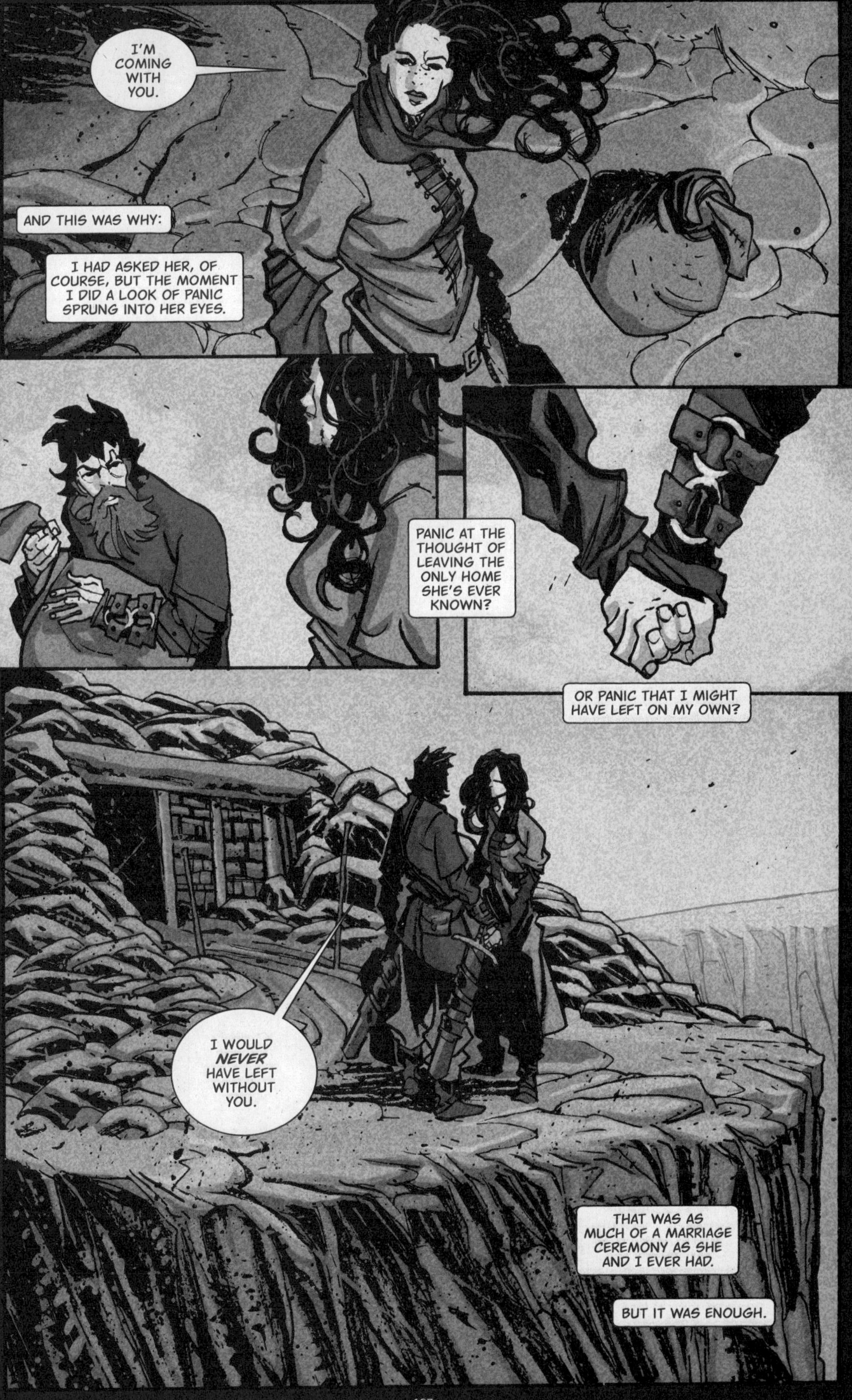
I'M COMING WITH YOU.
AND THIS WAS WHY:
I HAD ASKED HER, OF COURSE, BUT THE MOMENT I DID A LOOK OF PANIC SPRUNG INTO HER EYES.
PANIC AT THE THOUGHT OF LEAVING THE ONLY HOME SHE'S EVER KNOWN?
OR PANIC THAT I MIGHT HAVE LEFT ON MY OWN?
I WOULD *NEVER* HAVE LEFT WITHOUT YOU.
THAT WAS AS MUCH OF A MARRIAGE CEREMONY AS SHE AND I EVER HAD.
BUT IT WAS ENOUGH.

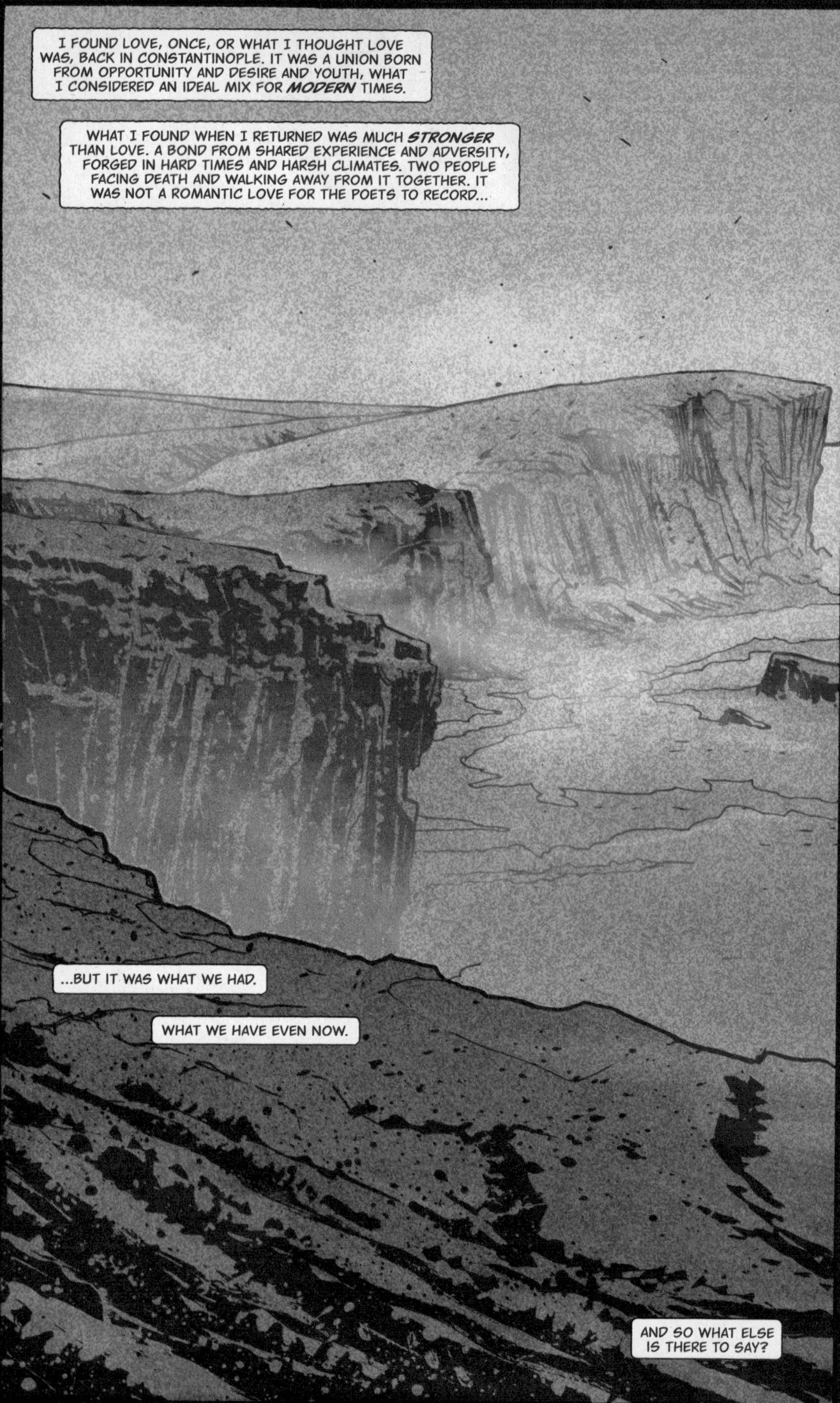
I FOUND LOVE, ONCE, OR WHAT I THOUGHT LOVE WAS, BACK IN CONSTANTINOPLE. IT WAS A UNION BORN FROM OPPORTUNITY AND DESIRE AND YOUTH, WHAT I CONSIDERED AN IDEAL MIX FOR *MODERN* TIMES.
WHAT I FOUND WHEN I RETURNED WAS MUCH *STRONGER* THAN LOVE. A BOND FROM SHARED EXPERIENCE AND ADVERSITY, FORGED IN HARD TIMES AND HARSH CLIMATES. TWO PEOPLE FACING DEATH AND WALKING AWAY FROM IT TOGETHER. IT WAS NOT A ROMANTIC LOVE FOR THE POETS TO RECORD...
...BUT IT WAS WHAT WE HAD.
WHAT WE HAVE EVEN NOW.
AND SO WHAT ELSE IS THERE TO SAY?

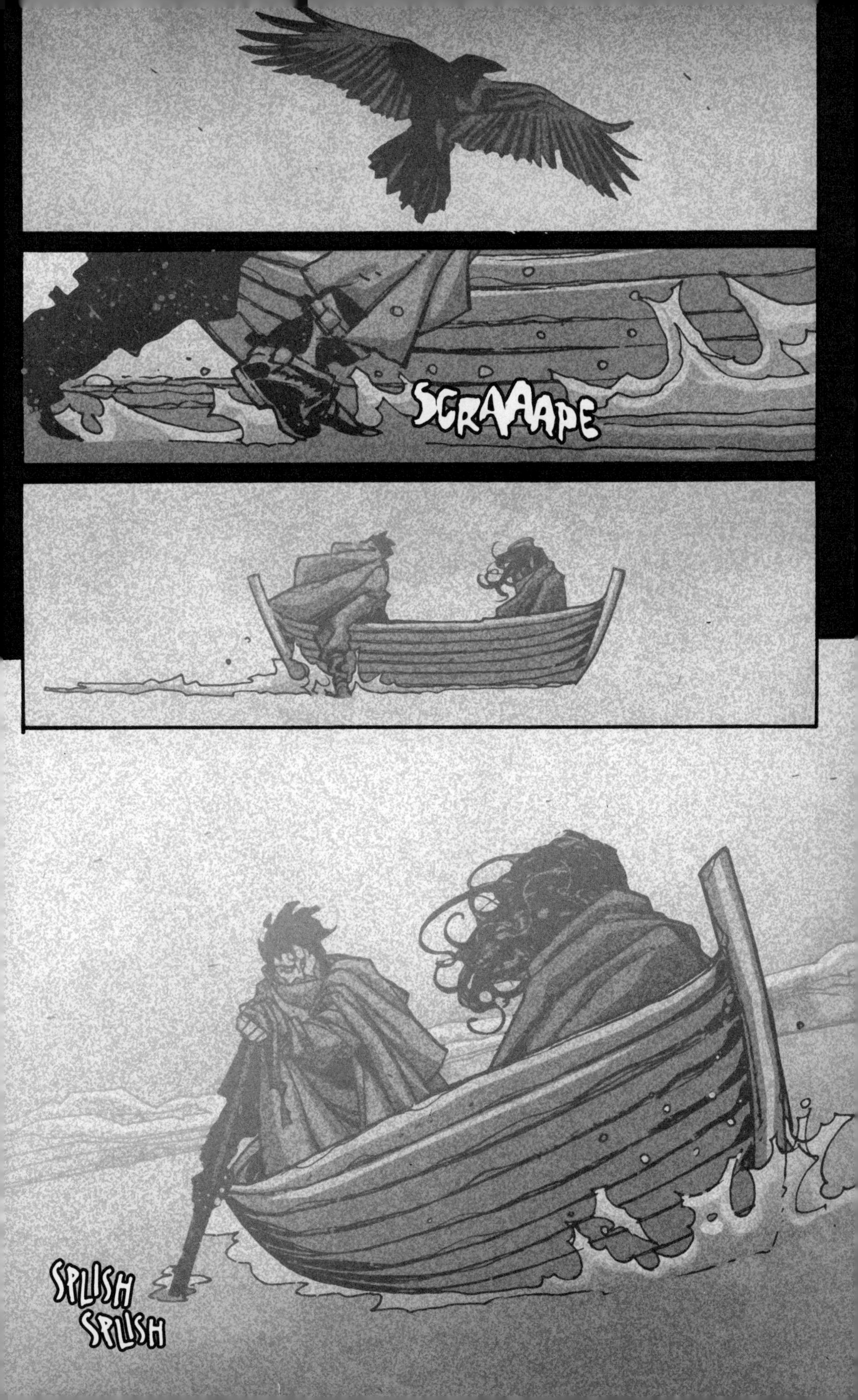
SCRAAAPE
SPLISH
SPLISH

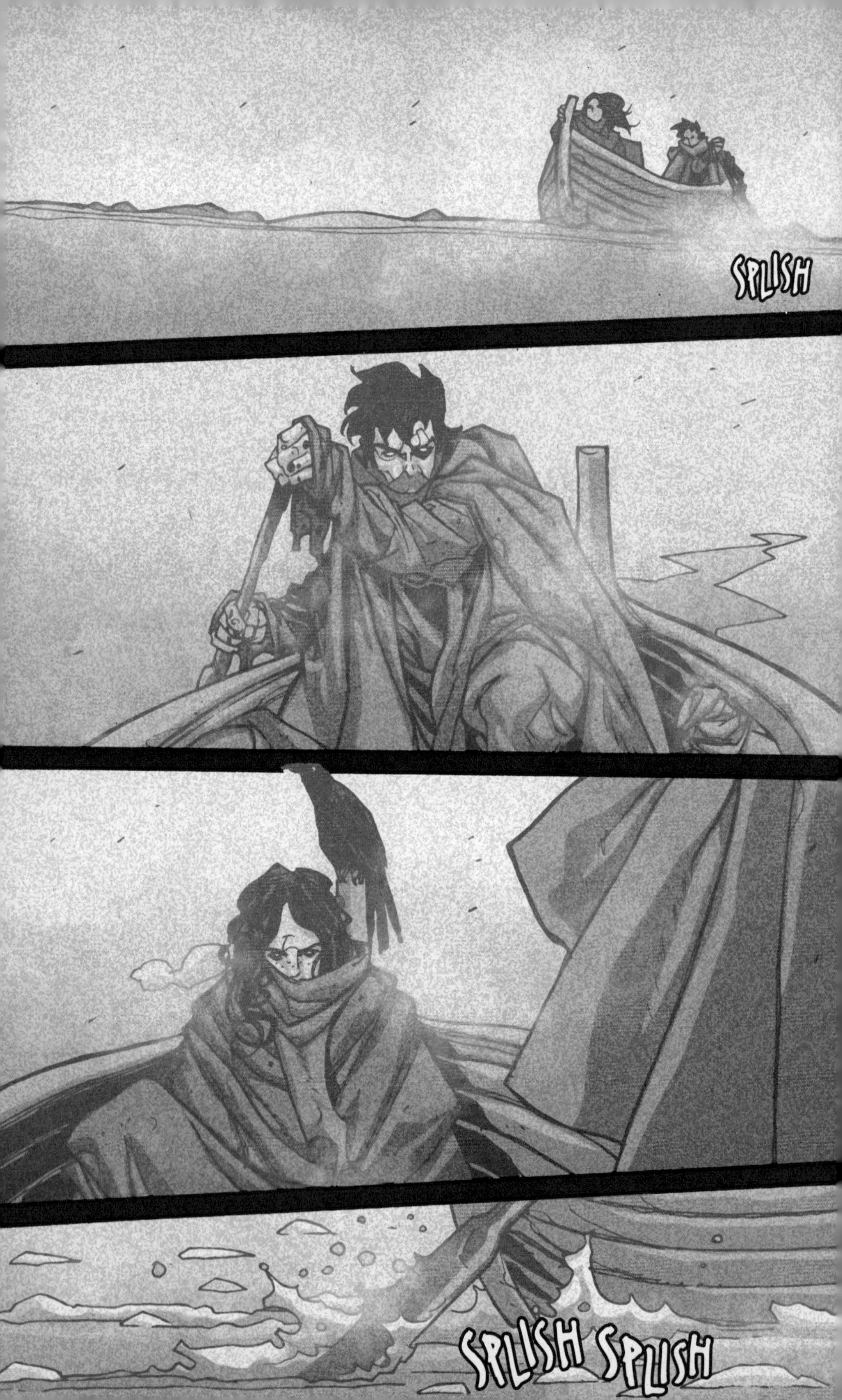
SPLISH
SPLISH SPLISH

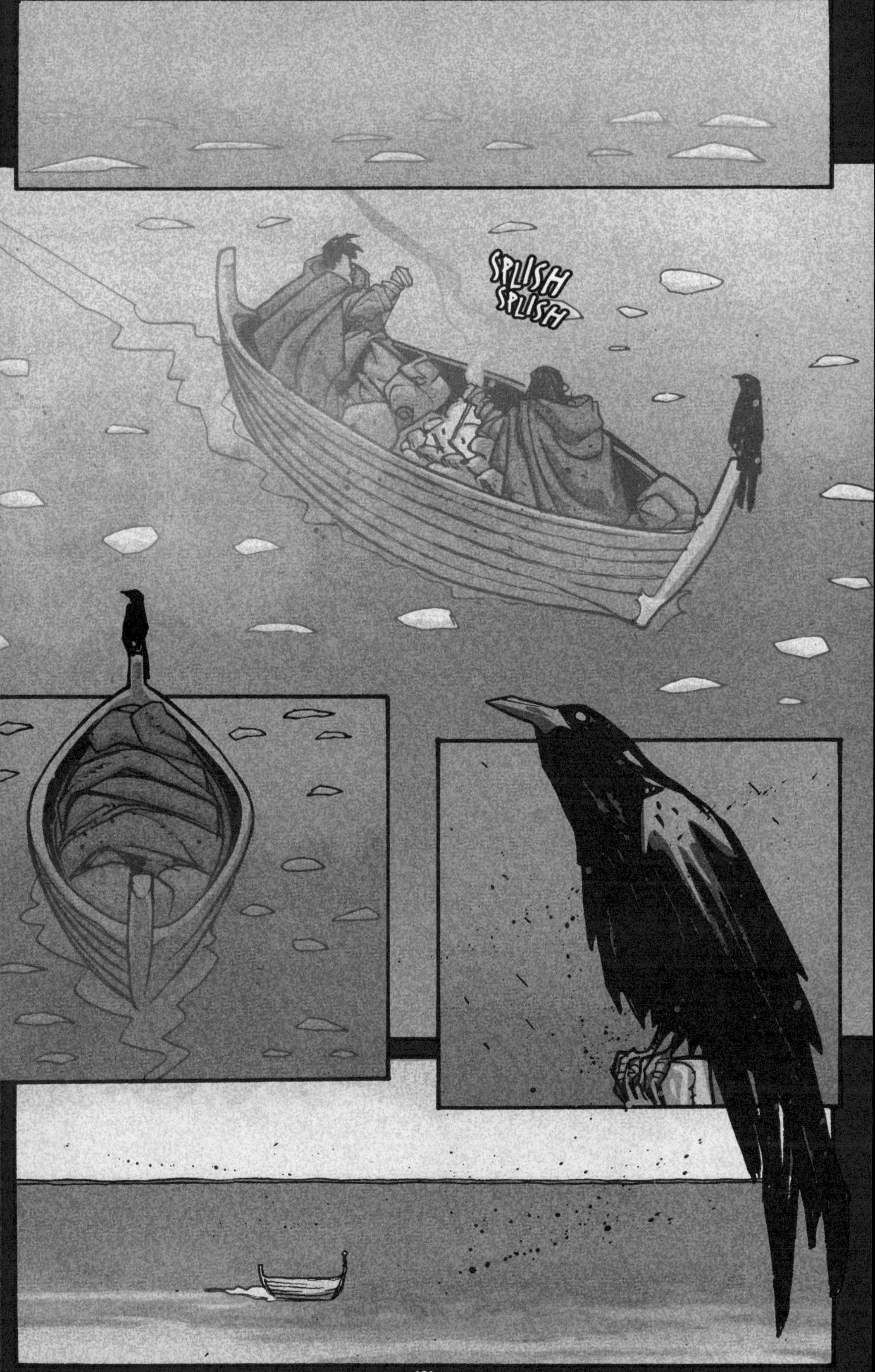
SPLISH
SPLISH

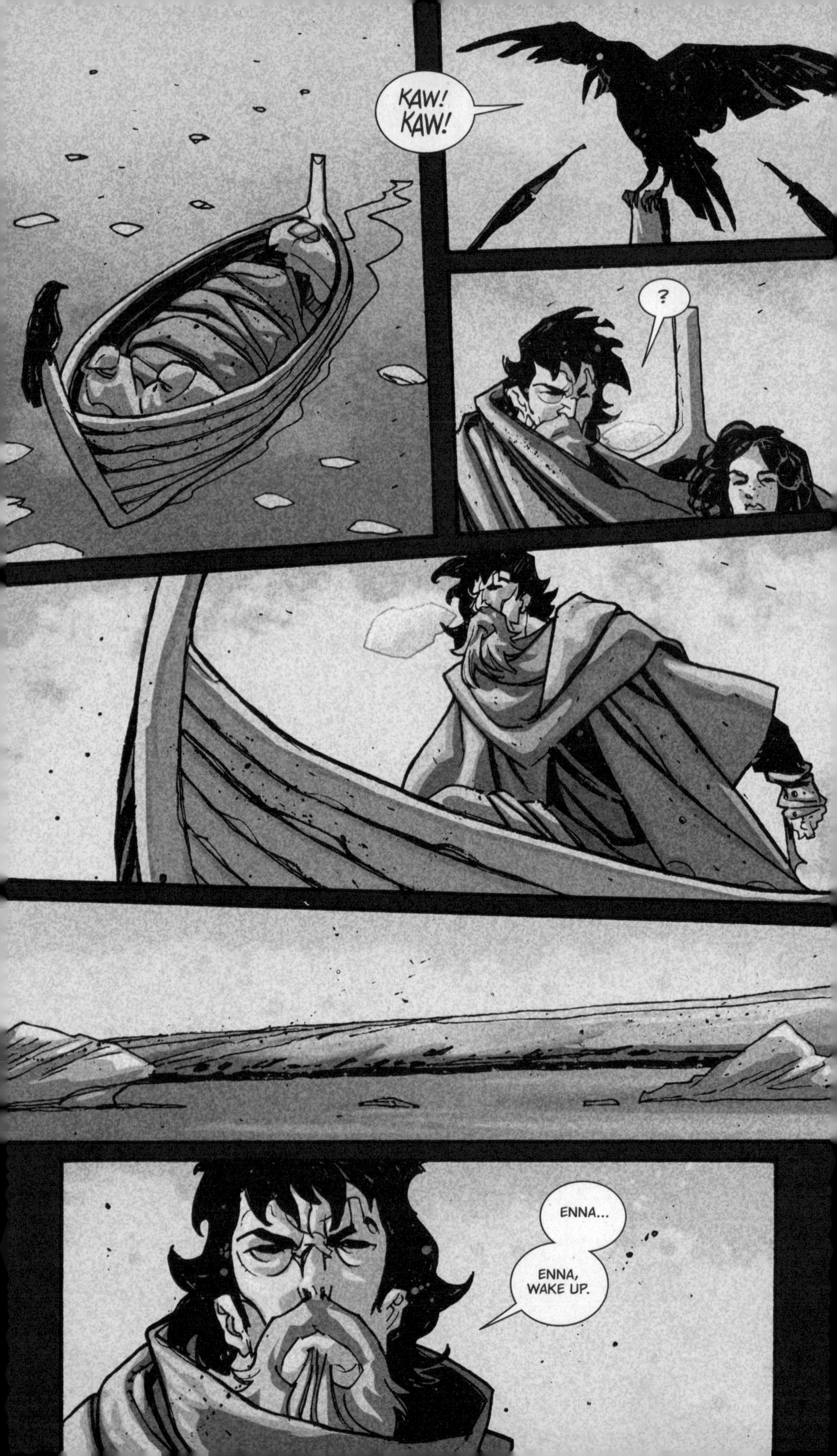
KAW! KAW!
?
ENNA...
ENNA, WAKE UP.

VARIANT COVERS

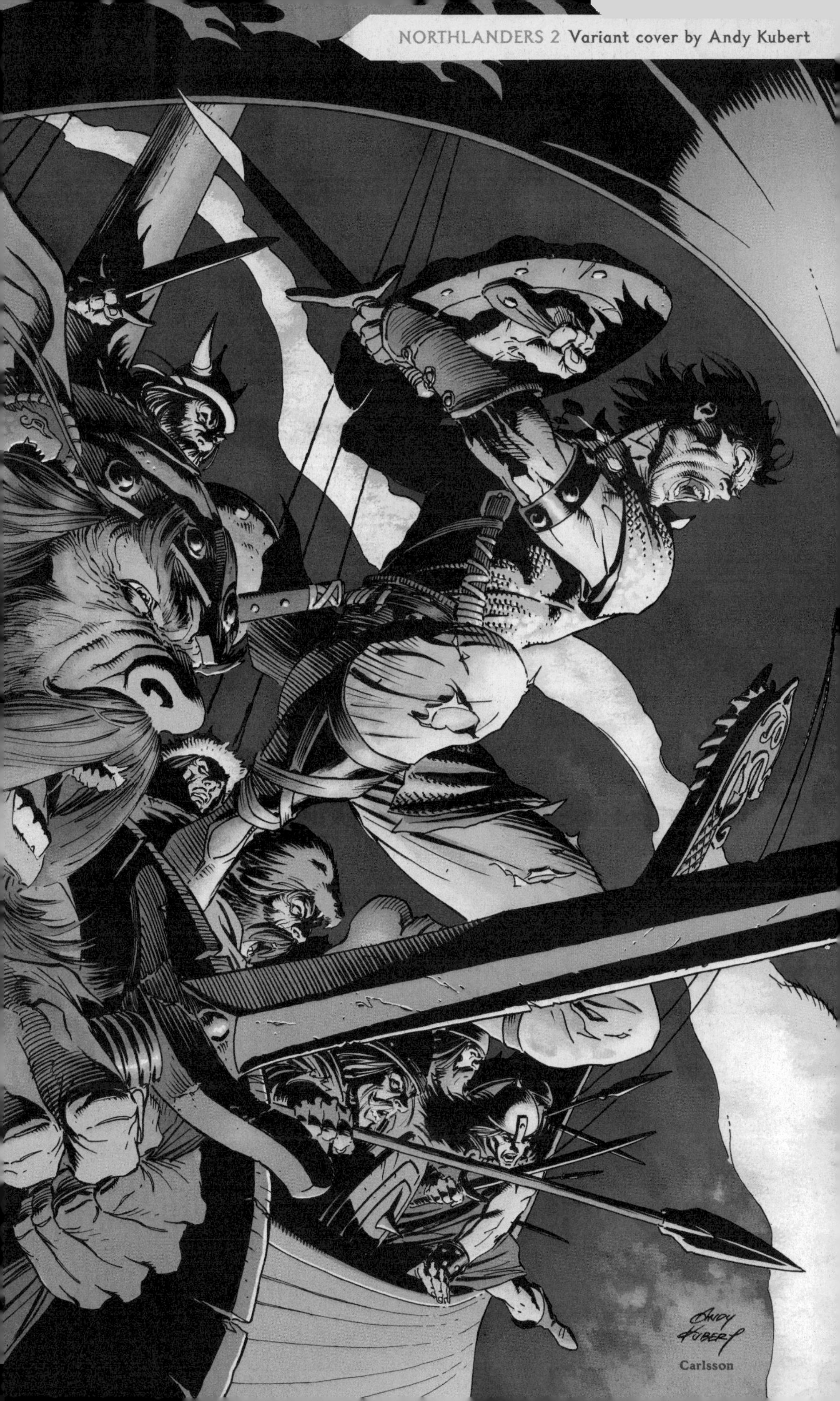
ANDY KUBERT
Carlsson
NORTHLANDERS 2 **Variant cover by Andy Kubert**

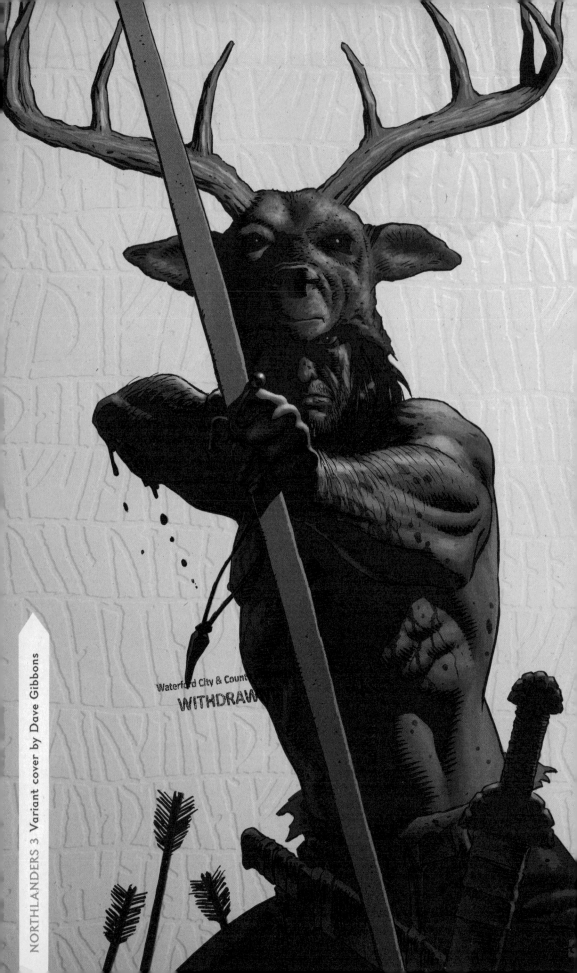

Waterford City & Count
WITHDRAW